Images: Readings for Writing

Images: Readings for Writing

Emil Roy
University of South Carolina—Aiken

Sandra Roy
Dalton College

Harcourt Brace College Publishers
Fort Worth   Philadelphia   San Diego   New York   Orlando   Austin   San Antonio
Toronto   Montreal   London   Sydney   Tokyo

Vice President, Publisher:	Christopher P. Klein
Acquisitions Editor:	Carol Wada
Development Editor:	Michell Phifer
Project Editor:	Matt Ball
Art Director:	Don Fujimoto
Production Manager:	Serena Manning
Product Manager:	Ilse Wolfe West
Copy Editor:	Joni Harlan
Proofreader:	Karen Keady
Indexer:	Leoni McVey
Cover Image:	Abrams/Lacagnina/Image Bank
Text Type:	Clearface 10/12

Address for orders:
Harcourt Brace College Publishers
6277 Sea Harbor Drive
Orlando, FL 32887
1-800-782-4479 or 1-800-433-0001 (in Florida)

Address for editorial correspondence:
Harcourt Brace College Publishers
301 Commerce Street, Suite 3700
Fort Worth, TX 76102

Harcourt Brace College Publishers may provide complimentary instructional aids and supplements or supplement packages to those adopters qualified under our adoption policy. Please contact your sales representative for more information. If as an adopter or potential user you receive supplements you do not need, please return them to your sales representative or send them to:

Attn: Returns Department
Troy Warehouse
465 South Lincoln Drive
Troy, MO 63379

ISBN: 0-15-503166-X

Library of Congress Catalog Card Number: **96-77397**

Credits appear on page **296–297**

Printed in the United States of America

6 7 8 9 0 1 2 3 4 5   067   9 8 7 6 5 4 3 2 1

To our children, Rosalind and Portia

Preface

Images: Readings for Writing has been written for teachers of basic writing who need a book that their students find both interesting and helpful. It uses clear, understandable prose which students can read easily. This book offers a clearly defined step-by-step approach to reading professionally written and student paragraphs and essays. It presents simple, usable advice directly to the students. In doing so, this text simplifies the difficult jobs of teaching and learning. Thus, it makes the basic concepts of reading and writing easier and more enjoyable for everyone. Its approach combines the following:

- Practical advice on writing,
- Professional and student writing samples, and
- An organization that reflects rhetorical types.

Moreover, it fits into either a one-semester or one-quarter course.

The first part of the book shows the students how to write basic paragraphs and essays. The chapters that follow treat each of the rhetorical approaches from simple to more demanding. Finally, an attached handbook treats commonly found problems in grammar, mechanics, punctuation, and spelling.

The first two chapters help students understand and apply the principles of clear, well-organized writing. Chapter 1, "Basic Paragraph Writing," takes a process approach. It advises students how to extend the thesis of an essay to paragraph-creation. It also directs them to focus the main idea of the paragraph in a topic sentence. In addition, it suggests ways to choose and arrange the paragraph's supporting subject matter. Exercises are strategically placed in the chapter, which are designed to lead students to identify aspects of good paragraph writing. They are followed by assignments that invite the students to use these skills in actual writing.

Chapter 2, "Basic Essay Writing," helps students write brief essays of up to 400–600 words long. Like the initial chapter, it takes a process approach, leading students through the following steps:

- Finding a topic, purpose, focus, and audience for an essay;
- Prewriting;
- Planning, organizing, and developing their ideas;
- Drafting and revising essays; and, finally,

- Proofreading their essays for errors in grammar, mechanics, spelling, and punctuation.

Like the initial chapter, its exercises not only identify aspects of good writing, they also help students create and improve their essays.

The following nine chapters focus on rhetorical modes, ranging from simple to more complex:

- Description
- Narration
- Examples
- Classification and Division
- Comparison and Contrast
- Process
- Cause and Effect
- Definition
- Persuasion

All these chapters follow a common format. Each one

1. Provides students with guidelines about particular modes of writing,
2. Applies these patterns to paragraph- and essay-length versions of the mode,
3. Supplies marginal comment analyzing these versions,
4. Reprints a number of carefully-selected, high-interest selections that include short and long examples of professional and student writing,
5. Precedes each writing selection with a brief précis, prereading queries, and vocabulary words,
6. Suggests queries for understanding the content and the writer's technique, along with writing suggestions following each selection,
7. Traces sample student essays from a prewritten draft, to questions for student and peer evaluation, to drafts annotated for organizational and proofreading improvements, to a final draft, and
8. Intersperses queries for writer-and peer-evaluation of student writing.

The discussions of guidelines for writing individual modes are presented in highly readable language. Then, a wide range of specific examples supports them. The brief and longer professional writing is straightforward and clearly explained. These models guide the students in shaping their own writing. Student essays appear among the models of writing and are later traced through successive drafts. They show students that they to can write perceptive, well-composed paragraphs and essays. Whether professional or student-written, the writing in this text is meant to be provocative, multi-cultural, and wide-ranging. These selections not only reflect rhetorical approaches, they will also stimulate class discussion of their content and techniques.

This book is primarily intended to improve the reading skills of basic students. At the same time, it will help students apply their learning to their writing. By thinking not only about what the readings say but how they say it, the students will not only read more capably, they will improve their writing.

The book also includes a brief handbook. It provides simple, amply-illustrated explanations of common problems in grammar, mechanics, punctuation, and spelling.

Finally, an Instructor's Manual accompanies this text. It includes responses to the exercises, queries and problems raised in the book.

ACKNOWLEDGMENTS

I would like to thank the following reviewers whose valuable insights helped to shape *Images:* Wendy Patterson, Buffalo State College; Vivian Brown, Laredo Community College; Eileen Schwartz, Purdue Calumet; Betty Dixon, Rancho Santiago College; Sarah Dye, Elgin Community College; Jane Maher, Nassau Community College; Stanley Coberly, West Virginia University at Parkersburg; and Elaine Chakonas, Triton College.

Images: Readings for Writing

Chapter Six:
Classification   103

Chapter Seven:
Comparison and Contrast   133

Chapter Eleven:
Persuasion   231

Handbook:
Grammar and Mechanics   259

Thematic List of Readings

Nature and the Environment

Ethics

History

CHAPTER ONE

Basic Paragraph Writing

Each of the following chapters in this book will describe ways of writing special types of paragraphs, such as narrative, descriptive, example, and so on. This chapter, however, will describe how to write good **body** paragraphs of all kinds; introductions and conclusions will be dicussed in Chapter 2.

> *Your body paragraphs need a topic sentence and specific, concrete supporting examples.*

THE TOPIC SENTENCE

Nearly all body paragraphs need a topic sentence. This sentence has three purposes:

- It **supports the thesis** of your essay by dealing with one of its main ideas.
- It tells the reader the **main point** of your paragraph.
- It helps you (the writer) **choose and arrange the subject matter** of your paragraph.

Writing a **thesis** for your essays will be discussed in Chapter 2. A thesis statement tells your reader

What you're writing about ("the best restaurant in the world," "caring for a household pet," "vacationing without our children");

why you have chosen this topic ("to reveal friendly, professional service," "to preserve their companionship and affection," "to keep our marriage alive"); and

how you hope your readers will react to your essay ("dreaming of great meals of the past," "avoiding visits more traumatic than the illness," "finding time to make romantic gestures").

Think of each of your paragraphs as a short essay. Each topic sentence develops an aspect of the thesis. In the rest of the paragraph, you will describe or explain what this idea means. Here is an example of a paragraph whose topic sentence focuses on part of a thesis. The supporting details in the paragraph, in turn, develop its topic sentence:

Essay Thesis   The two most important things you can do for your face are to keep it clean and protect it from the sun. (Two ideas: one for each paragraph.)

Topic sentence ——————▶

The use of examples is ——▶
limited by the topic sentence

The conclusion applies to *all*
the examples ——————▶

Any number of products will do a fine job of washing the face, including bar soaps or cleansers that come in tubes. Some soaps, such as Dove, leave a moisturizing residue. That's fine for people with dry or irritated skin, but people with oily skin or acne should avoid such products. Deodorant soaps or cleansers specifically for acne-prone skin are more appropriate for them. Abrasive scrubs are also sold for oily skin, but they can irritate the skin and may aggravate acne. **Whatever soap or cleanser is used, any moisturizer should be applied right after washing, when the skin is still slightly wet, so the moisturizer traps some of the water.**

"Caring for Your Skin," *Consumer Reports*

Here's another paragraph whose topic sentence carries out a thesis; examples within the paragraph also develop the topic sentence:

Essay Thesis   Home computing is suddenly the fastest-growing segment of the PC market. At least five factors are spurring sales.

Topic sentence takes ——▶
up one factor mentioned
by thesis

Details support ——————▶
topic sentence

Prices are falling. Today, after several years of price warfare, $1,500 buys an IBM-compatible PC with a huge amount of data storage. It also has a fast processor chip that can run Microsoft's Windows operating system. An equivalent PC would have cost at least $3,500 in 1991.

Stanley Engelbardt, "Get Ready for Virtual Reality"

Take care to link your topic sentences closely to your thesis. Each of your topic sentences should restate an aspect of your thesis, giving your reader confidence that you are controlling the direction of your writing.

Thesis Keeping weight off may involve different skills than taking it off.

Topic Sentences

1. Alternate dieting with regular eating until your weight stabilizes.
2. Slowly increase the amount of food you eat.
3. Taking weight off will make you feel better.

The third sentence makes a general statement about **taking** weight off, not **keeping** it off. Thus, the writer should delete it, perhaps replacing it with a statement like, "When you **do** indulge, compensate."

Look over the following sentences:

Thesis Building a large vocabulary is the best way to boost your SAT verbal score.

1. Make a habit of reading challenging publications and books.
2. Turn the dinner table into a classroom.
3. Don't be a slave to your calculator.
4. Look at word roots.

Topic sentences 1, 2, and 4 all deal with ways to build a large vocabulary. However, the third topic sentence deals with another topic—mathematical skills—and should be omitted or replaced.

WRITING PRECISE TOPIC SENTENCES

Your topic sentence should not be too **general,** for example:

My car's fuel economy is fairly good. (What **kind** of car? How good?)

Neither should it be too **specific,** for example:

My 1994 Toyota Corolla gets 34 miles per gallon on the highway and 26 miles per gallon in the city. (This level of detail should come after the topic sentence, **supporting** it.)

Rather, strike a happy medium, for example:

My 1994 Toyota Corolla pleases me with its stingy use of fuel. (The writer might support this topic sentence with numbers on highway and city mileage, dollar amounts spent on gas, and other details.)

The following are some examples of precise and weak topic sentences:

Precise: Renewable batteries are alkalines, so you get longer life from each charge.

Weak: Renewable batteries are totally different. (This sentence needs to name both kinds of batteries. Then it should tell what difference the writer wants to stress.)

Precise: Fire fighters are learning how to battle airport blazes.

Weak: Fire fighters are getting good training. (This sentence needs to tell **what kind** of training fire fighters are getting, for **what kinds** of fires.)

Precise: Most earthquakes are caused by strain building up along the earth's fault lines.

Weak: Earthquakes are pretty scary. (This sentence should tell **what causes** most earthquakes, instead of referring vaguely to the writer's feelings: "scary.")

In the precise topic sentences above, the writer clearly tells **what** or **why** or **how**:

- "are **alkalines**"
- "**how to** battle"
- "by **strain building up**"

Avoid the vagueness reflected in weak topic sentences. The next section will deal with the position of topic sentences in the paragraph.

WHERE TO PUT TOPIC SENTENCES

The simplest paragraph, and often the most effective, begins with a topic sentence; the topic is then developed with specific, concrete details or examples. However, topic sentences may often come second in the paragraph, following an interesting lead-in. At times, however, a paragraph may present a series of examples. In this kind of paragraph, the topic sentence will come last, summing up.

In the following paragraph the topic sentence appears **second**, after a lead-in:

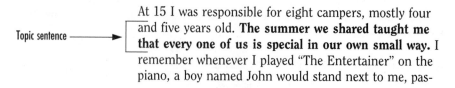

Topic sentence ⟶

At 15 I was responsible for eight campers, mostly four and five years old. **The summer we shared taught me that every one of us is special in our own small way.** I remember whenever I played "The Entertainer" on the piano, a boy named John would stand next to me, pas-

sionately rocking his head back and forth to the music.
And there was Gloria, who every time I saw her was
singing "Lean on me."

Richard Dyer, "Going Home"

In the following paragraph the topic sentence is positioned **last:**

In Utah, eccentric millionaire Thomas W. Bicknell offered to donate a library to a town that adopted his last
name. Residents of Thurber quickly changed their town
name to Bicknell—but so did residents of Grayson, who
wanted in on the deal, too. A Solomonic judgment ended
the stalemate. Thurber remained Bicknell, while Grayson
changed its name to Blanding, Mrs. Bicknell's maiden

Topic sentence ⟶ name. **The towns divided the books equally.**

Dana Milbank, "What's in a Name?"

Here's a paragraph with its topic sentence **first** and conclusion **last:**

A hush settles over the house. I tuck in Robert and
John in the cozy bedroom they share, a protected south-
facing room with a fine view of the woods. There are a
few final sleepy questions—where snakes live in the winter and whether a balloon set adrift will float all the way
to outer space. Then their eyelids flutter and their breath
comes soft and deep. **I am left with the darkness and**

Conclusion ⟶ **the peace.**

Alice Steinbach, "Summer Dreams"

The next section takes up ways to develop the topic sentence with specific, interesting details and examples.

BUILDING THE PARAGRAPH

In addition to a topic sentence, each of your body paragraphs needs plenty of details, facts, and examples. These elements develop the topic sentence, explaining
what it means to your reader. Before actually drafting your paragraph, make a list
of supporting details. Then test them by asking yourself questions, such as will
readers be able to visualize each of the details in their minds? Do the details actually name or measure some fact or object?

Here is an example of a weak paragraph:

Life is like a game I once played as a kid. When some new Scouts joined up, we lined up some furniture. Then we blindfolded them and told them to find their way around. We took away the chairs. (The writer fails to tell exactly **who** does **what, when,** or **why.)**

Here is the same paragraph, but well developed:

Life is like a game I played as a young boy. When I was a Boy Scout, we played a game when new Scouts joined the troop. We lined up chairs in a pattern. This created an obstacle course through which the new Scouts, blindfolded, were supposed to maneuver. The Scoutmaster gave them a few moments to study the pattern before our adventure began. But as soon as the victims were blindfolded, the rest of us quietly removed the chairs. Perhaps we spend our lives avoiding obstacles which exist only in our minds.

Sam Chazin, "Player of the Game"

The second paragraph develops the idea of the game with a list of details:

- Chairs lined up in a pattern
- Creating an obstacle course
- New scouts blindfolded, supposed to maneuver
- Removing the chairs
- Avoiding imaginary obstacles later in life

The well-developed paragraph is not only clearer, but more interesting. Readers can visualize the main idea by grasping the specific details that develop it.
Here is another example of a vague paragraph that includes no detail:

I saw the launch of a large rocket a while ago. After the countdown, it was launched. It was very impressive, we all thought. (The writer doesn't describe what the launch **looks** or **sounds** like.)

Here is the same paragraph supported more concretely:

I was an observer at the night launch of Apollo 17 in 1975. The countdown came and then the launch. The first thing you see is this extraordinary orange light, which is just at the limit of what you can bear to look at. It takes a few seconds for the sound to come across: "WHOOOOOSH! HHHH-MMMMM!" The first stage ignites this beautiful blue flame. And then there's total silence. People just get up quietly, looking at one another, speaking quietly and interestedly.

Susan James, "All I Ever Wanted"

This well-supported paragraph not only tells **what** ("night launch of Apollo 17") and when ("night . . . 1975"), it also appeals to **vision** ("extraordinary orange light") and **sound** ("WHOOOSH!" . . . total silence"). These details impress readers because we can "see" and "hear" the rocket launch.

HOW DOES THE WRITER GATHER EVIDENCE?

Gather supporting details in these ways:

- By observing situations closely and taking notes if needed.
- By recalling memories and re-running them in your mind like a video.
- By making lists.
- By remembering appeals to senses such as vision, sound, touch, taste, and smell.

In addition to supporting a topic sentence, details within paragraphs should belong together, which is the topic of the next section.

UNIFYING PARAGRAPHS

Each of the details in a paragraph must support the main idea in the same way. Listing your supporting details helps you test your examples for consistency. You don't want to drift away from your main idea part way through the paragraph. After drafting your paragraph, ask yourself if the details actually relate closely to the topic sentence. If not, you may need to discard the example or even change your topic sentence.

Here's an example of a paragraph whose details all support the same main idea:

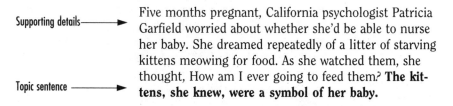

Supporting details———▶ Five months pregnant, California psychologist Patricia Garfield worried about whether she'd be able to nurse her baby. She dreamed repeatedly of a litter of starving kittens meowing for food. As she watched them, she thought, How am I ever going to feed them? **The kit-**
Topic sentence ———▶ **tens, she knew, were a symbol of her baby.**

P. J. O'Rourke, "Beware the Professional Worriers"

Here's an example of a paragraph whose initial details support the topic sentence, but the supporting details wander away to treat another topic:

Topic sentence ———▶ **Criminals know that punishment works,** and they use it every day all over America. Criminals demand absolute obedience. If corporal punishment doesn't work they will use capital punishment. They know that fear of death is the best deterrent for disobedience. Actually the words *penalty, restrict,* and *violate* appeared more times in President Clinton's health care bill than in his crime bill.

Wanders into new topic ⎤

Most of the detail in the preceding paragraph deals with crime and criminals. However, it adds a detail that treats these topics only incidentally: language in a health bill.

The following paragraph begins with a topic sentence followed by several supporting details.

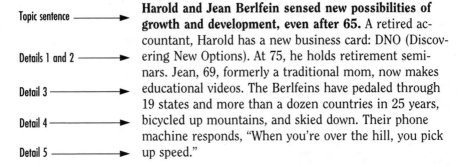

Topic sentence ➤ **Harold and Jean Berlfein sensed new possibilities of growth and development, even after 65.** A retired accountant, Harold has a new business card: DNO (Discovering New Options). At 75, he holds retirement seminars. Jean, 69, formerly a traditional mom, now makes educational videos. The Berlfeins have pedaled through 19 states and more than a dozen countries in 25 years, bicycled up mountains, and skied down. Their phone machine responds, "When you're over the hill, you pick up speed."

Details 1 and 2 ➤

Detail 3 ➤

Detail 4 ➤

Detail 5 ➤

Jay Hovde, "Journey to the Winner's Circle"

All the details in the preceding paragraph show how the Berlfeins have grown and developed, even after the age of 65.

The following paragraph also begins with a topic sentence, supported by closely related details. However, midway through the paragraph, the details wander away in another direction:

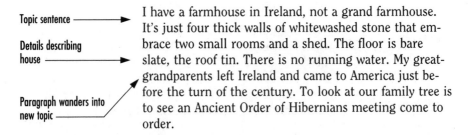

Topic sentence ➤ I have a farmhouse in Ireland, not a grand farmhouse. It's just four thick walls of whitewashed stone that embrace two small rooms and a shed. The floor is bare slate, the roof tin. There is no running water. My great-grandparents left Ireland and came to America just before the turn of the century. To look at our family tree is to see an Ancient Order of Hibernians meeting come to order.

Details describing house ➤

Paragraph wanders into new topic ⎓

Here is another example of a paragraph that begins well, with a clear topic sentence and supporting details, but moves in a new direction midstream, confusing the reader.

Topic sentence ➤ **Some earthly beings grow quite old.** The oldest animal ever was a tortoise that died in 1918. The reptile had

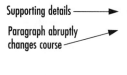

Supporting details   ⟶

Paragraph abruptly changes course

been captured—already full-grown—in 1766, nine years before the American Revolution began. It died 152 years later as World War I came to a close. The mayfly typically lives only a matter of hours once it emerges from its nymphal shell. Few mayflies live longer than a day. They devote their brief lives to a single, desperate mission: finding a mate.

The above paragraph takes up two unrelated ideas, one crowding in upon the other. The writer needs to invent a new topic sentence dealing with both. Or the paragraph should be broken into two new ones, developing each one more fully.

    Finally, the next paragraph develops an initial topic sentence with several closely linked details describing a $100 bill. However, the conclusion has nothing to do with the main idea of the sentence: the appearance of a forged bill:

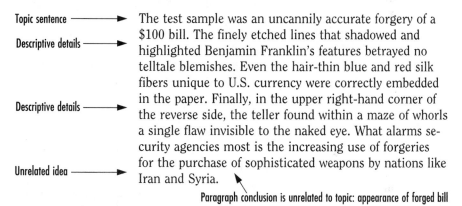

Topic sentence   ⟶

Descriptive details   ⟶

Descriptive details   ⟶

Unrelated idea   ⟶

The test sample was an uncannily accurate forgery of a $100 bill. The finely etched lines that shadowed and highlighted Benjamin Franklin's features betrayed no telltale blemishes. Even the hair-thin blue and red silk fibers unique to U.S. currency were correctly embedded in the paper. Finally, in the upper right-hand corner of the reverse side, the teller found within a maze of whorls a single flaw invisible to the naked eye. What alarms security agencies most is the increasing use of forgeries for the purchase of sophisticated weapons by nations like Iran and Syria.

Paragraph conclusion is unrelated to topic: appearance of forged bill

Make sure your paragraphs include the following parts:

- A topic sentence that sums up the paragraph's main idea—usually the first sentence, but not always.
- Supporting details, examples, facts, or reasons all closely linked to the topic sentence.
- A conclusion (optional) that sums up without bringing in a new topic.

The next section deals with connecting the ideas within paragraphs, helping to unite them.

HOLDING PARAGRAPHS TOGETHER

Many paragraphs flow more smoothly if you connect their ideas with transitions. The following transitions will help you link sentences together within paragraphs:

Presenting examples: another, for example, for instance, in particular, namely, specifically.

Showing comparison: in comparison; not only, . . . but also; similarly.

Showing contrast: although, but, however, in contrast, on the other hand, while, whereas.

Indicating sequence: after; and; also; and finally; first, . . . second, . . . third; before; furthermore; next; so; then.

Summing up results: as a result, consequently, therefore, thus.

Here's an example of a paragraph with transitions, which are shown in **boldface**:

> Americans spend some $4 billion for 4 billion pounds of fresh tomatoes every year—**but** we don't necessarily enjoy what we're eating. To get their crop to the supermarket whole and unbruised, growers pick tomatoes green, firm, and flavorless **so** the fruit can be washed, sorted, and packed without damage. **Then,** before shipping, packers expose the tomatoes to ethylene gas to spur ripening and redden the skin. **But** the crash-course doesn't work very well. **The result is** the hard, pale, flat-tasting supermarket tomato we're all familiar with.
>
> Lisa Delaney, "Design a Diet That Works for You."

Notice how choppy the same paragraph sounds without transitions::

Need contrast here ——— Americans spend some $4 billion for 4 billion pounds of fresh tomatoes every year—we don't necessarily enjoy what we're eating. To get their crop to the supermarket whole and unbruised, growers pick tomatoes green, firm, and flavorless. The fruit can be washed, sorted, and packed without damage. Before shipping, packers expose the tomatoes to ethylene gas to spur ripening and redden the skin. The crash-course doesn't work very well. We're all familiar with the hard, pale, flat-tasting supermarket tomato.

Show sequence

Indicate sequence

Sum up results

Show contrast

As these examples show, transitions make your meaning clearer. However, don't overuse them.. You will also want to link ideas together by using synonyms or words that mean the same (for example, "When **illness** clouds your thinking, you can't assess your **disorder**" [**disorder** refers to the same thing as **illness**]. Or you may refer to an earlier word with a pronoun ("After your **doctor** checks your throat, **he** checks your glands.") Read your sentences aloud to make sure that the connections between them will be clear to your readers.

EXERCISES

1. Identify the topic sentence in each of the following paragraphs. If the paragraph has a conclusion, identify that too:

To negotiate the best deal, you've got to understand how leases work. A lease is not a rental but a contract in which you finance the car for a short period of time. When that time is up, you can either give the car back to the dealer or buy it for a specific price. That figure, which you and the dealer agree on before the lease begins, is the car's "residual value." When negotiating a lease, most dealers focus on the monthly payment and steer consumers away from the car's purchase price.

Are older husbands more satisfied than their wives? In a survey conducted at Long Island University's Southampton College, men described their marriages in more positive terms than did their spouses. Sixty percent said they were very happy versus 51.5 percent of the wives; 73 percent of the men said they *always* liked their wives, while only 50 percent of the women said they *always* liked their husbands. Many of the couples had persevered through myriad troubles—e.g., alcoholism, infidelity, chronic illness, and bankruptcy—to regain happiness and satisfaction together. These are just a few findings of the most comprehensive survey of long-term marriages ever made in the United States.

2. Add topic sentences to the following paragraphs. Indicate whether they belong at the beginning, end, or somewhere in between:

In many areas, especially during a dry season, farmers and ranchers say kangaroos have become a plague. Some Australians are even shooting the "roos" without permits. They say hunting quotas are too low to lessen the animals' damage, estimated at more than $130 million a year. "There are more kangaroos than ever before," said Graham Berry, a farmer. "They eat for up to 15 hours a day. They eat all night."

That's why Carl Lewis, who already holds eight Olympic gold medals, plans to compete again at 36 in the 1996 Games. It's why discus thrower Al Oerter, after winning gold medals in four consecutive Olympics, tried again for the Olympic team at age 47. Swimmer Janet Evans, who won three gold medals in Seoul in 1988, embodied that same desire to win four years later. The class valedictorian, the corporate CEO—those who rise to the top in any endeavor—must have the same drive.

Now the FDA's label "low fat" (except for milk) means that the product has no more than three grams of fat per serving. "Fat free" means less than half a gram of fat per serving. A "reduced fat" product, such as mayonnaise, has at least 25 percent less fat than regular mayonnaise. Finally, a "light" mayo has 50 percent less fat than regular.

3. Rewrite the following paragraphs, changing general statements to specific details. Look for general terms like *good, terrific, bunch*, and *right*. Replace them with terms that show how big, heavy, colorful, valuable, or fitting (and so on) an entity is.

Having just a lot of good qualities, these really terrific Cherished Eddies have made an appeal to folks everywhere who want them. Now, the Hamilton Collection is presenting the *Monthly Friends to Cherish* figurine collection, with a whole bunch of these toys. Just look at "Seth," carrying school things. "Alan" is all ready for rain, and "Denise" is ready for a holiday. This group of toys will make you happy. With good clothes, the right things around them, and adoption papers, each one of these dudes is one of a kind. To get all of their appeal, each one of them has been put together with lots of attention. And somebody colored them real nice.

A nice lady who lives somewhere in the Southwest read something somewhere about my wife's strong feelings about my overcoat, which is old and worn out, with lots of things wrong with it. However, I think the coat's still put together well and keeps off the weather. In other seasons, I don't wear it anyway. It's like most of my other clothes: I like them raggedy that way. It's a waste of money to buy new clothes when the old ones still suit me. Clothes have one purpose: to keep me from walking around without anything on. When I wear this old overcoat, people don't come up to me asking for money. Sometimes, they think I'm another beggar and say things. These old clothes are just as good as those designer threads. This widow who read about my coat sent me one of her late husband's, which was in really good shape.

---

4. In the following paragraphs, underline devices that help link ideas together: transitions (*thus, so*), synonyms (*doctor, physician, medical expert*), or pronouns (*food groups, they*).

Magnesium (Mg) is an essential mineral for the overall health of your heart, muscles, and nervous system. But, unlike calcium, Mg is not found in a few easy-to-target food groups. And some things that *do* contain Mg are high in sugar or fat. Furthermore, a 1994 Gallup survey revealed that about 72 percent of Americans report an inadequate intake of this vital mineral. And that's not good, for Mg deficiency has been found in patients with diseases like hypertension and diabetes. So, many doctors recommend an oral Mg supplement for their patients.

"Line dancing is a great way to meet people," says Ollie Mae Ray. "And it gives you a terrific psychological boost because learning a new dance provides a wonderful feeling of accomplishment." "It's also great exercise," says Ray, whose studies indicate that line dancing provides cardiovascular benefits. Plus, it improves flexibility, balance, and coordination. "In addition, it's so much fun that many people don't realize what a workout they're getting," Ray notes. "But when you do fast dances like Slappin' Leather, it gets your heart rate up, and dances like the Tush Push really work the muscles in your legs and lower body." When she teaches at senior centers, Ray encourages people in wheelchairs to join in by moving their upper bodies. She also teaches "hand-jive" dances like the Ding Dong Daddy.

5. Sentences in the following paragraphs are not linked together closely. Fill in each blank with a transition word or phrase.

Annual flowers are the showy extroverts of yard and garden. They live for only one season, _____ it's a long one—from mid-May to late October. _____ other flowers, such as perennials that bloom and then wither, annuals keep getting better. To start an annual bed, _____ choose a location and select the right flowers for the exposure. _____, with a can of orange marker spray paint, spray a spot of paint every few feet along the hose. _____ remove the hose entirely and connect the dots. This will give you the design for your bed, which you will _____ need to spray with a herbicide.

_____ I was stationed at Myrtle Beach, S.C., I spent my spare time fishing in the backwaters of the Intracoastal Waterway. _____ I became a guide of sorts for some senior non-commissioned officers. _____, a chief master sergeant hooked a 20-pound striped bass. _____ he reeled the fish onto the boat, he slipped the hook out of its mouth. _____ he released it back into the water. _____, he noticed the puzzled look on my face. "Rank does have its privileges. I can't keep a fish that has more stripes than I do," he explained.

CHAPTER TWO

The Basic Essay

The previous chapter discussed ways to plan, organize, and fill out a body paragraph. This chapter will help you do the following:

- Find a topic for your writing.
- Find a purpose and focus for your essays.
- Find an audience for your writing.
- Plan, organize, and develop your ideas.
- Draft your essays.
- Revise your writing.
- Proofread.

In this chapter you will also learn how to write introduction and conclusion paragraphs for your essay, as part of the drafting process.

FINDING A TOPIC

Unlike poetry or a personal journal, two assumptions are associated with the writing you do for class: you have something important to say, and your reader should be able to understand it without serious effort. When beginning to write, do this: visualize your readers (your instructor, your peers, and your classmates). You are required to write. However, your readers have no duty to struggle with vague, poorly formed sentences and disorganized thoughts. If need be, tell yourself at the outset, "I'll let George (or whomever) read over my draft. He'll tell me if I'm on the right track." These preliminary steps will help you get your ideas across to your readers.

Once you've decided to write, consider the following suggestions about handling a topic.

CHOOSE A TOPIC YOU'RE ENTHUSIASTIC ABOUT

Consider an interesting aspect of your job, an eccentric co-worker or relative, or your hobby or favorite sport. Your readers may know or care little about your interests. Yet your burning focus on those interests will carry them along, especially if you load your writing with vivid details.

LIMIT YOUR TOPIC

Often, your assigned or chosen topic may be too large to handle in a 400- or 500-word essay. Limit it. If, for example, you have chosen to handle a topic like electronics in your life, you know it's too general. After all, electronics covers everything from your car engine to your cellular phone to your computer. To narrow it down, you may decide to discuss your stereo. However, your topic may still be too broad. You may need to limit your topic even further to assembling your stereo in your room or installing it in your car.

START EARLY

While you may be tempted to delay, begin exploring your topic by making some notes, talking it over with a friend, and setting a schedule for finishing your essay. Grappling with the job early will help you avoid those late nighters or last-minute rushes to finish your paper.

Exercise A. Selecting and Narrowing Essay Topics

Look over the following list of topics. Some of them could be treated adequately in a 400- to 600-word paper, whereas others would need to be limited. For those that are too broad, think of ways to narrow them. Then write a **thesis**—a crucial statement that identifies your topic and your purpose.

- Buying a used car for commuting to and from work
- My favorite reading material
- The person who influenced me to become a medical technician
- The best movies of the 1990s
- Recycling
- Requiring motorcycle helmets in my state
- Getting started in my favorite sport

- My favorite relative
- An exciting vacation
- Collecting the stamps of Western Europe

FINDING A PURPOSE AND FOCUS FOR YOUR ESSAY

Once you have limited the scope of your essay, think why you're writing about the topic. What do you want to emphasize about it? To answer these questions, consider using some helpful prewriting devices such as listing, freewriting, and clustering. Experiment with each of them, trying to find out which ones work best for you or for a chosen topic.

LISTING

If you're especially well organized, try **listing** your ideas. This is a device that busy people use to limit the clutter in their lives. To make this work, put your topic at the top of a piece of paper. Then write down all the thoughts it suggests. At this stage, throw nothing away. Add details to your list for five or ten minutes. A list on planning a vacation might look like this:

pack the minimum: wear the rest	keep kids busy with games
give kids bag of goodies	supply kids with I.D.
take a first-aid kit	pack prescription drugs
have a phone credit card	hide valuables
arrange time alone	make backup arrangements
avoid hassle: relax the day before	provide unwinding time afterwards
carry luggage to see how it feels	give kids something to look forward to daily
get names of local physicians	watch for thieves

Once you've put together a list, look for links between items. The preceding list includes ideas that involve managing children—keeping them busy, safe, and interested, for example. Other ideas involve ways to avoid unpleasant surprises or medical emergencies, like taking medications along or preparing a list of physicians at your destination. This exercise, like the ones that follow, will help you detect your interests as well as generate supporting details.

FREEWRITING

If you need a way just to get started, try freewriting. Begin with a clean sheet or two of paper. Giving yourself ten or fifteen minutes, write randomly on your topic. The important goal here is to keep writing. Don't stop to check your spelling, punctuation, or mechanics. If you are unsure how to write something correctly, guess at it and mark it with a symbol (* or ±, perhaps). Try not to lift your pen from the page. Write "I can't think of anything more to say" if you get stuck. Here's an example of freewriting:

The talk-shows today often deal with bonding, as though only people can do it. What they mean is forming a tie between people maybe through shared experiences, perhaps growing up together. However, I have bonded with my dog Bullet, something we did during the last two years. I picked him out on Easter Day, 1992, when he was a four-month-old, long-legged Jack Russell puppy. Bullet had a wiry white coat and a black mask on his face. (I named him later when he raced around the yard.) He didn't watch where he was going when he ran, so he crashed into a cement park bench. When I rushed him to a vet, they pinned the bone together surgically. That meant we had to confine Bullet to the house for the next six weeks and carry him up and down three flights of stairs.

In this freewrite, the writer thinks of a concept, "bonding," and then applies it to herself and her dog. She redefines a term on the basis of her own experience. Your own freewriting may not hang together as well as this example. However, it gives you an opportunity to explore your own experiences, finding out what matters to you.

CLUSTERING

Another device is **clustering.** To use it, put your topic in the center of a blank sheet of paper and circle it. As you think of related ideas, write them around your central topic, connecting them with it and to each other with lines. Keep filling in your cluster as you move toward the perimeter, becoming more and more specific and detailed as you move along. There are no rigid rules for clustering—people find their own ways to make clustering fit their purposes. Below is an example of fifteen minutes of clustering on Anita's bell collection. It leads her into a trial thesis and a question about her plan.

Trial Thesis

Collecting bells is a sentimental hobby for me because every one is bought for a unique reason.

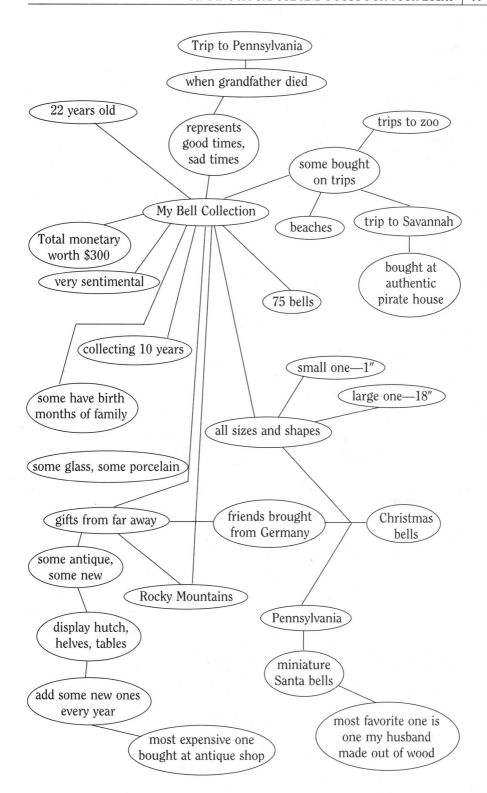

Plan:

Divide items into three or four categories (for example, sizes and shapes, origins, display).

Exercise B. Using Prewriting Techniques

Choose two of the following topics. Use one of the prewriting techniques—listing, freewriting, or clustering—to narrow it down. While doing so, generate details that would help you develop a 400- to 600-word essay.

my favorite person	sports
a dream house	music
vacationing	a career
cars	family
television	politics

After you have explored your topic, found your focus, and generated some details, you can go on to write a **thesis,** a statement of your position in the paper that also answers the question, "So what?" for your reader.

FINDING AN AUDIENCE FOR YOUR WRITING

Before drafting an essay, think a moment of your audience's needs. A high school student, a parent, and a business person may all be planning a vacation in Spain. But each would prepare differently from the others. If you have not been assigned a particular audience, try to imagine the reception given your writing by an audience of classmates or peers. As you write, consider the following pointers.

GET AND KEEP YOUR READERS' ATTENTION

Readers like appeals to human interest or oddities of behavior. Write to stimulate them and make them want to read further. Consider the bicycle shop that attracted patrons' attention by naming itself "Won-A-Go Biking" and a delicatessen called "Salvador Deli." Like these signs, will your writing catch your readers' attention and keep it?

READERS WANT TO BE INFORMED AND INTERESTED

In the course of their reading, readers want to be educated, to learn new things. In the freewrite example given earlier, for instance, we're intrigued to learn not only that a pet owner treats her dog like a child, but that surgical techniques developed for humans are used on animals, too. We would read more of her essay to learn how the dog recovers with its owner's help. Readers of an essay that grew out of this freewrite would feel they received a fair shake, that they had been enlightened.

READERS WANT TO SEE FROM YOUR VANTAGE POINT

By supporting your writing with pungent, vivid details, you capture your readers' attention and keep it. You may dismiss as forgettable a young couple's first look at a maternity ward. But you'd remember a young father's comment, "Look, honey, their first slumber party." Readers not only want to walk in your shoes; they like evidence that you're credible, an authority they can trust.

USE A NATURAL SPEAKING VOICE

In your writing, choose language that sounds conversational and reasonable. To test the naturalness of your style, read your writing aloud, or ask a friend to do so. You may hope to impress your instructor by using three-dollar synonyms gleaned from a thesaurus, but you're likely to lose your reader's interest—and that of your classmates—long before the end of your paper.

Exercise C. Meeting Readers' Needs

B. Spencer Sutton of Brooklyn, New York, recently sent out a brochure called "Telephones and Your Health." Sutton is studying the market feasibility of a line of "sanitary handset covers" in ten colors and ten fragrances, including "wild rose" and "banana-coconut." The brochure states that telephone receivers are "disease-and-germ-covered," and adds, "considering the damage [they] can cause [they] should be at the top of the list of things to use with caution and protection." Read over the questions in Sutton's brochure, and respond to the assignments that follow.

ONE MAN'S HANG-UP

1. If you observed a person coughing or sneezing on a telephone mouth cup, or blowing his nose into a sanitary tissue while using a phone, would you use it?

2. Would you use a handset with an accumulation of earwax and hair oil on the ear cup or saliva and food particles on the mouth cup?

3. If you observed a person with lip or mouth blisters using a phone, would you let the cup touch your lips or place it near your mouth?

4. If you noticed a person with red crusty ears or a facial or scalp rash using a telephone handset, would you use it?

5. When you or a member of your household is infected with a cold or flu, is the phone disinfected after each call by the infected person?

6. Is the infected person required to use a separate phone until the cold is gone?

7. When you drive, take a train, or fly into another city or country and need to use a public phone, do you place the public handset on your ear and mouth without any concern?

8. Do you try to hold it away from your head?

9. Would you buy an inexpensive, portable, compact, sanitary handset cover for your personal hygiene, disease-prevention, and health-maintenance efforts?

10. How soon would you want to purchase the sanitary handset cover?

Harper's, June 1995

Each of the following writing assignments involves a different audience, all of whom use telephones. Consider what kind of writing supported by what details would be the most persuasive.

1. Write a brief newspaper ad for Sutton's sanitary handset cover. Which of his points would most effectively persuade readers to buy or order one of his products?

2. Assume that you are a regional distributor for Sutton's sanitary handset covers. Write a letter to your local city council asking for a license to demonstrate in front of City Hall in favor of wider use of sanitary handset covers. What evidence would be most likely to persuade city council members to grant your request for a license?

3. Assume that you are a former phone user who blames your medical problems on the use of unsanitary phones. Write a letter to the city health department demanding that they regularly test and officially certify all public telephones as sanitary and germfree.

PLANNING, ORGANIZING, AND DEVELOPING YOUR IDEAS

At this stage in your writing, you have chosen or been assigned a topic. You have developed a reason to write about it and focused on a limited, particular aspect to fill out with supporting details. In addition, you have considered your audience's needs, even visualized your readers. You are now ready to state a working thesis, a statement of your limited topic that answers the question, "So what?"

To create your working thesis, begin by writing a simple sentence that answers one or more of these questions: What's this paper about? What is my opinion on this topic? How do I want my readers to react to the paper? For example, you may begin with a working thesis like, "Our college night program needs more activities, such as a jobs fair." This working thesis tells what you think about the topic (students need more activities in the night program) and tells what your essay will do (argue for events like a jobs fair).

If you made a list earlier about ways to flatten your stomach, you might write a working thesis that looks like this: "To flatten your stomach permanently, you need to begin by losing fat." This working thesis not only tells what you think and why (reasons for dieting), it also aims your writing at a particular group (those with fat around their middles). To stay on your topic as you write your essay, start with a working thesis. Then look back at it from time to time. This will keep you from drifting away into a sidepath. To write a good working thesis, use the following guidelines.

CLEARLY STATE AN OPINION

Tell your reader not just your topic but where you stand on it. Take note of the bumper sticker that reads, "I don't care who's on board, what you love, who you brake for, or what you'd rather be doing." If you decided to tell your readers that even a factory job can be a learning experience, the first two working theses below wouldn't express your opinion on the topic:

> **Weak:** Some people have different ideas about whether it's a good thing to work in a factory for the summer. I'm going to look at both sides of this issue. (The reader can't tell what point the writer intends to make.)

> **Weak:** I want to say what I think about working in a factory for the summer. (This apparent attempt at firmness falls flat. The reader doesn't know what the writer's opinion is. You're not writing a whodunit. State your viewpoint here, not later.)

> **Improved:** By working in a factory during the summer, I learned to respect the honest factory worker, man or woman. (Readers know the writer's opinion. They expect the writer to support it with reasons in the essay.)

PICK ONLY ONE MAIN IDEA

Many writers try to narrow their topic, but they don't go far enough. They may limit the topic to two ideas, but each one heads in a different direction. If you encounter this problem, pick one of your ideas, and put the other aside to develop in another essay.

> **Weak:** Kids with mental disabilities ought to be treated with friendship; along with this they should be given projects they can succeed at. (This thesis has two main ideas—friendly treatment of youngsters with mental disabilities and worthwhile projects. Each one calls for different supporting evidence.)
>
> **Improved:** To help children with mental disabilities relate to peers and adults better, they should be taught to care for farm animals. (This essay will show how children with mental disabilities learn to nurture farm animals.)

Keeping your working thesis down to one sentence will help avoid the two-idea problem.

TAKE AN ORIGINAL APPROACH TO YOUR TOPIC

Before you develop a topic, ask yourself whether you have taken an especially interesting or unpredictable approach. Have you had a quirky or unusual experience with the topic that would draw your readers' interest? Avoid bland or overused treatments like the following:

> **Weak:** Criminals ought to be locked up and the key thrown away. (This essay is likely to be filled with tired slogans about punishing burglars and murderers.)
>
> **Weak:** My used car often breaks down. (While the writer might include some horrifying examples of hair-raising breakdowns, the topic is fairly humdrum.)
>
> **Weak:** My girl (or boy) friend is my best pal. (This approach may meander aimlessly among obvious generalities.)

If you write about yourself, think of ways to broaden the paper's appeal. Help your readers put themselves in your place or learn something new about the subject. Take a new or debatable approach to your topic.

LIMIT YOUR THESIS TO PART OF A LARGER TOPIC

When you begin to draft your essay, remember that it will be quite brief, often no more than 500 or 600 words. In four to six paragraphs, you can't handle ways of becoming wealthy by investing in the stock market. Nor can you deal adequately with the causes of World War II in a page or two. Limit yourself to an important part of your chosen topic.

Weak: Medical science can enrich our lives. (This topic could hardly be handled well in a book, let alone a two- or three-page paper.)

Improved: To improve her mobility, Aunt Susan had her hip replaced. (This narrowed topic could be covered in a short cause-and-effect essay.)

Weak: Communications at this school are terrible and ought to be improved. (An essay dealing with communications at even a small school would involve the telephone system, the school newspaper, class handouts, the classroom delivery of professors, and a number of other ways of exchanging information. Thus, the thesis is too broad for a brief essay.)

Improved: To help students get assignments, turn in papers, and take tests, this school should assign them Internet mailboxes. (This thesis limits the problems it would solve and proposes a single, clearly limited solution. Therefore, a student could cover it adequately in a 400- to 600-word essay.)

Weak: If you're bored with your present job, start your own business. (This topic has appeal, but it is too general and unfocused, without regard to its audience.)

Improved: The businesses most needed in the renovated Midtown section are a coffeehouse, a dollar bargain store, and a movie multi-theater. (This thesis is specifically defined.)

BE SPECIFIC

Try to avoid vague, often emotional words in your thesis, such as *big, good, better, awful, terrible,* or *bad.* It's fine to make value judgments in your theses if you clearly spell out the standards for your judgments.

Weak: People who include seafood in their diets often make a bad choice.(It's hard to tell what kind of seafood, who has chosen it, or why.)

Improved: Tuna is not as heart-healthy as we thought, especially when diners flavor it with mayo and other high-fat dressings. (This spells out the seafood choice and the conditions that make tuna high fat rather than low fat.)

Weak: Building your own house can be an exciting learning experience.(The writer doesn't make clear whether the learning experience is positive or negative.)

Improved: Building your own house can save the owner up to 50 percent of the cost of buying one already built. (Sets up an essay detailing the savings.)

STATE YOUR THESIS NEAR THE BEGINNING OF YOUR ESSAY

You owe it to your readers to tell them your topic and attitude at the outset of your paper. Don't confuse them or make them guess. While professional writers sometimes imply their theses, tell your readers early, in the first paragraph (until you sell your first piece of writing). Once you have mastered the ways of putting together and stating a thesis, move on to creating a plan for your essay.

Exercise D. Creating Thesis Statements

Decide whether each of the following thesis statements is weak or adequate. If you decide a statement is weak, show how it can be improved.

1. I think that *Forrest Gump* is a really super movie with an inspiring messáge for everyone.
2. Which is the best place to buy a computer, at a store or through mail order?
3. Some people think that women in the military should not be exposed to combat.
4. My paper will show you the best way to register for classes.
5. Being forced to write a satisfactory essay before being allowed to graduate is a terrible imposition on students.
6. To provide individual attention to public school children, authorities should enact Deborah Meier's 20-20 vision: 20 students per class, 20 teachers per school.
7. In order to renew their drivers' licenses, residents of Florida who are over 75 should be required to pass a physical exam.
8. It's great to be able to talk things over with your parents.
9. To provide troops with appetizing meals in the field, the military should outfit kitchens on wheels to serve hamburgers, hot dogs, pizzas, and other short orders.
10. A good father ought to share parenting responsibilities with his wife.

Exercise E. Writing a Plan

Look over the thesis statements you wrote for Exercise A. Write a plan for each thesis statement. You may state your plan after the thesis statement or make it part of your thesis. Then label the thesis and plan separately.

CREATING A PLAN FOR DEVELOPING YOUR ESSAY

As already indicated, a good thesis needs a clear topic, purpose, and focus. Along with the thesis, you'll need a plan to develop your essay. Think of a plan as a clearly marked road map to get you from Paducah to Columbus. Your plan often grows out of your early listing or clustering. Suppose, for example, that you have chosen to describe the people who take part in hot air balloon contests. You have written a lead-in: "While this fraternity of free spirits might appear ordinary in person, they show their flashy gypsy colors in the flamboyant balloons they fly." (A lead-in attracts your readers' interest to your topic and launches your introductory paragraph.)

You have focused on a topic (hot air balloonists) and a purpose (balloons reveal their owners' personalities). However, your reader can't tell from your thesis why pilots fly hot air balloons or what points your essay will cover. You need to focus on a thesis, perhaps on the ways balloonists support themselves. Moreover, by writing an essay plan, you will tell your reader how you intend to develop your essay. You will also give yourself a handy reference point to keep you on track. In the following examples, the essay plan is underlined.

Many balloonists are so swept away that they make the sport a full-time passion. Many give rides to support themselves, run off-shoot businesses, or work where they can leave their jobs long enough to attend balloon races.

Helped by your essay plan, the reader knows you will talk about the work lives of balloonists: they give rides, run off-shoot businesses (like manufacturing, selling, or repairing balloons), or work close enough to attend week-long and weekend races. While the essay plan sometimes comes after the thesis, it is sometimes combined with it, as in these examples:

The information highway will change your life through video conferencing, home shopping, and video on demand. (The three items in this list prepare your reader for paragraphs on each one.)

Fire ants are extremely destructive because they crowd out other insects and animals, make farm land unplowable, and even chew through electric cables. (These three items prepare your reader for paragraphs on each one in the body of your essay.)

Along with telling your readers how you intend to develop your essay, the plan guides you in arranging the body of your paper by telling how ideas will flow from one to the other in the essay. You will probably want to write a body paragraph for each idea in your plan (see Chapter 1 for pointers on writing body paragraphs). The plan will help you limit your approach to those ideas you can cover fully in a 400- to 600-word essay. In writing your thesis and plan, be careful to blend them smoothly to avoid awkward transitions.

> **Weak:** *The Bridges of Madison County* succeeded at the box office for the following three reasons. It had a well-written screenplay, deft direction, and accomplished acting. (The list of reasons is brief; thus, saying "for the following three reasons" adds nothing.

> **Improved:** Its well-written screenplay, deft direction, and accomplished acting combined to bring *The Bridges of Madison County* success at the box office.

At this point in the development of your paper, you have prewritten and preplanned it. You have found (or been assigned) a topic, for which you have created a purpose and focus. You have prewritten, perhaps using listing, clustering, or freewriting. Based on this preliminary work, you have designed a thesis and plan. Now you are ready to draft your paper, to get your ideas down on paper in organized form.

Exercise F. Locating the Thesis and Essay Plan

Find the thesis and essay plan in the following sentences by underlining the plan.

1. Students should all use NerdWare for Windows because it helps them to persuade others more easily, improve their school performance, and enrich their conversational skills.

2. To make Christmas happy and hassle free, divide the duties among friends and relatives, do what you really like, and keep physically fit.

3. A recent revival of *West Side Story* succeeded because of the exuberance of its dancing, its treatment of street gangs, and the vividness of its comic moments.

4. Soap operas have managed to boost their ratings through the use of unusual story lines, social relevance, and viewer nostalgia.

5. Giant squids interest marine biologists because no one knows where they live, they have given rise to stories about sea monsters for centuries, and new submarines will help scientists capture the giants on film.

6. Grant's tomb in New York should be left alone because he was not from there, he had a bad reputation, and he revealed a heart of gold.

7. Five million children will attend 8,500 camps in the United States this summer to improve their ability in sports, become more sociable, and lose weight.

8. The prices of bottled mineral and spring water depend largely on bottle shapes, the distances the bottles travel, and the health claims they make.

9. Scientists claim that the earth needs protection against asteroids because the dinosaurs were wiped out by the impact of a comet, the earth is a large target, and a swirl of asteroids and comets surrounds the earth.

10. Smaller classes in the schools let teachers devote more time to their lessons, help them follow their students' progress more closely, and lead to better communication with parents.

DRAFTING YOUR ESSAY

Once you have completed your prewriting and pre-planning, draft your essay. All essays have three parts: an introduction, a body, and a conclusion. (Chapter 1 contained a discussion of the middle part of your paper—body paragraphs.) When drafting your essay, include your thesis and essay plan in the first paragraph of your essay.

LEAD-INS

To interest your reader in your topic and purpose, begin your introduction with a **lead-in.** Your thesis and plan usually follow your lead-in. Your brief lead-in should intrigue and attract your reader. Here are some types of lead-ins:

An anecdote:

For five years Linda Stillman's eyes and ears functioned for those of Michelle Smithdas, a deaf-blind woman. At age 36, Michelle had enrolled in the master's program at Columbia University's Teachers College in New York City. Linda volunteered to become Michelle's "miracle worker."

A set of statistics:

My newspaper office recently became part of the Internet, a computer network that links some 25 million people in 140 countries.

A question:

After hanging up on an annoying phone call, I said to my spouse, "Honey, do you remember when the ringing of a phone didn't make us cringe? When even wrong numbers were fun?"

A quotation:

Last October Senator Daniel Moynihan (D-New York) held a Finance Committee hearing on social behavior and health care costs. Moynihan cited the explosion of illegitimacy—currently five times what it was thirty years ago. "Now then," Moynihan asked, "what are we going to do?"

A joke:

A grasshopper walks into a bar. The bartender looks at him and says, "Hey, they named a drink about you!" "Really?" replies the grasshopper. "There's a drink named Stan?"

A little-known fact:

Editor H. L. Mencken traced the word *southpaw* to Chicago sportswriters in the late nineteenth century. They used it while writing about the city's west-side ballpark. Pitchers faced west into the setting sun, so that their left arms were to the south.

INTRODUCTION

When writing an **introduction,** keep these guidelines in mind:

- **Create a good first impression.** Like meeting a person for the first time, your readers will want to keep reading—or stop—on the basis of your first paragraph.
- **Link your lead-in to your topic.** The grasshopper joke might lead to a paper on social drinking, whereas the story about southpaws could connect with an essay on sports jargon.
- **Keep your lead-in short.** Don't string out your appetizer; you want to move your reader to your main course: the body of your essay.

CONCLUSIONS

After finishing the body of your essay, write a conclusion. For this final paragraph, consider these possibilities:

Sum up your main points:

As results of new medical studies come in, women will have an easier time deciding whether to take hormone supplements. In the meantime, a woman should pay lifelong attention to her hormones, raise questions with her doctor, and get the exercise and nutrition that will keep her fit.

Suggest taking action:

Why would anyone want to be second or third or tenth? Why not at least try to realize your dream, what deep down you would truly love to achieve?

State a moral:

Plato believed such small beauties were a privilege of nature. I know that by spending a few dollars on flowers each week, I make my spouse smile; I smile too.

Strike a note of hope or despair:

For parenting to be joyless is tragic. My simple wish is that parents have fun with their kids.

GUIDELINES FOR DRAFTING YOUR ESSAY
SCHEDULE YOUR WRITING

Give yourself enough time to write, rewrite, and polish your essay. Knowing your paper is not due until 9:00 Friday, next week, or whenever takes the pressure off your first draft. The prewriting exercises suggested earlier in the chapter will help start the creative process. If you still have trouble getting started, try some tricks. Talk over your topic with a friend or classmate; sometimes, they will have ideas you can work into your paper.

REMIND YOURSELF THAT YOUR DRAFTS ARE DISPOSABLE

If you don't like them, tear them up and throw them away. Pretend your essay is a letter, addressing it to an absent friend or relative. Once you've written it, you can reshape it in essay form. Then write the easiest part first, promise yourself a reward after fifteen minutes of writing, or dictate it into a cassette recorder. To reassure yourself that you don't need to write deathless prose, read some of the first drafts included in later chapters in this book. Give yourself permission to write garbage.

PLAN YOUR FORMATTING

When you put pen to paper, write on only one side of lined paper and leave wide margins. If you need space to write in new thoughts or rewrite, double space your drafts. However, double spacing may fool you into believing you've written more than you actually have. A single-spaced essay also keeps your ideas closer together, helping you keep your eye on your earlier plan or design. Invent some symbols to help you along the way, starring words you've guessed at (*), underlining ideas that need support, putting a checkmark in the margin beside ideas that seem fuzzy or poorly stated. Leave blanks in your essay to fill in later.

USE A COMPUTER WITH A WORD-PROCESSING PROGRAM

You can write your first draft faster on a computer than you can write it by hand. (If you don't type well or at all, consider scheduling time in your school's computer lab or attending workshops for students who need these skills.) The computer also lets you store your prewriting, notes, or good ideas until you need them. You can also add, delete, copy, and move parts of your text easily without rewriting the entire draft. If you can't spell a word or think of a synonym, the program's dictionary and thesaurus are available by pressing a couple of keys or clicking your mouse. Save your drafts regularly, and print out your drafts as a record in case your computer crashes or just to read over if your inspiration weakens. When you have a draft, you've made progress. However, you aren't finished until you revise and proofread your essay.

REVISING YOUR WRITING

If you planned your writing in advance, set your writing aside for awhile before attempting to revise it. Revision means more than minor tinkering. As you read over your draft, new ideas will occur to you, as well as new ways of arranging them. When you change later ideas, look back at the earlier parts of your paper, changing them too, if necessary. You may even need to start over.

Although we've taken up revision after drafting, you'll be changing and developing your ideas from the moment you choose—or are assigned—your topic. You'll rethink your approach in your head, in conversations with others, and as you make notes. At times, you'll rewrite here or there randomly; at others, you'll concentrate on a "chunk" of prose. You may even put part of your paper aside to work on another part, only to think of new ideas to use elsewhere.

Revision can happen at any time—in other words, it is difficult to avoid. You'll guess at the best words, sometimes crossing out, sometimes writing in. Sometimes you'll add complete sentences or move sections from place to place. Revision may happen randomly, or you may plan it carefully.

As in your drafting, use a computerized word processor to revise. Most writers like working with a printed copy of their work while keeping the draft on-screen for changes. You may like splitting the screen into two windows, helping you look back at the first paragraph as you change later ones. If you repeated the same word too often, boring your reader, you can replace it easily with your word processor's thesaurus.

When you revise, don't try to fix everything in one or two passes. Break the job into parts. Here's a process that may work for you:

1. Consider topic, purpose, and audience.
2. Consider thesis, plan, and organization.
3. Consider ideas and evidence.
4. Consider style and clarity.
5. Consider grammar, punctuation, and spelling.

To help you revise, apply the following checklist to your writing:

1. How is my treatment important to both my reader(s) and to me? Have I kept my readers in mind, even formed a mental picture of them as I wrote?
2. Which of my readers' needs have I met? To educate, inform, persuade, or amuse?
3. Have I written or implied a clear, focused thesis early in the paper, usually in the introductory paragraph?
4. Have the paragraphs in the body of my paper grown directly out of my thesis?
5. Do each of the body paragraphs follow a logical order, such as order of importance?
6. Do topic sentences at or near the beginning of each paragraph sum up each paragraph's main idea?
7. Have I developed each paragraph's main idea with two or three supporting examples or details?
8. Are all the sentences in my paper clear and understandable, especially when read aloud?
9. Have I chosen the most accurate, clearest words to express my ideas?

PROOFREADING

Once you've finished your draft, you've almost met your readers' expectations. However, one set of tasks remains: straightening out your paper's grammar, mechanics, punctuation, and spelling. Keep your readers' attention and trust by making sure you don't distract them with errors. To polish your paper, consider the following tips.

LOOK FOR ONE TYPE OF PROBLEM AT A TIME

Rather than trying to find all your errors in one reading, make a mental check-list, looking first for spelling problems and typos, then punctuation, and then grammar. You can also use your computer's grammar checker, usually located in the "Tools" menu of the word-processing program. If necessary, get some help with this step from your college's writing lab.

LIST COMMON PROBLEMS YOUR INSTRUCTORS HAVE FOUND BEFORE IN YOUR OWN WRITING

If skilled readers have found problems in your writing before—for example, subject–verb agreement errors or tense problems—pay close attention to these areas. Look for confusions between look-alike and sound-alike words, such as its/it's, there/they're/their, and who's/whose. Most grammar handbooks have lists of these easily confused words.

USE SOME TRICKS TO FIND PROBLEMS

Read your draft aloud, have a friend or classmate do this, or record yourself reading it with a cassette player and then listen to it. If you have trouble reading or understanding your prose, move the language around so it sounds clearer. Some people like to read their papers backwards, a sentence at a time, so their minds won't silently fill in missing words or meanings.

PREPARE A CLEAN, READABLE DRAFT

Be sure to follow your instructor's formatting instructions: Do you need a title page? Should the paper be single or double spaced? Numbered pages? Should your name appear on every page? If your syllabus doesn't tell you, be sure to ask. If you use a typewriter or dot-matrix printer, put in a fresh ribbon. If possible, print your drafts with a laser printer for professional-looking papers.

Exercise G. Proofreading

The following selection includes many errors of grammar, spelling, mechanics, and punctuation. Correct them.

Jist imajine: no jangly cions in your pants,

no crinkld bills in yur wallet. To by a soda,

you simly insret somethin called a stored

valu crad into teh vening mashine. A test

disply above the slot were you once droped

quaters tells you whow much are bein de-

duced and the reminaing vale on the

card.you pul out the sam card to bard a bus,

do your landray, or buy a nwspepper. You ad

value to the card buy inseting it in a Au-

tomadic Teler Machne. You'll even be able to

relode the card over an spetial tellephone—

elimating at last the magor encumbance of

hume binking: the inabilty to draw csah.

once e-muney is excepted as universal as

grenbacks, dont be suprised if a disheveled

mna on the stret stebs up to you and says,

Bother, can you spar a liddle stored valu?"

CHAPTER THREE

Description

You will often write brief descriptions in a sentence or two. At other times, you will write paragraphs or complete essays filled with description. You may want to describe objectively to show what anyone might see. Depending on your purposes, however, you might also want to convey an attitude or set of feelings. The following example combines **subjective** values with **objective** details to describe a person's house and appearance:

Objective description —

Subjective description —

Objective description —

> The Randy Weaver who answers the doorbell of the two-story house with the flaking brown paint and squeaky front door on a corner lot in Grand Junction, Iowa (pop. 880), is dwarfed by his own legend. He is about 5 feet 7 inches, with neatly styled salt-and-pepper hair. He wears a pressed pair of jeans, black T-shirt, and clean white socks.

Anyone reading this could visualize Randy Weaver's house and person **objectively** as the writer does. The writer used unbiased terms to describe the house, such as *flaking brown paint* and *squeaky front door*. The writer also describes Randy objectively with terms like *5 feet 7 inches* and *neatly styled salt-and-pepper hair*. However, the words *dwarfed by his own legend* bring in **subjective** feelings and personal judgment. Readers may or may not agree with the writer. In your own writing, you will often describe people and objects in clear, unbiased detail. At the same time, however, your own feelings and values will sometimes color these descriptions. When writing descriptively, keep the following guidelines in mind.

DECIDE ON YOUR PURPOSE

You are not only helping your reader visualize a place, object, or person. You may also be conveying an attitude, persuading your reader to take some action, or offering an explanation. Here are two descriptions of the same town, one objective and the other filled with emotion:

Objective ⟶ In April, Needles settles into silence, punctuated by the roar of tractor-trailers along the highway. "This is a place for people who are running from something," says

Value judgment ⟶ Bruce Weekely, the former police chief.

You must think through your purpose, whether it's to see like a camera or pronounce judgment, or both.

PICK DETAILS THAT SUPPORT YOUR PURPOSE

Many of your descriptions will seek to create an overriding impression, a single conclusion that all the details must fit exactly. For example, if you were describing your favorite car, you'd stress its comfort and appearance, not the fact that its tires often went flat or that its balky carburetor sometimes caused it to stall. In the following ad copy, a writer lists details that support closely linked impressions:

European styling combines with stainless-steel technology to make Steelex Frames one of the lightest frames around. They're ultra light and thin, but extremely durable.

The writer's purpose could be summed up in the words "Strong as Steel . . . Light as a Feather." He said nothing about cost or availability—details that are trivial or unrelated to the purpose. In your own writing, include only the facts or examples that are connected to your purpose. Leave out the details that distract your reader or seem unimportant.

USE CLEAR, SPECIFIC DETAILS

When you present a description to readers, give readers vivid images rather than a vague, misty impression. If, for example, you were describing people who were down on their luck, you would go beyond words like *down-and-out drifter* or *homeless, wandering bum*. You might, instead, picture one of them as a 59-year-old retired welder with a long, white beard and trembling hands, who lives on Social Security and drinks a bottle of 151-proof Baccardi a day.

Similarly, to describe a favorite vacation hideaway, you would say more than

"That's what a vacation was always meant to be." Rather, you'd point out its giant iguanas, three species of endangered sea turtles, 200-foot sea cliffs, and the largest marine-originated cave system in the world. Similarly, a church descriptively called a group of singers their "prison quartet: behind a few bars and always looking for the key." In your descriptions, be specific and detailed.

PLACE DETAILS IN ORDER

Descriptions often follow organizing patterns. They may move clockwise around an area, from bottom to top or top to bottom, from here to there, from one side to another, or from beginning to end. When describing a person, for example, choose the most striking detail of his or her appearance. Then move up or down from there. For example, a writer emphasizes the face in her description of Angel Corella, a 19-year-old ballet dancer from Spain: "As he reaches down to scoop up the white peonies flung to him, his face is illuminated by a smile, and his dark eyes gleam." Or, in another example, rather than saying the outdoor terrace was "incredibly striking," the writer used a memorable image: "A single palm tree rises in the patio against the blue sky of tropical paradise. But there's a snake in this garden, a red spiral staircase coiling up behind the palm as if to pluck something from its fronds." This description moves from below in an upward movement. As you appeal to your readers' senses, move logically to make sure your readers can follow your choice of details.

READINGS

Chapter 1 showed how topic sentences sum up the main idea in a paragraph. Details develop this main idea or topic sentence. In your descriptive paragraphs, hold your readers' interests by supporting a clear purpose with vivid, memorable details, as in the following example:

PRECIOUS DANGERS

Melissa Holbrook Pierson

Topic sentence ⟶ At precisely this moment someone, somewhere, is getting ready to ride. The motorcycle stands in the cool,

Details setting: feeling, sight, smells ⟶ dark garage, the air smells of gas and grease. The rider approaches from outside. The light goes on. A flame, everlasting, seems to rise on a piece of chrome. The rider zips leather sleeves down tight on the forearms, pulls the helmet on, buckles the chin strap. Leather

Details action in order ⟶ gloves with studded palms go on last. The key is slipped into the ignition at the top of the steering head. Then the rider mounts, swinging a leg over the seat.

In her description of a motorcycle rider, Pierson first describes the setting: the feel, look, and smells of a garage. It feels "cool" and looks "dark." The air "smells of gas and grease." Then she describes the rider's actions, each one neatly and briefly, in time order:

- The rider first "approaches."
- Then she "zips" her sleeves,
- "pulls" on her helmet,
- "buckles" the chin strap,
- "puts on" leather gloves,
- "slips" in the ignition key, and
- "mounts" the motorcycle.

Chapter 2 described how a **thesis** sums up the main idea for an entire essay, much as a **topic sentence** sums up the main idea in a paragraph. In the following descriptive essay, the title and then the thesis *seem* to sum up the writer's main idea, but they do not. After describing himself—as well as strike-bound baseball—in the essay, Mr. Behn develops his implied three-part thesis: ways the team owners could make money by using replacement players. To conclude, Behn sums up with a final bit of whimsy.

THE NEXT TED WILLIAMS? I'M YOUR MAN

Robert D. Behn

Major League Baseball started spring training this week with "replacement players." But who qualifies? Either a former major leaguer—someone who is over the hill—or someone who will never make the majors.

Thesis: writer's qualifications as "player" ➤ That's me! I am both over the hill and guaranteed never to make the big time. So I am doubly qualified.

Now I'm waiting for my offers. After all, the salary is *Details "salary" in dollars* ➤ the usual major-league minimum: $115,000 for the season. And if they settle the strike before the end of the season, I'll get $20,000 in termination pay.

Topic sentence as question: why should owners hire him? ➤ But who will come out to see me—or any other replacement player? If the fans want to see minor leaguers, they can go to see minor leaguers, they can go to a minor league ball park. If they want to watch over-the-hill ball, they can just stop by their hometown field. Even at

<table>
<tr><td>First answer: charge replacement players for playing ⟶</td><td>only $115,000 per player, the owners are going to lose money. But why pay for replacement players at all? After all, they charge middle-aged guys like me several thousand dollars for a week at fantasy camp. Just think of how much they could charge for the real thing.</td></tr>
<tr><td>Specific example: wearing Yankee uniform in game ⟶</td><td>The Yankees could easily command five-figure fees for a 10-day West Coast trip. And imagine how high the bidding would go to put on the pinstripes in Yankee Stadium for a single game against the Red Sox.</td></tr>
<tr><td>Second, detailed answer: friends and relatives would watch ⟶</td><td>The crowds would come out, too. Friends and relatives would flood the ballparks to see their would-be heroes perform. Wouldn't you turn out to see your college roommate, your neighbor, or your boss fulfill that childhood dream of replacing Don Mattingly at first base?</td></tr>
<tr><td>Extends second answer: wife and daughter would play ⟶</td><td>And how about your wife or daughter? How much would you pay to watch her play a position long denied her? With this simple step, the major-league owners could burnish their badly tarnished image.</td></tr>
<tr><td>Third answer: sell rights to play, with specific examples ⟶</td><td>But what if the owners are worried that no one will want to see such replacement players? Then make it a package deal. The Red Sox could not only sell the right to play Ted Williams's spot in left field; as part of the package they could also sell the replacements all the seats in section 30.</td></tr>
<tr><td>More specific examples: business incentives telling who, why, and where ⟶</td><td>High-tech corporations in Silicon Valley could buy a place for their CEOs on the roster of the Giants or the Athletics. Or a business could buy a roster position and award it to an employee as part of an incentive package. That would be more of a motivator than even a winter vacation in the Caribbean.</td></tr>
<tr><td>Returns to first answer with details: many former students will pay to watch ⟶</td><td>Obviously, the people with the most friends would be the ideal replacement players. That's what makes me ideal. I've been teaching for 22 years. Thousands of former students would pay real money to watch a ball roll between my legs.</td></tr>
<tr><td>Conclusion sums up: everyone wins from idea ⟶</td><td>So I've written John Harrington, CEO of the Red Sox, to offer my services. If he insists, he can certainly pay me $115,000. I'll bring out the fans. And I'll bring back the memories—of Bill Buckner.</td></tr>
</table>

The New York Times

Behn's essay describes both himself and a transformed game of baseball: moneymaking has completely replaced the game's sporting aspects. His essay pretends to begin with a two-part thesis: how the writer fits the mold of "replacement baseball player." Having established the essay's humorous tone, Behn then develops three reasons for owners to hire replacement players. In conclusion, he pretends to have applied for the job. To develop his essay, he uses numerous specific details to display his knowledge of both business and baseball, naming a number of famous players who supposedly cared more about playing than the money.

> *To develop your own descriptive writing, list details suggested by a topic or main idea, or freewrite sentences for five or ten minutes. Later on, you can draw on these ideas for a more sharply focused paragraph or essay.*

In the following excerpt, Marlon Brando's family problems contrast sharply with his long-time success as an actor. To emphasize this conclusion, the description focuses sharply on details that describe Brando's inability to understand—let alone carry out—the responsibilities of fatherhood.

Words to Define

saga: tale or story

autobiography: history of a life told by the author

offspring: child

dysfunctional: unable to carry out ordinary tasks

clan: closely related group, family

Prereading

1. To what extent do your own traits reflect your parents' child-rearing methods? Describe both the methods and your own traits.

2. If you know children of gifted or prominent parents, how would you describe their talents and shortcomings?

LOST HOPE

Al Prince and Jeffrey Ressner

While art often imitates life, it's unlikely a movie could ever be made of the Brando family saga, because it's too complex and twisted for any screenwriter to handle. Where to start? In Brando's recent autobiography, *Brando: Songs My Mother Taught Me*, he described his mother as "an off-the-shelf drunk" and his father as physically abusive. Where to end? The two-time Oscar winner (*On the Waterfront, The Godfather*) partly dedicated the book to "my children, who brought me up" yet he barely mentioned his 11 (at least) offspring by his three wives and numerous lovers. Christian, 36, once said of his dysfunctional clan, "My family's so weird and spaced out . . . I'd sit down at the table with all these strange people and say, 'Who are you?'" Brando alternately spoiled, ignored and bullied his children; as even he tearfully admitted at Christian's sentencing, "I think perhaps I failed as a father."

Time

Queries for Understanding

1. How were Brando's parents flawed?
2. What information is included on Brando's quality as an actor, and why?
3. How many children has Brando had with how many wives and lovers?
4. Why do the writers include this information?

Queries on the Writer's Techniques

1. The writers quote first from Brando's autobiography, then from his testimony at his son's trial. Why do they quote in this order?
2. Brando's son Christian was sentenced to prison for killing his sister's lover. What effect on the reader do the writers hope Christian's comments on his relatives will make?
3. Why do the writers conclude with Brando's admission of failure regarding one child?

Writing Topics

1. Describe the values that every good parent should have, drawing on your knowledge of people you know well for your supporting details.
2. Describe the standards by which you yourself could be considered a good parent.

The following obituary of Britain's last surviving hangman emphasizes the horror of the man's actions, while contrasting the details of his macabre profession with the ordinariness with which he treated it.

Words to Define

execution: putting to death

posthumously: after one's death

reintroduction: bringing back

qualms: second thoughts, guilt feelings

operational: actually working

souvenirs: remembrances, tokens

Prereading

1. What jobs now considered distasteful have disappeared as a result of changes in society?

2. Describe some ways of changing people's behavior other than punishment.

BRITAIN'S LAST SURVIVING HANGMAN DIES

Britain's last surviving hangman, who took part in the execution of 25 people—including one who was posthumously pardoned—is dead. Sydney Dernley, 73, died Tuesday of a heart attack at home in Mansfield, 120 miles north of London, his family said. "He was a craftsman, like a carpenter, if you like. He took a pride in his job, but he wasn't a callous man. Nobody suffered; he was very quick," his 73-year-old widow, Joyce Dernley, told reporters. Dernley was assistant to chief executioner Albert Pierrepoint, who hanged 450 people and died in a nursing home in 1992 at age 87.

Britain abolished the death penalty in 1969. Pierrepoint came to believe that capital punishment was useless as a crime deterrent and campaigned against calls for reintroduction. But Dernley, his assistant from 1948 to 1953, kept his belief in it. Dernley continued to maintain that Timothy Evans, whom he helped Pierrepoint hang in 1950, was guilty of wife murder even after Evans was granted a posthumous pardon. "He never had any qualms about hangings," Joyce Dernley said.

Dernley was particularly proud of carrying out, with Pierrepoint, the fastest hanging on record. They hanged James Inglis in seven seconds from his arrival at the gallows to the trapdoor opening. Inglis was convicted of murdering a prostitute.

The *Daily Telegraph* said Dernley kept a fully operational gallows in the cellar of his home plus souvenirs including ropes, straps used to bind the hands and feet of the condemned, and the hood placed over their heads. In his 1989 book, *The Hangman's Tale*, Dernley said he decided at age 11 he wanted to be a hangman.

The Associated Press

Queries for Understanding

1. Sum up the selection's main idea.

2. What contrast does the selection draw between Dernley and Chief Executioner Albert Pierrepoint?

3. What record was Dernley particularly proud of?

4. For how long had Dernley held his career goal? What evidence of it did he keep in his home?

Queries on the Writer's Techniques

1. The writer describes Dernley's quickest hanging. How might this description affect the reader?

2. In the writer's quote of Dernley's wife, which of his personal qualities does she stress? Does the quote increase our admiration or disgust (or both?

3. The selection gives numbers (ages, numbers of victims, time, and so on). Do these numbers increase our admiration or horror of Dernley and the death penalty?

4. The selection includes a key irony (contrast between apparent and intended meanings): a career spent putting people to death. What other ironies does the selection include?

Writing Topics

1. Trace your own plans for a career to their beginnings, linking them to your personality traits.

2. Describe the job or career of a close friend or relative, emphasizing ways in which their actions, dress, or other evidence reveal this career.

The following selection discusses video-on-demand. Although video-on-demand is difficult to include on the information highway, it may be one of the highway's most talked-about features.

Words to Define

technologically: resulting from scientific progress

intervals: regular periods of time

electronically: working by the movement of electrons

Prereading

1. If video-on-demand were available to you, how, why, and when would you make use of it?

2. Describe the electronic aids or tools that you find most useful, and why.

VIDEO-ON-DEMAND

Video-on-demand is the most talked-about service on the information highway, and one of the most difficult to pull off technologically. In its simplest version, video-on-demand would be a more advanced form of the pay-per-view service now available to most cable-TV subscribers. The same movie would be sent to different channels at intervals staggered a few minutes apart. For example, you might be able to watch *The Terminator* starting at 10, 10:20, 10:40 or 11.

Eventually, true video-on-demand would be like having a video library in your basement: you'd be able to electronically browse through a list of movies, choose one, then start the flick whenever you wanted. You could even press "pause."

Popular Science, May 1994

Queries for Understanding

1. Describe pay-per-view as it presently exists.
2. How would video-on-demand differ from pay-per-view?
3. What benefits would users gain from video-on-demand?

Queries on the Writer's Techniques

1. The selection mentions both positive and negative aspects of video-on-demand. Does it balance them, or does it lean strongly one way?
2. What details of video-on-demand describe how it would work?
3. What actions would users of video-on-demand take to operate the service?

Writing Topics

1. What kinds of people would be most likely to find video-on-demand attractive?
2. Describe the reasons why you would subscribe to video-on-demand.

The following selection describes how, in adulthood, an African-American woman believes her father's virtues outweigh his character flaws.

Words to Define

zoot suit: a man's suit popular in the late 1940s, with full-legged trousers and a coat with wide lapels and heavily padded shoulders

cashmere: a fine wool from goats

equivalent: in a one-to-one linkage

berated: criticized, attacked

restriction: limitation on movements

Prereading

1. What person from an older generation has influenced you or someone you know?

MY FATHER, SARGE, A LIVING MEMORY

Student Essay (Annita)

At age 66, Horace Phillips was very tall and lean. One would recognize him a mile away by the gangster-style hats he wore. Under them sprouted the longest eyelashes surrounding the prettiest brown eyes ever seen on an older man. With his large nose and small ears, he smelled trouble and heard silence. When the kids fell quiet, this signaled instant investigation, as far as he was concerned. Moreover, like Will Rogers, he never met a stranger. His friendly smile instantly broke the ice. A very sexy dresser, he wore zoot suits, with cufflinks on his shirts. In cold weather, he'd wear a cashmere coat, leather gloves, and a pair of galoshes.

Everyone liked Sarge. The neighborhood kids swarmed around his house, and ladies whispered about their boyfriends in his ear; the fellows all sought his advice for making women happy. When his kids were young, they always had sleepovers because everyone enjoyed his humor. He would amaze the children by cooking food and serving it in pyramids. When his oldest son needed spending money for a field trip, Sarge suggested holding a waist party: charging the dollar equivalent of one's waist size as an admission fee. His son raised more than enough money.

He knew his children better than they knew themselves. If one of his kids came home and brought unfinished homework from school, he'd ask if they needed something, some help, perhaps. If an errand needed running, he would say to his wife, "Someone wants to go somewhere" when no one had said a word. If his daughter needed to go to the store, he gave her the exact change and told her to come back right away. He knew that if he didn't warn her, she'd spend the extra money on her friends.

With all his likability, Sarge had his flaws. He hated to be wrong, and he made rigid rules. He allowed no outsiders in the house, no going outside if parents were away from home. For example, one night when Sarge passed his house, his daughter was talking to someone on the porch, a girl named Dolores, with her back turned. She wore a blue jean jacket with the collar turned up, making her look like a boy. When Sarge came home later, he berated his daughter for flirting with a boy. When she protested, he refused to believe her, even demanding, "Are you telling me I'm wrong?" When she said yes, he put her on restriction for talking back. His daughter felt deeply hurt by his refusal to accept the truth from her.

Despite his occasional bull-headedness, he was a good father. On balance, his children treasured their childhoods and the lifetime lessons their father taught them.

Queries for Understanding

1. What aspects of her father's appearance does the writer stress, and why?
2. What makes Sarge so likable to both family and others?

3. How does Sarge reveal his interest in his children?

4. What negative aspects of her father's character does the writer note?

Queries on the Writer's Techniques

1. To what extent does the writer describe her father with concrete, visual detail?

2. Why does the writer deal with outsiders' impressions of her father before dealing with his family relationships?

3. Does Sarge's "character flaw" have any positive aspects?

Writing Topics

1. In American society, what is—and what should be—the father's role in bringing up children?

2. In American society, is the influence of the family on children's values stronger or weaker than outside influences, such as the media, schools, and so on?

As described in the following selection, by looking closely at 10,000-year-old water, scientists have found that the world's most recent ice age was caused by global cooling, not by a local chill caused by the movement of glaciers.

Words to Define

unique: particular, one of a kind

prevalent: the most common or frequently found

calibrate: adjust or modify

physical properties: traits revealed at the lowest atomic level

millimeter: a unit of length about four one-hundredths of an inch

periodic: happening at regular intervals

Prereading

1. Describe a problem that you once solved inventively. What was the problem, and what approach did you take to solve it.

2. In your observations of nature, have you wondered how particular aspects came about as they did? Describe them and speculate how they might have evolved.

SCIENTISTS FIND THERMOMETER TO TAKE ICE AGE TEMPS

Canadian scientists have discovered a unique thermometer to calibrate air temperatures that were prevalent during the last ice age. Their measuring stick: 10,000-year-old water.

Researchers at the University of Waterloo and Queen's University looked at water trapped in clay that formed at the bottom of Lake Agassiz, a huge glacier-formed lake that between 11,500 and 7,700 years ago covered most of Manitoba as well as parts of Saskatchewan, Ontario, the Northwest Territories, North Dakota, and Minnesota.

The scientists drilled 0.6-inch-wide wells 99 feet into the ground at four locations in Manitoba and North Dakota. Then they looked at the isotopic-oxygen content in water in the deepest clays, which would have been laid down about 10,000 years ago.

Most water—99.8 percent—is formed with ^{16}O (oxygen-16). However, there are two slightly heavier forms (isotopes) of water that are found in the remaining 0.2 percent (^{16}O has eight protons and eight neutrons, while ^{18}O has nine of each.)

Measurements on the Greenland icecaps, as well as the physical properties of the isotopes, have shown that as the temperature goes down, less ^{18}O will be found in water.

When the scientists looked at the amount of ^{18}O found in water trapped in the clay, they discovered that it was nearly half as much as is found in present-day rain and snow, according to a paper in the journal *Science*.

C. Vicki Remenda, a professor of geology at Queen's University whose doctoral thesis was the basis for the article, said that the old water had remained trapped because the clay was so dense that the water's flow rate was only a few millimeters a year.

She added that the ^{18}O findings confirm the theory that periodic ice ages result from generally colder world climate, and not, as some scientists have suggested, from cold micro-climates created by the glaciers themselves as they advance from the north.

Daily Citizen-News

Queries for Understanding

1. What area in North America did what scientists decide to study, and why?
2. How was the water studied by the scientists especially odd?
3. The scientists in this study know that cold water contains a different kind of oxygen. How did this knowledge help them?
4. What did the scientists conclude about periodic ice ages?

Queries on the Writer's Techniques

1. How does the selection group the scientific study in four steps?
2. What facts does the selection include to explain the difference between kinds of water?

3. What facts link changes in water to changes in temperature?

4. For what reason does the "old water" remain trapped? Why does the selection include this reason?

Writing Topics

1. Describe a memorable snowstorm, flood, tornado, or heat wave.

2. What dangers would be present in your home or workplace during a flood, earthquake, or fire?

THE WRITING PROCESS

For his early draft of a descriptive essay, Randy, the author of the following selection, focused on memories of his 1974 914 Porsche.

STUDENT DESCRIPTION ESSAY: FIRST DRAFT
RENOVATING MY PORSCHE

The car in my neighbor's yard was the most beautiful thing I've ever seen. It was raining but the car was still beautiful. The rain ran down onto the hood and beaded up and ran down the sides to the end of the car. The car was a two seater, low to the ground with shiney chrome bumers and silver wheels. I loved it. There was a sign in the window it said for sale. It took awhile but I bought the car. We took off the targa top and took it for a ride. I didn't notice anything burt the smell of the car. I expected it to be the smell of leather but it was the smell of moldy car mats. I didn't mind. The car started good. It took off okay. It shifted good except for a little grinding. We sped away. The car ran real good like it was glued to the road even. It stopped on a dime. I really like driving it. It's in my garage now. I don't drive it much, but its a real classic.

After writing this initial draft of his descriptive essay, Randy began the revision process by considering the questions in the following sections.

REVISING THE FIRST DRAFT

1. What words in the draft make the topic interesting? What sentences are well written?

2. What is the draft's main idea? Which of the details support the main idea best?

3. Which part(s) of the descriptive essay do you think were hardest to write? Why?

4. If the writer had more time to write this descriptive essay, what part(s) would or should get the most attention?

Randy's responses to these questions help him mark up the early version of his essay, as follows:

Writer needs to describe setting: where he is

The car in my neighbor's yard was the most beautiful thing I've ever seen. It was raining but the car was still beautiful. The rain ran down onto the hood and beaded up and ran

Need specific detail describing and identifying the car, details of neighbor's yard

Begin new paragraph with description of car's details

down the sides to the end of the car. The car was a two seater, low to the ground with shiney chrome bumers and silver wheels. I loved it. There was a sign in the window it said for sale. It took awhile but I bought the car.

New paragraph on purchase of car: need details on time of year

We took off the targa top and took it for a ride. I didn't notice anything burt the smell of the

Place material in more logical order: use a separate paragraph for sitting in car, warming up its engine, smelling its interior and exhaust fumes. Then, put first part of drive in its own paragraph.

car. I expected it to be the smell of leather but it was the smell of moldy car mats. I didn't mind. The car started good. It took off okay. It shifted good except for a little grinding. We sped away. The car ran real good like it was glued to the road even. It stopped on a dime. I

Begin new paragraph here with details about drive: writer's thoughts, speed of car, car's handling and sound, kind of brakes, writer's feelings

Expand conclusion: where is writer now, and how does he imagine his car

really like driving it. It's in my garage now. I don't drive it much, but its a real classic.

Based on his responses to the questions and his markings on the first draft, Randy writes an improved second draft of his descriptive paper. However, his essay is not yet complete. He needs to proofread it, asking the next set of questions.

Proofreading Queries

1. Have I corrected grammatical problems such as noun/verb agreement?
2. Have I corrected the spelling, particularly with words that sound alike and look alike but are not spelled alike?
3. Have I corrected the punctuation, separating word groups to clarify meaning?

STUDENT DESCRIPTION ESSAY: SECOND DRAFT

Need past tense "looked"

As I (look) out of my bedroom window on a

set off long introductory phrase with comma after "day,"

cold rainy day I saw the most beautiful thing

sitting in the rain. It was a 1974 black 914

Porsche with a red pinstripe. It sat in front of

use possessive "neighbor's" — *Separate modifiers with a comma*

my (neighbors) wet muddy front yard under a

misspelling: replace with "beautiful"

maple tree. It was the most (beautifull) piece

Set off introductory subordinate clause with comma: car, . . .

of art work I had ever seen. I just sat there

Comma splice: replace comma with semicolon; then comma after well

and looked, well it was more like a stare. As I

sat there and stared at this car all of my

senses started to get mixed up. The first

thing I noticed was the rain running off the

Comma splice: replace comma with semicolon: roof; . . .

roof, then it ran down the front of the car

over the windshield and onto the hood. After

Set off introductory subordinate clause with comma: hood, . . .

it reached the hood it was hard to follow that

first rain drop I saw. The hood was beaded up

with a trillion other drops. The rain fell of ◄— misspelling: should be "off"

wrong word: should be "designated"

the car like each had a (designed path) to fol-

wrong verb tense: should be "looked"

low. They (look) like they were racing to the

end of the car. The end in this particular

Misspelling: should be "beginning"

model was almost the (beinging.) The car was

only a two seater that sat no more than 2 to

Noun-verb agreement problem: should be was ——— 3 inches off the ground. The chrome around

Misspelling: should be shiny

capitalize: "Mom's"

the bumpers were as (shinny) as (mom's)

good china. Even the trim around the doors

Misspelling: should be "magnificent"

and the windshield was (magnifcent.) The

need past tense verb "noticed"

other thing I (notice) about this car was the

wheels. The tires were supported by glisten-

ing silver mags with four lug nuts that held

the mags to the car. There was more shine

Misspelling: should be "dimes"

on this car than a ton of (times) at the

Misspelling: should be "Franklin"

should be past tense "noticed"

Misspelling: should be sign ——— (Fraklin) mint. The last thing I (notice) was

should be possessive "passenger's"

this small (sing) in the (passengers) side win-

write as quotation: "For Sale."

dow that read (for sale.) After noticing this,

misspelling: should be "lit"

my eyes (lid) up like a Christmas tree. At that

misspelling: should be "knew"

point, I (new) that this car was going to be

mine somehow and someway. When the

should be "express"

"pony (expressed") finally reached my house ◄— Set off introductory subordinate clause with a comma:

it was a sunny, bright day. I quickly took off

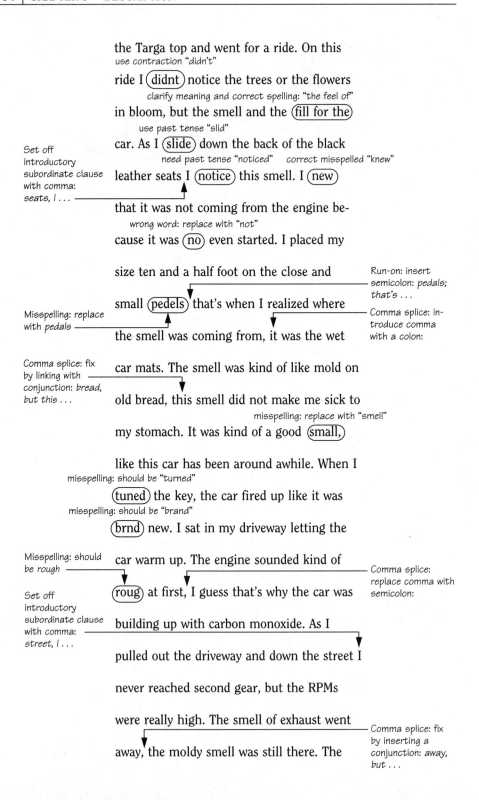

the Targa top and went for a ride. On this

use contraction "didn't"

ride I (didnt) notice the trees or the flowers

clarify meaning and correct spelling: "the feel of"

in bloom, but the smell and the (fill for the)

use past tense "slid"

car. As I (slide) down the back of the black

Set off introductory subordinate clause with comma: seats, I . . .

need past tense "noticed"   correct misspelled "knew"

leather seats I (notice) this smell. I (new)

that it was not coming from the engine be-

wrong word: replace with "not"

cause it was (no) even started. I placed my

size ten and a half foot on the close and

Run-on: insert semicolon: pedals; that's . . .

Misspelling: replace with pedals

small (pedels) that's when I realized where

Comma splice: introduce comma with a colon:

the smell was coming from, it was the wet

Comma splice: fix by linking with conjunction: bread, but this . . .

car mats. The smell was kind of like mold on

old bread, this smell did not make me sick to

misspelling: replace with "smell"

my stomach. It was kind of a good (small,)

like this car has been around awhile. When I

misspelling: should be "turned"

(tuned) the key, the car fired up like it was

misspelling: should be "brand"

(brnd) new. I sat in my driveway letting the

Misspelling: should be rough

car warm up. The engine sounded kind of

Set off introductory subordinate clause with comma: street, I . . .

Comma splice: replace comma with semicolon:

(roug) at first, I guess that's why the car was

building up with carbon monoxide. As I

pulled out the driveway and down the street I

never reached second gear, but the RPMs

were really high. The smell of exhaust went

Comma splice: fix by inserting a conjunction: away, but . . .

away, the moldy smell was still there. The

engine raced as we pulled up to a light

heading for a lonely back road. As the

misspelling: should be "red"

light turned from bright (reed) to a dull

— Set off introductory subordinate clause with a comma: *green, we . . .*

green we took off. When racing down this

back road, leading nowhere, I really started

misspelling: should be "appreciate"   *misspelling: should be "jamming"*

Misplaced modifier: clarify by adding *after I had been driving . . .*

to (apprecaite) this classic. I was (jaming)

awkward: replace with "except for"

through the gears nicely ~~for the exception of~~

a little grinding. After driving down this

tight, curvy back road, all of the smells went

— Fragment: connect with next sentence through *my mind was, . . .*

away. The only thing running through my

mind. Was "I wonder how fast I can get this

misspelling: should be "Grateful"

car to go" and some (Greatful) Dead tune

that I can't recall. The car felt like it was on

wrong tense: change to "reached"

air when the speedometer (reach) 85 MPH on

— Run-on: fix by inserting semicolon or period followed by capital: *It . . .*

Set off introductory subordinate clause with a comma: *turn, I . . .*

this bumpy straightaway, but it wasn't it was

still on the ground. As I entered a tight left-

should be past tense "dropped"

hand turn I (drop) the car from 5th to 4th

gear in a matter of seconds. The car felt

like it was on a track the way it took the

— Comma splice: fix by making second clause a phrase:

turn. The tires were humming a little, ~~it~~

~~sounded~~ like a hive of honey bees. After the

turn I started to wind it out. I saw the red

— Run-on: fix by beginning sentence with *When I . . .* and placing semicolon after STOP

octagon shape that read STOP I quickly

started to apply the brakes. These brakes

weren't anything special there was just the

Run-on: need semicolon after *special* or period with capital *There was*

misspelling: replace with "plain"   wrong word: replace with "they"

(plan) old pad on rotor brakes. But (there) did

misspelling: replace with "stopped"

the job well. The car (stoped) on a dime.

need past tense here: "pitched"

There was a little high-(pitch) sound coming

Misspelling: replace with "from"

Run-on: fix by connecting clauses with conjunction: *tire, but it . . .*

(form) the front right tire it went away. As I

Set off introductory subordinate clause with comma: *home, I . . .*

started to head for home I saw the sun

misspellings: replace with "slipping" and "barn"

(sliping) behind an old (bar.) I thought to my-

self, it doesn't get much better than this.

Proofreading Exercise

Proofread the following selection:

This black magnificent piece of art workis

still in my possion but its back home in my

parents garage. The car does not see much of

the road but when it does it is hard to bring

it back. The only thing different from the car

now is the driver side window. It was shat-

tered into a trillion pieces when my mother

forgot to close the door after getting in when

she pulled out of the garage. Sometimes I

catch myself sitting in my new bedroom

thing about that 1974 black, with a red pin-

stripe, 914 Porsche.

Based on his responses to the questions and his notes on his second draft, Randy writes a final draft of his descriptive essay:

Student Description Essay: Final Draft

As I looked out of my bedroom window on a cold rainy day, I saw the most beautiful object made by man. It was parked under a maple tree in my neighbor's muddy front yard. The 1974 black 914 Porsche with a red pinstripe took my breath away. As I watched, the rain ran off the roof, then over the windshield and onto the hood. Each drop blended with the next, getting larger, beading up with a trillion other drops on the hood as they raced toward the front bumper. Someone had spent many hours lovingly polishing that car.

Of course, it wasn't a large vehicle, only a two-seater. The car rode no more than 2 to 3 inches off the ground. The chrome on the bumpers and the trim around the doors and the windshield shined like Mom's good china. The tires were mounted with glistening silver mags, each held to the car with four gleaming lug nuts. My eyes lit up like a Christmas tree when I noticed a small sign in the passenger's side window: "For Sale." I was in love. This car was going to be mine somehow, some way.

Some dreams do come true. One bright, sunny afternoon, just a few months later, I took my wonderful Porsche for a drive. Although it was spring, I did not notice the trees or blooming flowers. All my senses sprang alive as I slid into the butter-soft leather seat. Suddenly, an odd smell, like mold on old bread, tickled my nose. It couldn't be coming from the engine, I knew, because I hadn't even started the car. However, when I placed my size ten-and-a-half foot on the small pedals, I realized the smell was oozing from wet car mats. Somehow, I didn't mind. It just reminded me this car had been around awhile. When I turned the key, the car fired up like it had just rolled off the assembly line. For a moment, I let the engine warm up. It sounded rough at first; that's probably why carbon monoxide filled the car interior.

As I pulled out of the driveway and drove down the street, I never reached second gear, but the rpms were really high. Even though the stench of carbon monoxide went away, the moldy smell still lingered. As I pulled up to a light, heading for a lonely back road, the engine raced. Obviously, the car needed a tune up. As the light turned from bright red to a dull green, I took off. Racing down this back road, leading nowhere, I really started to appreciate this classic.

After driving down a tight, curvy back road for a few minutes, all of the smells went away. Only two things ran through my mind: "I wonder how fast I can get this car to go," and some obscure Grateful Dead tune. When the speedometer reached 85 mph on a bumpy straightaway, the car seemed to float on air. As I entered a tight lefthand turn, the car held the road like a track. The tires hummed, sounding like a hive of honey bees. When a red STOP sign flashed to my right, I quickly applied the brakes. They weren't the high-tech, anti-lock variety, just the plain old pad-on-rotor brakes. But the car stopped on a dime. I knew life couldn't get much better.

I've got an apartment of my own now, and my magnificent piece of black artwork has stayed behind in my parents' garage. The car does not see much of the road, but when it does, I want to drive on forever. Sometimes, sitting in my new bedroom, I catch myself thinking about that 1974 black, red-pinstriped 914 Porsche.

DESCRIPTIVE WRITING TOPICS

The following are some possible topics for a descriptive paragraph or paper. Limit your topic to fit your instructor's requirements. Tell the reader *why* you have chosen your topic, and link your details closely to it.

1. An unusual relative, family member, or pet
2. Your best or worst belonging (a car, piece of furniture, article of clothing, jewelry, cabin)
3. A memorable vacation spot or workplace
4. A public place you like or avoid (store, waiting room, recreation area)
5. A memorable holiday or turning point in your life (graduation, birthday, move from place to place)
6. A set of equipment needed in your job, sport, or recreation
7. The ugliest or most beautiful place you have ever seen (park, building, dump, campus area)

CHAPTER FOUR

Narrative

Narratives describe events or actions, following the sequence of time. Unlike fictional narratives, however, you will describe incidents you have experienced, seen firsthand, or learned about. Your narratives often explain, persuade, or present as part of longer papers. At times, however, you will develop narratives as entire essays.

To write narratives effectively, use the guidelines in the following sections.

SPELL OUT YOUR PURPOSE

Whether your narrative is brief or paper-length, you need a clear purpose in mind. To give your reader a sense of direction, spell it out as a topic or thesis sentence. Or be sure your narrative makes your point through your choice of detail. You might, for example, begin your description of a difficult situation by saying, "It was a day filled with the little vexations of life." Or you might begin a narrative about a famous person with the words, "The 1990s are a toppling time. So it's nice to see a fallen idol get up, shake off the sludge, and battle back." These statements of purpose ready your reader for the kind of story you intend to tell.

ORDER YOUR INCIDENTS IN A CLEAR TIME SEQUENCE

Clarify **what** is happening **when** and **where.** Each event or incident should follow the next one chronologically. First one thing happens, then another, and then another. For example, a customer swears at a quick-shop clerk. A series of brief incidents follows:

Suddenly the clerk reached across the counter with both hands, grabbed the fellow by the collar, and literally plucked him off the floor. With fire in his eyes and passion in his voice, the clerk growled, "That is enough! You watch what you say in here, understand? There's a lady present!" Then he shoved the cusser away with obvious contempt. The foul-mouthed offender was stunned.

You can also help your reader follow your narrative by using transitions like these:

first	immediately	initially	next
second	third	after	in turn
then	momentarily	later	finally

In addition to using transitions, repeated words and synonyms help the reader move mentally from one action to the next.

VISUALIZE THE SETTING CONCRETELY

Each of your narratives will happen somewhere. If the location or a central object in your story matters to your readers, help them see it through your eyes. A professional finder, for example, needed to track down a cargo boat loaded with whiskey. It had sunk in the Missouri River in 1887. By comparing old and new maps, he noticed that the course of the river had changed. He eventually found the sunken boat twenty feet beneath a farmer's cornfield. These details vividly describe the **where** of the brief series of actions.

DESCRIBE PEOPLE IN SPECIFIC TERMS

As in your description of the setting, present your characters in easily grasped terms. Visualize a character in your own mind. Think of traits that strike chords in your readers' minds. For instance, the action hero Steven Seagal is depicted physically, visually:

He is a big man with a rather small head and small, well-cast features. His shiny black hair, only slightly receding, is always combed straight back, a cap of gel compelling the light to fall on it in a window. His little cool ponytail bounces when he chases evil with his lumbering, sloppy-legged run, which someone (not me, Steven) called "girlish." His high cheekbones and perpetual middle-distance squint give an Asiatic cast to his features.

In your own writing, describe your characters briefly, but in telling images.

USE CONVERSATION TO PRESENT YOUR CHARACTERS VIVIDLY

Allow your readers to hear, or overhear, your characters in your writing. This involves them more deeply in the action. Choose your words carefully, though. They should reflect your characters' age, status in life, or upbringing. For example, we quickly grasp the essence of a hold-up man in a brief dialogue. He tells a questioner where he makes his hits:

"Wherever I wanna go," Wilfred answered. "But mostly I hit the big malls an' shoppin' centers up in West Hollywood, Beverly Hills, Santa Monica, and what have you. I get one'a my girlfriends to rent me a car. Then I get all dressed up like this an' put on a runnin' suit, or maybe some funky clothes like you got on, over that. An' I always got me a hat or headband or somethin'. You know they could hardly ever pick you out of a lineup if you had sumpin' on yo' head."

In his own words, this small-time hold-up man tells what he learned in jail, revealing himself fully to the readers.

READINGS

The preceding brief examples of narrative are concrete, specific, and vivid. Chapter 2 showed how a **thesis** sums up the main idea for an entire writing; a thesis serves an **essay** as a **topic sentence** serves a **paragraph.** Here is a lengthier example of a narrative essay:

Sums up purpose of essay, the thesis ⟶

Revealing facts about ⟶ Penick's books

Details telling *what* and *when*

easy-to-see visual detail ⟶

For 90-year-old golf pro Harvey Penick, success has come late. His first golf book, *Harvey Penick's Little Red Book*, has sold more than a million copies, which his publisher believes makes it one of the biggest things in the history of sports books. His second book, *If You Play Golf, You're My Friend*, has already sold nearly three-quarters of a million. But anyone who imagines that Penick wrote the books to make money doesn't know the man. In the 1920s Penick bought a red spiral notebook

Brings in two other characters: writer and wife

Good transitions: "When" and "finally"

Indirect dialogue

and began jotting down observations about golf. He never showed the book to anyone except his son until 1991, when he shared it with a local writer and asked if he thought it was worth publishing. The man read it and told him yes. He left word with Penick's wife the next evening that Simon & Schuster had agreed to an advance of $90,000. When the writer saw Penick later, the old man seemed troubled. Finally Penick came clean. With all his medical bills, he said, there was no way he could advance Simon & Schuster that much money. The writer had to explain that Penick would be the one to receive the $90,000.

Terry Todd, "Morning Edition," National Public Radio

This narrative begins with the ending of Harvey Penick's success story. Then it returns to the beginning, charts Penick's hesitant move toward publication (and success), and ends with testimony that Penick remains unspoiled by success.

To develop your own narratives, freewrite sentences for five or ten minutes, stringing together concrete, specific details. Or make lists, using these ideas later in more carefully organized sentences and paragraphs.

The following selections are well-written examples of narrative writing, both paragraph-length and short essays. Your responses to the questions we raise will help you write narratives of your own.

In the following selection, two fishermen facing a life-threatening situation take fast but effective action.

Words to Define
alternated: took turns

Prereading
1. In what situations—real-life or fictional—have people or characters handled emergencies in unusual ways?

COULDN'T POSSIBLY BE TRUE

Chuck Shepherd

A fishing boat sank in rough, cold waters off Vancouver Island, leaving two men in a life raft that was tied to the sinking boat by a nylon rope. Neither had a knife to cut the rope. Had the ship sunk, it would have pulled the boat and the men down with it. For an hour, the two men alternated chewing the rope, with one man losing a tooth in the process. Minutes before the ship sank, the men finally chewed through the rope and survived.

Queries for Understanding

1. Who was stranded, where, under what conditions?
2. What factors caused the emergency?
3. What tool was missing, and why did it matter?
4. How did the people involved handle the emergency?

Queries on the Writer's Techniques

1. In what sentences does the writer describe the problem? The solution?
2. How does the writer keep the reader aware of passing time?

Writing Topics

1. When did you face a situation that struck you with fear, even panic? Describe the **when, where, why, what,** and **who** of the situation. What did you learn from this experience?
2. When have you traveled to an unfamiliar, even foreign place? How did you react at first? At what point in your visit did you begin to feel comfortable with your new surroundings, and why?

In the following selection, a courtroom experience involves some unexpected clashes between personal style and figurative language.

Words to Define
securities: financial notes or bonds

prosecuting: taking court action against someone

cascaded: flowed in waves (as in a rapidly flowing stream)

Prereading
1. Describe a situation that took an unexpected turn, surprising onlookers.
2. Narrate an action in which one or more characters reveal oddities of dress or other personal styling.

THIEVES USE HANGUPS TO OUTWIT OFFICIALS

New Jersey officials stopped a rash of purse-snatchings in restrooms along the Garden State Parkway by removing hooks from ladies' room stall doors. (Thieves would reach over the stall doors and remove purses, which women had hung on hooks while they used the toilet.) According to a *Philadelphia Inquirer* story, the thieves reinstalled the hooks, facilitating the theft rate's rise once again.

Atlanta Constitution

Queries for Understanding

1. At the beginning of the selection, **what** crime is occurring where, and **what** made it possible for thieves to carry it out?
2. How did local officials try to prevent these crimes?
3. How did thieves react to the officials' crime-prevention actions, with what effect?

Queries on the Writer's Techniques

1. What is the main idea of the paragraph?
2. Trace the cause-and-effect chain narrated by the selection, identifying each incident as cause, effect, or both.
3. What makes the selection comic?

Writing Topics

1. Write a narration of an event that changed midstream or turned out unexpectedly: how did you react to the unexpected turn of events?
2. What forced you to invent a new solution to a problem? How well did it work, or did your solution create new problems for you or for others?

In the following selection, a scientist, by observing closely, makes a surprising discovery about the effects of rainwater on stormy seas.

Words to Define

meteorologist: one who predicts the weather

batten down: to fasten down securely

confirmation: proof that something is true

phenomenon: an incident in nature

explanation: description why something has happened or is true

Prereading

1. Describe a discovery you or an acquaintance made by looking closely at something in nature or by watching a machine.

CALMING THE WATERS

One summer four and a half years ago, meteorologist David Arlas was sailing in Buzzards Bay, off Cape Cod. A storm suddenly came up. "The waves were about one and a half feet high at the time, and we thought we should batten down the hatches and get ready for intense rain," he recalls. "But to my utter surprise, as soon as the rain started, the sea became glassy and perfectly calm, except for the little ripples generated by the drops themselves." Arlas had witnessed something described by sailors for centuries: namely, that rain can calm choppy seas. But Arlas has now found scientific confirmation of the phenomenon—as well as a possible explanation. "The rain is simply stirring the water underneath, and when you stir the water, you kill the waves."

Discover

Queries for Understanding

1. At the beginning of the selection, **what** natural action is occurring. **What** did observers expect to happen next?
2. What unexpected action occurred?
3. Why does rain have the effect it does on ocean waves?

Queries on the Writer's Techniques

1. What is the main idea of the paragraph? Where does the writer state it?
2. Why does the writer quote Arlas directly? Why are these quotations effective?
3. Why does the writer tell readers that Arlas is seeing an age-old happening?
4. Why does the writer put the rain's effect on the waves in commonplace language?

Writing Topics

1. Describe a process in nature, giving both a commonsense and scientific explanation of why and how it happens.
2. Watch a weather channel on TV as it describes unusually cold, warm, rainy, or especially violent weather. Listen closely to the weather person's verbal description of the situation. How do these words resemble and differ from the pictures the channel shows?

Although legal barriers between the races have fallen, Mary Mebane recalls, in the following selection, a time when race powerfully affected even simple matters of daily life, such as seating in public transportation.

Words to Define

restrictive: limiting, confining

vigilante: unofficial, self-styled defenders of certain laws

industriously: hard-working, dedicated

complacently: self-satisfied, contented

affluent: wealthy, moneyed

furtively: secretively

apprehensive: fearful

insouciance: lack of concern, nonchalance

nondescript: lacking memorable traits

devastated: ruined, completely destroyed

frieze: like a decorative panel, unmoving

antagonist: enemy, contestant

devised: invented, created

Prereading

1. What customs or patterns of behavior discriminate against groups or classes of people? Tell how you saw or became aware of them.

THE BACK OF THE BUS

Mary E. Mebane

Historically, my lifetime is important because I was part of the last generation born into a world of total legal segregation in the Southern United States. When the Supreme Court outlawed segregation in the public schools in 1954, I was twenty-one. When Congress passed the Civil Rights Act of 1964, permitting blacks free access to public places, I was thirty-one. The world I was born into had been segregated for a long time—so long, in fact, that I never met anyone who had lived during the time when restrictive laws were not in existence, although some people spoke of parents and others who had lived during the "free" time. As far as anyone knew, the laws as they then existed would stand forever. They were meant to—and did—create a world that fixed black people at the bottom of society in all aspects of human life. It was a world without options.

Most Americans have never had to live with terror. I had had to live with it all my life—the psychological terror of segregation, in which there was a special set of laws governing your movements. You violated them at your peril, for you knew that if you broke one of them, knowingly or not, physical terror was just around the corner, in the form of policemen and jails, and in some cases and places white vigilante mobs formed for the exclusive purpose of keeping blacks in line.

It was Saturday morning, like any Saturday morning in dozens of Southern towns.

The town had a washed look. The street sweepers had been busy since six o'-clock. Now, at eight, they were still slowly moving down the streets, white trucks with clouds of water coming from underneath the swelled tubular sides. Unwary motorists sometimes got a windowful of water as a truck passed by. As it moved on, it left in its wake a clear stream running in the gutters or splashed on the wheels of parked cars.

Homeowners, bent over industriously in the morning sun, were out pushing lawn mowers. The sun was bright, but it wasn't too hot. It was morning and it was May. Most of the mowers were glad that it was finally getting warm enough to go outside.

Traffic was brisk. Country people were coming into town early with their produce; clerks and service workers were getting to the job before the stores opened at ten o'clock. Though the big stores would not be open for another hour or so, the grocery stores, banks, open-air markets, dinettes, were already open and filling with staff and customers.

Everybody was moving toward the heart of Durham's downtown, which waited to receive them rather complacently, little knowing that in a decade the shopping centers far from the center of downtown Durham would create a ghost town in the midst of the busiest blocks on Main Street.

Some moved by car, and some moved by bus. The more affluent used cars, leaving the buses mainly to the poor, black and white, though there were some business people who avoided the trouble of trying to find a parking place downtown by riding the bus.

I didn't mind taking the bus on Saturday. It wasn't so crowded. At night or on Saturday or Sunday was the best time. If there were plenty of seats, the blacks didn't have to worry about being asked to move so that a white person could sit down. And the knot of hatred and fear didn't come into my stomach.

I knew the stop that was the safety point, both going and coming. Leaving town, it was the Little Five Points, about five or six blocks north of the main downtown section. That was the last stop at which four or five people might get on. After the stop, the driver could sometimes pass two or three stops without taking on or letting off a passenger. So the number of seats on the bus usually remained constant on the trip from town to Braggtown. The nearer the bus got to the end of the line, the more I relaxed. For if a white passenger got on near the end of the line, often to catch the return trip back and avoid having to stand in the sun at the bus stop until the bus turned around, he or she would usually stand if there were not seats in the white section, and the driver would say nothing, knowing that the end of the line was near and that the standee would get a seat in a few minutes.

On the trip to town, the Mangum Street A&P was the last point at which the driver picked up more passengers than he let off. These people, though they were just a few blocks from the downtown section, preferred to ride the bus downtown. Those getting on at the A&P were usually on their way to work at the Duke University Hospital—past the downtown section, through a residential neighborhood, and then past the university, before they got to Duke Hospital.

So whether the driver discharged more passengers than he took on near the A&P on Mangum was of great importance. For if he took on more passengers than got off, it meant that some of the newcomers would have to stand. And if they were white, the driver was going to have to ask a black passenger to move so that a white passenger could sit down. Most of the drivers had a rule of thumb, though.

By custom the seats behind the exit door had become "colored" seats, and no matter how many whites stood up, anyone setting behind the exit door knew that he or she wouldn't have to move.

The disputed seat, though, was the one directly opposite the exit door. It was "no-man's-land." White people sat there, and black people sat there. It all depended on whose section was fuller. If the back section was full, the next black passenger who got on sat in the no-man's-land seat. Another thing about the white people: they could sit anywhere they chose, even in the "colored" section. Only the black passengers had to obey segregation laws.

On this Saturday morning Esther and I set out for town for our music lesson. We were going on our weekly big adventure, all the way across town, through the white downtown, then across the railroad tracks, then through the "colored" downtown, a section of run-down dingy shops, through some fading high-class black neighborhoods, past North Carolina College, to Mrs. Shearin's house.

We walked the two miles from Wildwood to the bus line. Though it was a warm day, in the early morning there was dew on the grass and the air still had the night's softness. So we walked along and talked and looked back constantly, hoping someone we knew would stop and pick us up.

I looked back furtively, for in one of the few instances that I remembered my father criticizing me severely, it was for looking back. One day when I was walking from town he had passed in his old truck. I had been looking back and had seen him. "Don't look back," he had said. "People will think that you want them to pick you up." Though he said "people," I knew he meant men—not the men he knew, who lived in the black community, but the black men who were not part of the community, and all of the white men. To be picked up meant that something bad would happen to me. Still, two miles is a long walk and I occasionally joined Esther in looking back to see if anyone we knew was coming.

Esther and I got to the bus and sat on one of the long seats at the back that faced each other. There were three such long seats—one on each side of the bus and a third long seat at the very back that faced the front. I liked to sit on a long seat facing the side because then I didn't have to look at the expressions on the faces of the whites when they put their tokens in and looked at the blacks sitting in the back of the bus. Often I studied my music, looking down and practicing the fingering. I looked up at each stop to see who was getting on and to check on the seating pattern. The seating pattern didn't really bother me that day until the bus started to get unusually full for a Saturday morning. I wondered what was happening, where all these people were coming from. They got on and got on until the white section was almost full and the black section was full.

There was a black man in a blue windbreaker and a gray pork-pie hat sitting in no-man's-land, and my stomach tightened. I wondered what would happen. I had never been on a bus on which a black person was asked to give a seat to a white person when there was no other seat empty. Usually, though, I had seen a black person automatically get up and move to an empty seat farther back. But this morning the only empty seat was beside a black person sitting in no-man's-land.

The bus stopped at Little Five Points and one black got off. A young white man was getting on. I tensed. What would happen now? Would the driver ask the black man to get up and move to the empty seat farther back? The white man had a businessman's air about him: suit, shirt, tie, polished brown shoes. He saw the empty seat in the "colored" section and after just a little hesitation went to it, put his briefcase down, and sat with his feet crossed. I relaxed a little when the bus pulled off without the driver saying anything. Evidently he hadn't seen what had happened, or since he was just a few stops from Main Street, he figured the mass exodus there would solve all the problems. Still, I was afraid of a scene.

The next stop was an open-air fruit stand just after Little Five Points, and here another white man got on. Where would he sit? The only available seat was beside the white man. Would he stand the few stops to Main Street or would the driver make the black man move? The whole colored section tensed, but nobody said anything. I looked at Esther, who looked apprehensive. I looked at the other men and women, who studiously avoided my eyes and everybody else's as well, as they maintained a steady gaze at a far-distant land.

Just one woman caught my eye; I had noticed her before, and I had been ashamed of her. She was a stingy little black woman. She could have been forty; she could have been fifty. She looked as if she were a hard drinker. Flat black face with tight features. She was dressed with great insouciance in a tight boy's sweater with horizontal lines running across her flat chest. It pulled down over a nondescript skirt. Laced-up shoes, socks, and a head rag completed her outfit. She looked tense.

The white man who had just gotten on the bus walked to the seat in no-man's-land and stood there. He wouldn't sit down, just stood there. Two adult males, living in the most highly industrialized, most technologically advanced nation in the world, a nation that had devastated two other industrial giants in World War II and had flirted with taking on China in Korea. Both these men, either of whom could have fought for the United States in Germany or Korea, faced each other in mutual rage and hostility. The white one wanted to sit down, but he was going to exert his authority and force the black one to get up first. I watched the driver in the rearview mirror. He was about the same age as the antagonists. The driver wasn't looking for trouble, either.

"Say there, buddy, how about moving back," the driver said, meanwhile driving his bus just as fast as he could. The whole bus froze—whites at the front, blacks at the rear. They didn't want to believe what was happening was really happening.

The seated black man said nothing. The standing white man said nothing.

"Say, buddy, did you hear me? What about moving on back." The driver was scared to death. I could tell that.

"These is the niggers' seats!" the little lady in the strange outfit started screaming. I jumped. I had to shift my attention from the driver to the frieze of the black man seated and white man standing to the articulate little woman who had joined in the fray.

"The government gave us these seats! These is the niggers' seats." I was startled at her statement and her tone. "The president said that these are the niggers' seats!" I expected her to start fighting at any moment.

Evidently the bus driver did, too, because he was driving faster and faster. I believe that he forgot he was driving a bus and wanted desperately to pull to the side of the street and get out and run.

"I'm going to take you down to the station, buddy," the driver said.

The white man with the briefcase and the polished brown shoes who had taken a seat in the "colored" section looked as though he might die of embarrassment at any moment.

As scared and upset as I was, I didn't miss a thing.

By that time we had come to the stop before Main Street, and the black passenger rose to get off.

"You're not getting off, buddy. I'm going to take you downtown." The driver kept driving as he talked and seemed to be trying to get downtown as fast as he could.

"These are the niggers' seats! The government plainly said these are the niggers' seats!" screamed the little woman in rage.

I was embarrassed at the use of the word "nigger" but I was proud of the lady. I was also proud of the man who wouldn't get up.

The bus driver was afraid, trying to hold on to his job but plainly not willing to get into a row with the blacks.

The bus seemed to be going a hundred miles an hour, and everybody was anxious to get off, though only the lady and the driver were saying anything.

The black man stood at the exit door; the driver drove right past the A&P stop. I was terrified. I was sure that the bus was going to the police station to put the black man in jail. The little woman had her hands on her hips and she never stopped yelling. The bus driver kept driving as fast as he could.

Then, somewhere in the back of his mind, he decided to forget the whole thing. The next stop was Main Street, and when he got there, in what seemed to be a flash of lightning, he flung both doors open wide. He and his black antagonist looked at each other in the rearview mirror; in a second the windbreaker and porkpie hat were gone. The little woman was standing, preaching to the whole bus about the government's gift of these seats to the blacks; the man with the brown shoes practically fell out of the door in his hurry; and Esther and I followed the hurrying footsteps.

We walked about three doors down the block, then caught a bus to the black neighborhood. Here we sat on one of the two long seats facing each other, directly behind the driver. It was the custom. Since this bus had a route from the black neighborhood to the downtown section and back, passing through no white residential areas, blacks could sit where they chose. One minute we had been on a bus in which violence was threatened over a seat near the exit door; the next minute we were sitting in the very front behind the driver.

The people who devised this system thought that it was going to last forever.

Mary, Viking Penguin, 1981

Queries for Understanding

1. Why is the writer's age, her generation, important for the experience that she narrates?
2. Why, according to the writer, was Saturday a good day to ride the bus?
3. Why does the writer think of Little Five Points as a "safety point"?
4. How is seating divided between blacks and whites on the bus? What behavior is expected when one section or the other is full?
5. When the well-dressed white man gets on the nearly full bus, how is a crisis avoided?
6. How does the bus driver react when a second white man gets on the bus and stands near the seat in no-man's-land?
7. How does "the little lady in the strange outfit" react to the stand-off?
8. How does the bus driver finally solve the problem?
9. What is the significance of Mebane's conclusion?

Queries on the Writer's Techniques

1. What contrast does Mebane draw between her experience and that of the white majority in segregationist North Carolina?
2. Why does Mebane include her description of Durham on an early Saturday morning in May?
3. Why does Mebane point out that the new shopping centers would empty the downtown in less than a decade?
4. Why does Mebane add her father's warning against looking back?
5. How does Mebane indicate the tension she felt while observing the events around her?
6. What contrast does Mebane draw between the first and last segments of her bus trip?

Writing Topics

1. Discuss a localized conflict involving race or religion that you have heard or read about. How did the people on both sides act and feel about it?
2. Discuss some contrasts between life as you know it now and life as it was a decade or more ago.

In the next selection, an initially frightening experience with a ghostly presence becomes comic.

Prereading

1. Describe a situation in your experience or knowledge whose outcome is unexpected or different.

THE WORST SCARE OF MY LIFE

Student Essay (Larry)

In November, 1969, I was working for the federal government in Champaign, Illinois, where I was a security guard at their Nike Hercules Missile Base. The base, located on Lake Shore Drive near Chicago, was surrounded by water and rock-filled banks. It was my job to check all the guard points, making sure the base was secure.

When I arrived late one afternoon at the security office for my shift, I noticed a warning posted on the boards: large parts of the fencing on the west side of the lake had been cut and not yet repaired. I immediately called my supervisor Colonel Stabler in Champaign to report the problem. In response, Colonel Stabler told me to act as a sentinel relief man and double-check all stations. As each guard reported in, I would re-walk the area to see if the guard had missed anything.

As night came on, it was misting rain, and the fog from the lake began forming a heavy cloud around the area, limiting vision to a few feet. At 11:45 p.m., one of the guards reported another section of the fence cut on the west side of the base. I immediately fastened on my pistol and headed for the area. When I arrived, a ghostly object startled me, moving along the shore line. Then a loud splash sounded in the water.

In a virtual panic, I locked and loaded my weapon. In the next instant, a white figure suddenly loomed up from the lake shore. "A ghost!" I thought. I was so upset and scared, I couldn't scream, and my gun slipped from my lifeless fingers. As I stood frozen in my tracks, the phantom moved steadily closer, signaling for me to approach. When it approached within a few feet, I bolted, fleeing the area as fast as I could run.

When I got back to the security post, I dialed the lake patrol with shaking hands, demanding that they search the area. Shortly afterward, they captured an escaped mental patient who admitted walking through the area. Under questioning , the man claimed he was a ghost from the past. In his escape, he had fitted a large bed sheet over his body, cutting crude holes for his eyes and mouth. Still a bit shaky, I called the mental institution to confirm the man's escape, and directed the security team to escort him back.

When I reported the incident to Colonel Stabler the next day, he said, "Larry, there's a show on tonight you should go see." I said, "What show?" He said, laughing, "Casper, the friendly ghost." From that day onward, whenever the colonel called, he would ask, "Is Casper the friendly ghost busy?"

Queries for Understanding

1. What is the setting for the student narrative, and what bearing does it have on the events that follow?
2. What initial emergency gets the action under way?
3. What instructions are given to the writer to deal with the situation?
4. How do the time of day and weather affect the writer's behavior?
5. How does the writer react to the apparent "ghost," and why?
6. How is the appearance of the "ghost" explained?

Queries on the Writer's Techniques

1. After reporting his supervisor's instructions, how does the writer divide his narrative into three parts?
2. How does the writer describe his feelings?
3. What makes the explanation of the ghost's presence and appearance credible?

Writing Topics

1. What situations in your experience or knowledge have turned out in unforeseen ways?
2. Have you encountered ghosts, phantoms, or the occult? Were these situations easily explained or not?

THE WRITING PROCESS

The writing topics that followed the preceding readings should give you ideas for your writing. You will need to limit them to fit your instructor's directions.

After choosing a topic for your narrative, do the following:

1. Describe your attitude or feelings toward this topic in a few words.
2. Explain why the topic interests you; are you involved personally or in the workplace with the topic? Give one reason for choosing this topic.
3. Why would others be interested in this topic? Describe readers who would find your topic entertaining or informative.
4. In a few words, tell what your readers might think, feel, or do after reading your narrative. Is this what you meant them to think or feel?
5. Briefly describe the purpose for writing the narrative, the specific and general setting, the characters, and any dialogue you might include.

6. What might make it hard for you to write a first draft of your narrative? Do you know enough about it to handle it well? Is your topic too broad or too narrow? Explain how you can solve these problems in a few words.

In the following first draft of a narrative, Daniel, the writer, recalls his wedding day as a disaster, even though he and his wife have remained happily married since. Because the day was crowded with incidents, he decides to retell it. To get started, he wrote the following first draft:

STUDENT NARRATIVE: FIRST DRAFT

My wedding day was the worse day of my whole life even though it was suppose to be the most important. Everything went wrong!

First, I was hung over from the bachelor party. Then everybody was late for the tuxedo appointments and mine was too tight. Also, I had to pay for everybody's tuxedo? This cost me $500. My brother, who was my best man, decided to get drunk before the wedding and he was late and he lost the ring. And then the preacher turned up and he was drunk too. When it was time to place the ring on my bride's finger, I had a pitiful substitute. Then the preacher introduced us as Mr. and Mrs. Daniels.

After that, my sister was putting us all down and my wife's father arrived drunk at the reception and wanted to fight everybody. Finally we discovered that the photographer had forgot to put film in his camera. This was the most terrible day ever.

REVISING THE FIRST DRAFT

After writing his first draft, Daniel begins the revision process by answering the following questions (with a friend to help him, perhaps):

1. What words in the draft make the topic interesting? What sentences are well written?
2. What is the draft's main idea? Which of the details support the main idea best?
3. Which part(s) of the narrative were the hardest to write? Why?
4. If the writer had more time to write this narrative, what part(s) would or should get the most attention?

Daniel's responses to these questions help him mark up the early version of his essay, as follows:

Sum up why day so important: marrying wonderful woman, brother best man, recording ceremony —→

Show cause and effect between incidents —→

My wedding day was the worse day of my whole life even though it was suppose to be the most important. Everything went wrong! First, I was hung over from the bachelor party. Then everbody was late for the tuxedo appointments and mine was to tight. Also, I had to pay for everybody's tuxedo? This cost me $500. My brother, who was my best man, decided to get drunk before the wedding he was late and he lost the ring. And then the preacher turned up, he was drunk too. When it was time to place the ring on my bride's finger, I had a pitiful substitute. Then the preacher introduced us as Mr. and Mrs. Daniels. After that, my sister was putting us all down and my wife's father arived drunk at the reception he wanted to fight everybody. Finlly we discovered that the photographer had forgot to put film in his camera. This was the most terible day ever.

←— Be more specific: "wedding day"

←— Tell how late

←— Develop effects of tight tuxedo in own paragraph, with specific details

←— Need more detail in separate paragraph: tell when, how he looked, what he said to explain

←— Need separate paragraph for preacher, specific details of action and speech

←— Group in same paragraph: wife walking down aisle, giving wife ring: tell what happened

Put minister's mistake, walking back down aisle, in own paragraph

Detail sister's behavior, wife's father's behavior —→

Develop conclusion more fully: what to do instead? Go to Justice of Peace?

Based on his responses to the questions and his markings on the first draft, Daniel writes an improved second draft of his narrative paper. After Daniel improves the organization and wording of his paper, his essay is not yet complete. He needs to proofread it, asking the following questions:

Proofreading Queries

1. Have I corrected grammatical problems such as noun/verb agreement?
2. Have I corrected the spelling, particularly with words that sound alike or look alike but are not spelled alike?
3. Have I corrected the punctuation, separating word groups to clarify meaning?

STUDENT NARRATIVE: FIRST REVISION

It was June 11, 1983. Just an ordinary day in

Chapel Hill, North Carolina, or was it? This

— Fragment: use comma after 1983, followed by lowercase just

day was to be the most important day in my

Comma splice: replace with colon as 1983: I . . .

entire life. My wedding day. There was one

— Fragment: connect as appositive to life, my . . .

misspelling: should be "single"

(sigle) task I did wrong on June 11, 1983, I

misspelling: should be wedding

woke up. My (weding) day was a pure, king of

all kings, world-record-breaking, super duper,

misspelling: should be catastrophe

chaotic (catrophe)! I awoke with a hangover

misspelling: should be bachelor

from the (bachlor) party. I found out that all

the men were late for our tuxedo apoint-

ments. The appointment was at 9:00 a.m. I

got the men together by 10:00 a.m. When I

arrived, I discovered two (prolems.) First,

misspellings: should be "problems" and "expecting"

everyone was (especting) me to pay for their

tuxes. Second, my tuxedo was too small. The

join words: "apiece"

tuxedos were fifty dollars (a piece). I had to

misspelling: should be "eight"

pay for (eigt) groomsmen and a best man.

When I left the store. I was five hundred dol-

lars poorer. I still had to wait until 12:00

p.m. for my tuxedo.

Fragment: fix by joining to next sentence: store, I

To the Student: Proofreading

Proofread the following paragraph:

Everyone dressed and waited until my tux ar-

rived Finally, my tux from Raleigh. After get-

ting dressed, we all went to the church. Well,

everyone but my brother Jimmy who was the

should be two words: "best man"

bestman. For some reason, Jimmy disa-

peared. Jimmy decided that it was a good

time. To stop and get a drink. He intended to

get his nerves up to be my bestman.

The wedding was to begin at 2:00 p.m.

Jimmy, my bestman, finally showed up at

2:17 p.m. He came to me and apologized for

the delay. Jimmy then told me something.

That a nervous groom does not wish to hear.

Fragment: connect to preceding: some- thing that a . . .

He said, "Uh, I lost the ring but don't worry

Bro. I've got you covered. I'm going to find it

cause it is around here somewhere." The

Run-on: make first sentence subordinate clause, by beginning with When . . . and placing comma after office, I . . .

preacher came into the office I shook my

head in disbelief. This man was drunker than

misspelling: should be "amazed"

Cooter Brown. This (mazed) me. At this

point, I decided to go with the flow. The wed-

ding began and everything was going great.

Comma splice: fix by making first clause subordinate: When my bride . . .

My bride-to-be entered the church, her

beauty captured the hearts of everyone.

The best man stood beside me as cool as a

misspelling: should be "cucumber"

(cucmber.) Until it was time for the ring. The

Fragment: joint to preceding by leaving out period and lowercase until

drunk peacher said, "The bride's ring please."

My brother's eyes grew as large as saucers.

He looked at me as he handed me the ring

Fragment: fix by joining to preceding sentence. ring, and then to . . .

and said, "Just go with it." I looked at the

ring. Then to my pitiful (bestman) and shook

my head. I placed the ring on my bride's fin-

ger begging her silently to take the ring. She

misspelling: should be "hesitantly"

took the ring (hesntly.) After our vows, the

drunk preacher presented us to the congre-

gation. He said, "I now introduce to you Mr.

no capital: should be "and"

(And) Mrs. Daniels." At that point, I made up

misspelling: should be "going"

my mind. I was not (ging) to pay this idiot

Run-on: fix by making first clause subordinate: When we . . . , with comma after church

one cent. We left the church I thought that

the worst was over. I discovered that I was

wrong. My "holier than thou" sister was

condemning everyone for being at a club.

Ironically, she was sneaking drinks, she ◄——— Comma splice: fix by making second clause a phrase: *drinks, thinking I didn't see her.*

thought I didn't see her. My wife's drunk fa-

ther came into the reception wanting to fight

everyone. He was upset because he did not

get to walk his daughter down the isle. He

misspellings: "everyone to"

wanted (everone too) know this. After getting

Fragment: fix with comma, then lower case: *upset, he*

my wife upset. He left the reception. To top

off the whole day, I found out that my

misspelling: should be "photographer"   misspelling: should be "film"

(photgrapher) did not have any (flim) in his

camera. What a total letdown for me. I real-

ized that my wedding day, the most impor-

Need comma after "life" to set off appositive

tant day of my life was a total disaster. My

wrong word: should be "advice"

(advise) to anyone planning to have a large

wedding is DON'T. Go to a justice of the

peace!

After correcting his second draft, Daniel writes the final version of his narrative.

STUDENT NARRATIVE: FINAL DRAFT

When I woke up on the morning of June 11, 1983, I was certain it was going to be the best day of my life. I was marrying a wonderful woman, my brother had agreed to be my best man, and I'd arranged to have the whole beautiful ceremony recorded on film for my future children and grandchildren. Unfortunately, my wedding day was an unforgettable catastrophe. To begin with, I woke up with a bad hangover. My friends and I had a memorable bachelor party the night before. It was so memorable, in fact, that all the men were an hour late for the tuxedo appointment. None of us felt too well as we struggled into our uncomfortable wedding clothes. To make matters worse, my friends assumed that I was going to pay for the rental of their tuxedos. The tuxes cost fifty dollars each. With eight groomsmen and a best man, the bill for all of the clothes came to five hundred dollars. Nevertheless, I kept telling myself, the beautiful, memorable wedding would be worth all the cost and effort. And then I tried on my tux. Apparently, the manager mixed up my measurements with someone else's because my tux was exactly two sizes too small. However, the manager promised to have the correct size in the store by noon. Everyone dressed and waited for my tux to arrive from Raleigh. As soon as it did, I dressed in a rush and we all headed for the church. Unfortunately, the wait for my tux unhinged my brother Jimmy completely. To quiet his nerves, he slipped off and went to a nearby bar. The wedding was supposed to start at 2:00 p.m., but we didn't see Jimmy again until exactly 2:17, when he staggered into the church office, red-eyed and apologetic. He had a lot to apologize for. "Uh, Bro, I lost the ring, but don't worry. I've got you covered. I swear I'll find it around here somewhere." Just then the preacher arrived. Apparently, he and Jimmy had been drinking together. The man of God slurred his words and didn't even know my name, Daniel Holmes. But I couldn't do anything to change the situation, so I decided to stop worrying and relax. That was a mistake. My beautiful wife-to-be walked down the aisle escorted by her stepfather. She hadn't spoken to her father in five years, and we both liked and respected this man who had raised her like his own daughter. The ceremony went well up until the preacher muttered, "The bride's ring, please." Jimmy broke out in a sweat, reached into his pocket and handed me a cigar band. "Please," he whispered, "Just go with it!" I stared at him and then at the "ring." Carefully, so that it wouldn't tear, I placed it on my bride's finger. Although her mouth dropped open in disbelief, mercifully, she said nothing. After our vows, the drunken preacher introduced us to the congregation. "I now introduce to you Mr. and Mrs. Daniels." Our friends giggled as we walked back down the aisle. I vowed silently that I was not going to pay that idiot one cent. When we left the church, I thought the worst was over. I was wrong. For one, my stuck-up sister condemned everyone for visiting a club. Ironically, she sneaked drinks, thinking no one saw her. Not only that, but my wife's drunken father crowded into the reception, trying to pick a fight. Enraged because no one asked him to walk his daughter down the aisle, he angrily shouted his irritation, upset my wife, and left in a huff. Finally, my photographer had neglected to load film in his camera. What a total disaster. My advice to anyone planning a large wedding is "Don't." Go to a justice of the peace.

NARRATIVE WRITING TOPICS

The following are some possible topics for a narrative paragraph or paper. Limit your topic to fit your instructor's requirements. Tell the reader *why* you have chosen your topic, and link your details closely to your topic.

1. An influence on you by an older or younger person
2. An important turning point in your life

3. A memorable act of affection or disdain

4. A lesson you learned in your family or workplace

5. An episode that helped you gain poise, self-confidence, or assurance

6. A family story about a member of an earlier generation

7. A move, vacation, or trip that affected your life

CHAPTER FIVE

Examples

Examples appeal to the senses—sight, sound, touch, smell, or taste. Examples can also use measurements. They describe what kind, how high, how long, how many, in what direction, or at what time of day or year. They are the simplest, most effective way to develop your ideas in most of your writing.

Writers often develop a **topic sentence** or **thesis** with **examples:**

Topic sentence: Alix Lambert's most ambitious art project invited active bodily involvement

Example: She got married and divorced four times in six months.

Example: She titled this performance "Wedding Piece."

To write examples well, use the following guidelines.

STICK TO YOUR SUBJECT

Make sure all of your examples fit your topic or purpose. If you're discussing the way an artist works, don't wander off into a description of the tattoo subculture in Russian prisons if it has nothing to do with your topic.

CHOOSE THE MOST CONVINCING EXAMPLES

If you are discussing the making of an art work, stick with examples of its look, sound, or feel. Avoid an interesting but irrelevant side-path, such as an oddball series: "She shaved her hair off, other than tufts at the side, and then photographed herself in a suit and tie." Make sure your examples are up-to-date, not drawn from the distant past.

USE AN ADEQUATE NUMBER OF EXAMPLES

One example may seem to your reader to provide thin support. Use several examples. It's better to overexplain than to leave your reader wanting more information. If you want to give examples of how an artist looks the part, you might list details like these:

> tall and perfectly built, with cropped convict hair and tattoos
>
> posters of himself stripped to the waist, gun in hand
>
> close-up images of the skull-and-crossbones ring he wears
>
> a replica of his trademark pistol
>
> movie marquee cutouts of him performing high kicks.

USE TRANSITIONS, PRONOUNS, AND REPEATED WORDS

At times, link examples to the paragraph with transitions, pronouns, and repeated words. Words such as *for example, in addition*, and *for instance* unify the paragraph and keep your reader on track. Sometimes a simple listing does the job; if your examples sound choppy, add transitions. However, if you do use transitional words, be sure that an entire sentence follows the transition.

> **Mistake:** Dada artist Marcel Ducham had himself photographed. **For example, in women's clothes.** (The second word group lacks a subject and verb; thus, it is a fragment.)
>
> **Correction:** Dada artist Marcel Ducham had himself photographed, for example, in women's clothes.

READINGS

As Chapter 1 pointed out, **topic sentences** sum up a paragraph's main idea. You will use examples to make this general concept clearer, more vivid to your reader. By filling out this general idea, your paragraph will draw word pictures in your reader's mind. The following paragraph develops topic sentences with interesting, concrete examples:

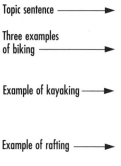

Topic sentence ⟶

Three examples of biking ⟶

Example of kayaking ⟶

Example of rafting ⟶

Ride, kayak, and raft like the devil in the Australian island state of Tasmania. On bikes, you'll cruise along the roads of Evandale's farming country, descend through the towering peaks of Ben Lomond National Park into the Fingal Valley, and explore the quaint fishing village of Bicheni. After five days you'll ditch the bikes for sea kayaks and paddle along the blue-green waters of Honeymoon Bay, picnicking and sleeping on sandy white beaches each night. After a short hike up Mount Graham, the trip concludes with a rafting expedition through the Tasmanian rainforest on the rapids of the Picton River.

Chapter 2 showed how a **thesis** sums up the main idea for an entire writing; it serves an **essay** as a **topic sentence** serves a **paragraph.** Sometimes a writer begins an essay with an example, following it with a **thesis.** The following essay begins with an example meant to catch the reader's attention:

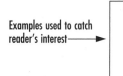

Examples used to catch reader's interest ⟶

At 7:15 a.m., all is quiet in the hallways of Frank W. Ballou Senior High, a tired sprawl of brick and steel in the most crime-infested ward of Washington, D.C. It's long before classes start. The only sound comes from the computer lab, where 16-year-old Cedric Jennings is at work on an extra-credit project.

Tall, gangly, and unabashedly ambitious, Cedric arrives this early every day, often not leaving until dark.

Topic sentence ⟶

The high school junior with the perfect grades has big dreams: he wants to go to the Massachusetts Institute of Technology.

Topic sentence ⟶

Cedric is one of a handful of honor students at Ballou, where last April just 80 of 1,350 students could boast an average of B or better. Students attend school sporadically, some read at only a fifth-grade level, and some must repeat lower grades. "So much of what goes on here is crowd control," says a math teacher.

Thesis statement ⟶

Street culture has invaded the school to the point where those seeking to do well academically are the objects of bullying and derision. Last school year, one student was shot dead near the school by a classmate during lunch period, a boy was hit on the head with an ax, a girl was wounded in a knife fight a few blocks away.

Ros Suskind, "Tormented for Learning,"

Your supporting examples will often prove a point, convincing your readers to share your views. As in the preceding selection, your thesis may be novel or somewhat controversial. You should choose details or facts that are vivid and convincing. As they read your writing, readers should be able to *see* your images in their mind's eye. The driver of a truck full of onions once told an arresting officer he was forced to speed: If he didn't stay ahead of the smell, his eyes would fill with tears, and he couldn't see to drive.

Both you and your reader should find your examples interesting and concrete. They may not only add variety to your topic, they may also extend its range, sometimes for several paragraphs. The following essay takes this approach to sightseeing in Iowa, along the upper Mississippi River. The writer is more interested in helping us visualize these scenes than in persuading us to make a visit.

Title hints at thesis ————————▶

Up the Big River

Burlington, Iowa, is a picturesque, late-Victorian town built into bluffs 150 feet above the upper Mississippi River. Here German immigrants got rich making wagons and plows for Great Plains homesteaders. **Driving north along the river, you'll find dozens of such charming old towns.**

Thesis: introduces example extending ——▶ to end of essay

Examples of vegetation and birds ——▶ one might see

At Sabula, a small island village, cross the bridge into Illinois. Bluffs rise several hundred feet from the flood plain. North of Sabula, white pines edge the tops of these craggy cliffs. River islands are nesting grounds for egrets, wood ducks, and great blue herons. In winter and summer, too, of late, you might also spot bald eagles.

Examples of houses and boats along ——▶ the way

Take State Highway 84 into Galena, one of the best-preserved river towns. A short, steep climb from Main Street leads to grand Italianate, Queen Anne and Greek Revival homes built 150 years ago. A footbridge across the Galena River takes you to Ulysses S. Grant's home. Only 15 miles northwest is Dubuque, Iowa. At the riverfront, see the Fred W. Woodward Riverboat Museum. There's a life-size log raft you can walk on, a model steamship created in flawless detail, and a flat-bottomed johnboat once used to harvest river mussels, the shells of which were used for buttons.

Examples of gambling opportunities ⟶

If you have the nerve of a riverboat gambler, you might head for the *Dubuque Diamond/Jo*, a casino boat on the Iowa side of the Mississippi. Or cross back into Illinois, where they'll also happily let you lose your life savings on boats like the *Silver Eagle*, a sleek 205-foot cruise ship.

Minor examples of historical events ⟶

Up the road in Balltown is Breitbach's, a historic tavern where, according to the proprietor, you can see a horse blanket left by the James gang. About 50 miles north of Dubuque, the Pikes Peak overlook offers a view of the spot where explorers Louis Joliet and Father Jacques Marquette first saw the Mississippi in 1673.

More minor examples of the natural setting ⟶

A few miles farther, cross the bridge into Prairie du Chien, Wisconsin, established by French fur traders around 1685. Today the town caters to campers and fishermen. On the drive from Prairie du Chien to La Crosse, young birches arch gracefully over the two-lane road, which hugs sheer bluffs crowned with oaks. A nearby lock and dam make the Mississippi as wide and placid as a lake.

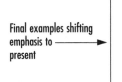

Final examples shifting emphasis to present ⟶

The bridge at La Crosse takes you into Minnesota. What may be the oldest town, Wabasha, a half-hour north, has almost its entire downtown in the National Register of Historic Places. From there you are only a couple of hours from the Twin Cities and the 20th Century.

"Great Vacation Drives," *U.S. News and World Report*

This essay clearly traces sights seen along a journey following the course of the upper Mississippi. While doing so, it also indicates the history of the area. Its past is still reflected in nature and present-day activities.

To develop your own sets of examples, freewrite sentences for five or ten minutes, stringing together concrete, specific details. Or make lists, using these resources later in more carefully organized sentences and paragraphs.

The following selections will present well-written examples of example writing, both paragraph-length and short essays. Your responses to the questions we raise will help you write versions of your own.

How They Did That

Ron Magid

Before ILM could transform Jim Carrey as Stanley Ipkiss into *The Mask*, they had to first create the believable never-world setting of the film's action. For a prologue showing Vikings burying the magical mask in the New World, ILM transformed a California beachfront into the East Coast of some 2,000 years ago. "We did a matte painting on the computer to augment the beach and add a Viking Edge City, the comic book setting for *The Mask*. A very grungy, polluted Chicago was created via four big vista paintings on the computer. The first was that identical beach locale, 2,000 years later, which utilized the same background as the Viking landing, only this time, ILM added huge toxic waste dump spouts on the sand with the city itself looming darkly in the distance. The three other plates were shot on location in the city of Los Angeles, where the computer matte artists added double-decker freeways, computer graphics (CG) cars, and modernistic buildings.

The MASK Collector's Magazine

Queries for Understanding

1. What did ILM have to do before working on changing the mild-mannered Stanley Ipkiss in *The Mask*?
2. How did the technicians create the Viking Edge City?
3. How did the scene change in 2,000 years?
4. All together, how many paintings did the people at ILM create? (Read carefully.)

Queries on the Writer's Techniques

1. What is the main idea of the paragraph?
2. What specific examples does the writer use to describe how ILM changed the Viking beach scene to the modern scene?

Writing Topics

1. Have you ever imagined how some location looked in the past or how it will look in the future? Write a paragraph describing one particular scene. Then, either describe it as you imagined it was or as you think it will be in the future. Be sure to use two or three specific examples.
2. Have you ever visited a place and then tried to describe it to someone who has never been there? Write a paragraph about a specific scene, de-

scribing it to someone who has never seen it (don't try to describe, for example, the whole city of Atlanta; instead, simply describe one aspect of it, such as the confusing exits on Interstate 75).

Most people have dealt with frustrating computerized answering services. Now many are trying to bank by phone. In the following selection, the writer describes how, in response to consumers' frustrations, two large companies are trying to make life easier.

Words to Define

synonymous: similar to

fumbling: to touch awkwardly, handle nervously

enable: to make possible

debit: an item of debt

PHONING IT IN

Suzanne Kantra

Banking by phone has become synonymous with fumbling your way through a maze of push-button choices from your telephone's dialing pad. But better phones and services may soon ease the frustrations of tele-banking.

Banking giant Citibank and on-line service operator U.S. Order are each employing so-called screen phones in separate attempts to make banking by phone an easier, more visual experience. Both efforts combine on-line banking options and LCD screens. Those computer-like features enable you to see and select from a menu of banking functions including paying bills and transferring funds, while you receive audio feedback through a speaker in the phone.

In addition to these basic services, Citibank's Enhanced Telephone (made by Philips), and U.S. Order's PhonePlus phone each feature a card reader—a slot in the Citibank phone for debit and automatic teller machine (ATM) cards, and a credit-card style magnetic code reader in the U.S. Order phone for debit, ATM, or credit cards. The card readers will enable you to take advantage of options such as shopping by catalog, ordering food, or buying airline tickets through the screen phone.

Citibank (800-285-3000) will be offering the Enhanced Telephone to its customers in the Chicago area this spring and in the New York area later on in the year. U.S. Order (800-947-3000) works through selected ATM networks, including the Mac, Most, and Money Station networks thus far. U.S. Order hopes to add more networks this year. The Enhanced Telephone and PhonePlus phones each cost about $200.

Popular Science

Queries for Understanding

1. Why is banking by phone so frustrating at present?

2. Which companies are employing screen phones to make it easier?

3. List the features that make the screen phones convenient.

4. What are the differences between the Citibank and U.S. Order phones?

Queries on the Writer's Techniques

1. The writer uses four paragraphs to explain her ideas. What is the topic of each paragraph?

2. How does the writer capture the reader's attention at the beginning of the essay?

3. What examples in the second paragraph support the writer's ideas?

Writing Topics

1. Think of one computerized element of modern life that you find extremely frustrating. How could the manufacturers make it easier to use?

2. If you could design a phone for your home, what extra services would it provide? Why would you want these services? Use specific examples to explain why they would be useful.

3. Are you comfortable using computers? What do you find most helpful or most frustrating about them? Give specific examples from your personal experience to support your ideas.

In the following selection, a nontraditional student remembers her first car in vivid detail but with limited nostalgia.

Words to Define

obliterate: blot out, totally get rid of

remnants: vestiges, parts left

in lieu of: in place of

Prereading

1. What early possession have you outworn or outgrown, but still remember vividly?

MY FIRST CAR

Student Essay (Suzanne)

When I was only fifteen years old, my parents gave me my first car, a 1982 Dodge Colt hatchback. Although I was happy to get my own wheels, both the exterior and interior were in terrible physical shape.

To begin with, the exterior sported greyish-silver paint with red pin stripes running down each side. Unlike the rest of the car, a slightly different shade of silver graced the front right fender; someone must have wrecked the car before it fell into my hands. Once brightly chromed, rust now held the front bumper together. Although I often cleaned it, I could never obliterate the tiny little bumps that the rust had made. While the cheap plastic hub caps on each side matched, the right side ones clashed with the left side ones. Finally, pine tar had nearly ruined the rear bumper, which once been chrome.

If the exterior was scary, the interior was a real fright. At first glance, one would notice that fuzzy sheep skins covered the tattered seats. An imitation leather cover protected the steering wheel. The carpet was clearly original: nothing in that bad shape could have been a replacement. It used to be maroon, but quite a few stains spotted its faded appearance. On the dash, a few indicator lights still worked, giving essential information like "Low Battery," "Check Engine," and— the one I became well-acquainted with—"Low Fuel." Folded down, the back seat revealed the remnants of a rear window defogger. Several strands of wire running horizontally across the back glass had once heated and defogged the windows. For some time, evidently, some of the strands had failed to heat. As a result, the back glass looked striped on foggy mornings.

In spite of all its eyesores, inside and out, the "Coltster" never failed me mechanically, though I never changed the oil. Three years later, I traded in the Colt in lieu of a $1,500 down payment on a Mazda pickup—getting a fantastic deal for this ragged-out car because my uncle was a salesman at the dealership. Although I miss the Colt at times, I wouldn't trade anything for my truck.

Queries for Understanding

1. What flaws affecting the exterior of her car does the writer remember?
2. What flaws affecting the interior of her car does the writer remember?
3. Why does the writer remember the car warmly despite its flaws?

Queries on the Writer's Techniques

1. In what order does the author list the exterior flaws, and why?
2. In what order does the author list the interior flaws, and why?
3. Why does the writer have mixed feelings about the trade of her Colt?

Writing Topics

1. Discuss this issue: would it be better if cars lasted ten or fifteen years, or it is best that they be traded every two or three years?
2. Make a list of mechanical objects that we depend upon, but wear out: which are worth repairing, and which must be replaced?

Although Americans theoretically have more leisure time today, they spend their time at a much more rapid pace. The author of the following selection wonders if the change is for the better.

Words to Define

essence: the most important part

nanosecond: one billionth of a second

megahertz: one million cycles per second

warp speed: speed of light or faster

waxing: to become gradually more intense

nostalgic: longing for things of the past

YOUR PACE OR MINE?

Michael Cohn

Quick! Read this! Hurry up! We've got to move fast. The whole world is moving fast. Fast, fast, fast! Speed is of the essence.

Was it always like this? This crazy? This hectic? I don't think so. In fact, the old days were slow. . .way too slow. We took our time. We stopped to say hello. We chatted with the butcher. We collected stamps, did crosswords, and made soup from scratch.

How foolish! What were we thinking back then? Today, there's not a moment to lose! Certainly not at the office. There, we really move fast. *Mail* it to me? No way! Fax it to me! Better yet, 'Net it to me on that Information Superhighway! I need it *now*. I need it *sooner* than now! I need it fast!

And speaking of fast, boy am I fast. I got rid of that old clunker 486-chipped, 33-megahertz dinosaur of a personal computer. Too slow! Give me 66 megahertz! 75! 175! I can't waste a nanosecond!

Of course, I'm not sure how long a nanosecond is. I've no clue what a megahertz looks like. In fact, I wonder how many nanoseconds I waste just trying to figure out how to use half this stuff.

In our networked and information-overloaded world today, we've got no time to sit, or discuss, or decide. We think on our feet. We shoot from the hip, and shoot often. So what if we rush into a bad decision or 12 each day? Just make the call and move on; we'll worry about consequences another day.

All right, maybe all this "fast" stuff doesn't apply to rush hour. We move slowly. Horribly, painfully, fingernail-bitingly slow. But I've fixed that. I got a car phone! A car fax! A notebook computer! It's 5 p.m. on I-285 at Ashford-Dunwoody, and I move fast. . .cutting deals, reading memos, occasionally forgetting a turn signal.

Patience is a vice. Quick is the key. My workdays are fast. My evenings are fast. And of course, even my weekends are fast. Because I get everything done faster, I get one-hour dry-cleaning, a 30-minute workout, a 10-minute oil change for the car, and an instant lottery ticket. I pay my bills on-line. I get cash from an ATM.

We're all pretty fast, aren't we? Therein, however, may lie a small problem. How come, even though we're barreling through life at warp speed, we never get anywhere? How come we don't have more leisure time? Or quality time? How come we just have overtime? Are we moving at ultra-speed, or ulcer-speed? We may be faster, but we're also grayer. And tired. And we could really use a vacation. . .a long, *slow* vacation. I'm not waxing nostalgic. I like my world today. But what have we gained from our fast-forward lifestyle? Do we all feel like 60 the day we turn 40?

Wouldn't it be a little better if we all just slowed down, took a deep breath, smelled the roses, and had a tall, cool glass of iced tea?

Maybe. But make mine instant.

Atlanta Journal/Atlanta Constitution

Queries for Understanding

1. What social niceties have been lost because of the stress on speed?
2. What personal problems have developed because of fast lifestyles?
3. How does the author feel about life in the fast lane?
4. What are some of the problems in business that result from the fast pace?
5. How does he cope with slow traffic?

Queries on the Writer's Techniques

1. What examples does the writer give to describe the lost social and personal pastimes, and why?
2. Why do you think the author wrote this essay?
3. Why are the terms *ultra-speed* and *ulcer-speed* effective?

Writing Topics

1. Does your life move fast or slow? What are you gaining or losing by living at the speed you do?
2. Would you prefer to live in the "slow old days" or today? Why?
3. What would be gained if we all slowed down and took life easier?
4. What would be lost if we all slowed down and took life easier?

THE WRITING PROCESS

After choosing a topic for your paragraph or essay, answer the following questions:

1. Describe your attitude or feelings toward this topic in a few words.

2. Explain why the topic interests you: are you involved personally or in the workplace with the topic? Give one reason for choosing this topic.

3. Why would others be interested in this topic? Describe readers who would find your topic entertaining or informative.

4. In a few words, tell what your readers might think, or feel, or do after reading your paragraph or essay. Is this what you intended them to do?

5. Give two or three examples that develop or explain your main idea. Are they part of an extended example, or are they rather diverse?

6. What might make it hard for you to write a first draft of this topic? Do you know enough about it to handle it well? Is your topic too broad or too narrow? Explain how you can solve these problems in a few words.

Mark, the writer of the next selection, felt he knew a lot about baseball. To narrow his topic, he decided to exemplify the skills needed by players, whether amateurs or professionals.

STUDENT EXAMPLE ESSAY: FIRST DRAFT

There are a lot of baseball games played in high school, college and professionally. After watching all of these it is easy to pick out a good player because he has many certain qualities; hands, speed and a strong arm. Hands are real important. The plays all involve the use of hands and it is a good thing to be able to use your hands real quick. Pitchers throw real fast and you need good hands to do that. Will Clark has good hands. He can wait until the ball is almost in the catchers hands' before he hits it and this is good hands because he needs to be able to hit it far if he wants to keep his job. Also he is fast and that's good because you have to run fast to get a score you have to run fast past all the bases. At least 4.3 second. Pete Rose could do this. Lastly of all a good arms is necessary. You have to throw the baseball real fast like almost sixty foot going maybe 82 mph. You also have to do a lot of other stuff. Like throw the ball with an arch. Lots of players can't do this its real hard to do because it takes a lot of strong arms and lots of them don't always have this. I think if you have all these three things you can be a good if not great baseball player.

REVISING THE FIRST DRAFT

After writing the draft of his example paper, Mark began the revision process by answering the following questions on the organization of the draft:

1. What words in the draft make the topic interesting? What sentences are well written?

2. What is the draft's main idea? Which of the examples support the main idea best?

3. Which part(s) of the essay do you think were hardest to write? Why?

4. If you (the writer) had more time to write this essay, what part(s) would or should get the most attention?

Mark's responses to these questions help him mark up the early version of his essay, as follows:

Indicate personal experience specifically ──────►

There are a lot of baseball games played in

high school, college and professionally. After

Combine these ideas in single, brief sentence

watching all of these it is easy to pick out a

good player because he has many certain

Begin new paragraph here: combine mention of hands with reasons why, in all ──────

qualities; hands, speed and a strong arm.

Hands are real important. The plays all in-

volve the use of hands and it is a good thing

to be able to use your hands real quick.

Describe need for pitching speed in more specific detail ──────►

Pitchers throw real fast and you need good

hands to do that. Will Clark has good hands.

Wordy and repetitious: sum up more briefly, with specific details ──►

He can wait until the ball is almost in the

catchers hands' before he hits it and this is

good hands because he needs to be able to

Begin new paragraph here, clearly moving from quick hands to quick feet. ──────►

hit it far if he wants to keep his job. Also he

is fast and that's good because you have to

Develop paragraph more fully with specific facts and reasons ──────►

run fast to get a score you have to run fast

past all the bases. At least 4.3 second. Pete

Define good arm with ────── more specific details

Rose could do this. Lastly of all a good arms

is necessary. You have to throw the baseball

real fast like almost sixty foot going maybe

82 mph. You also have to do a lot of other

stuff. Like throw the ball with an arch. Lots

of players can't do this its real hard to do be-

cause it takes a lot of strong arms and lots of

them don't always have this. I think if you

have all these three things you can be a good

if not great baseball player.

Replace stuff with specific tasks and skills, defining with an arch

Place conclusion in a separate paragraph, summing up more specifically: what "three things"

Based on his responses to the questions and his markings on the first draft, Mark writes an improved second draft of his example paper. However, his essay is not yet complete. He needs to proofread it, asking the following questions:

Proofreading Queries

1. Have I corrected grammatical problems such as noun/verb agreement?
2. Have I corrected the spelling, particularly with words that sound alike or look alike but are not spelled alike?
3. Have I corrected the punctuation, separating word groups to clarify meaning?

STUDENT EXAMPLE ESSAY: FIRST REWRITE

Misplaced modifier: preceding phrase should refer to "I," then read have learned what . . .

After seeing over one thousand high school,

misspelling: should be "college"

(colege) and professional baseball games, (it)

has become somewhat easy to share what it

takes to be considered a quality player. In

essence, a quality baseball player must

misspelling: should be "possess"

(posess) quick hands, average speed and a

strong arm. First ~~of all, let us discuss why it~~

Wordy: omit, as it is said better in the next sentence

~~is so important that a player have quick~~

omit misspelled, unneeded word

~~hands.~~ Since most of the actions ~~incorperated~~

replace with more specific: "require quick . . ."

in baseball ~~involves the use of the~~ hands,

Misspelling: replace with maneuver

catching, hitting, fielding and throwing. ~~It is~~

Wordy: replace with "To succeed, players must . . ."

~~important that he/she be able to~~ (manover)

replace with less awkward "their"

~~his/her~~ hands quickly and with ease. For ex-

ample, if a pitcher was throwing fast balls at

85 mph or better, a quality hitter must be

misspelling: replace with "possible"

able to wait on the ball as long as (posible)

before he/she swings the bat. The most im-

portant factor in accomplishing this

misspelling: replace with "particular"

(particlar) task is simply having quick hands.

Will Clark of the Texas Rangers sets a perfect

misspelling or typo: should be "He"

example of this task. (Hew) seems to be able

show possessive: "batters' "

to sit in the (batters) box and wait until the

pitcher's pitch almost reaches the

show possessive & correct misspelling: "catcher's mitt"

(catchers mit) before he hits the ball over the

fence. His hands seem to attack the baseball

omit apostrophe in possessive: should be "its"

like a cobra attacks (it's) victim. Second of

Not parallel: rather, compare "baseball player" to other professionals

all, like many other sports being played to-

day, a quality baseball player must (posess) at

misspelling: should be "possess"

least average speed. One of the biggest as-

misspelling: should be "definitely"

pects of baseball is (definetly) scoring runs.

wrong word: should be "players"

replace vague word with *quickly*

Consequently, teams must have (plays) who

can (sufficently) run the bases. ~~With this in~~

wordy: leave out

~~mind, it is important to distinguish what is~~

~~meant by average speed.~~ By major league

standards, an average player must ~~be able to~~

run from home plate to first base in at least

should be plural "seconds"

4.3 (second.) ~~A great example of~~ this quality ← Weak and wordy: replace with *Pete Rose best exemplified this quality*

rather than repeating, use pronoun "He"

~~would have to be~~ Pete Rose. (Pete Rose) was

not the fastest player to ever play the game of

baseball. However, Pete possessed 4.3 speed

Break up overlong, wordy sentence: *base. Many still consider him . . .*

to first base ~~and is still considered by many~~

~~to be~~ one of the greatest players to ever play

the game of baseball.

Proofreading Exercise

Proofread the following paragraph:

Third in order, a quality baseball player must

have a strong arm. By major league stan-

dards, a player to be considered to have a

strong arm, he/she must be able to throw the

baseball 60 ft 6 inches at least 82 mph by

radar gun calibrations or throw the ball 240

ft with an 8 ft or less arch. Keeping in mind,

not only these standards, but he/she must be able to do these particular tasks on a consistant basis. One such person seems to stick out of mind is Dave Parker. Dave Parker was an outfielder for the Pittsburgh Pirates. He could literally throw the ball from the 360 ft fence on a line to home plate. Watching him throw the ball from the outfield was like watching a canon ball being shot from a canon. Consequently he was called the "canon

In conclusion, in order to be considered a quality baseball player, a player must pos-

misspelling: should be "average"

sess quick hands, (avage) speed and a strong arm. These are simply the main ingredients

misspelling: should be "successful"

it takes to be (successfull) in the game of baseball.

After rethinking his second draft, Mark writes a final version of his example paper.

STUDENT EXAMPLE ESSAY: FINAL VERSION
BECOMING A QUALITY BASEBALL PLAYER

When I was three, my grandfather began taking me to baseball games. The excitement quickly took hold, and I imagined becoming a player like those I saw on the field. In kindergarten, a teacher asked me, "Joe, what's one and one?" All the other kids laughed when I said, "A ball and a strike." In my lifetime, I've not only played in Little League, public school, and college, I've seen over one thousand high school, college, and professional baseball games. As a result, I've learned what it takes to become a quality player: quick hands, average or better speed, and a strong arm.

First, most of the action in baseball requires quick hands: catching, hitting, fielding, and throwing. To succeed, players must maneuver their hands quickly and easily. For example, if a pitcher throws a fast ball at 85 mph or better, a quality hitter must wait as long as possible before swinging the bat. By waiting, the hitter can better judge the speed and arc of the ball. With this skill, a player is more likely to get a hit or home run. The best example of quick hands, combined with perfect judgment, is Will Clark of the Texas Rangers. He can sit in the batter's box and wait until a pitch almost reaches the catcher's mitt. Then he hits the ball over the fence. His hands attack the baseball like a cobra attacks its victim, making his play a model of talented hands.

Second, like professional athletes in many other sports, a quality baseball player must possess at least average speed. To win, baseball teams must score runs. Consequently, teams need players who can not only hit but run the bases quickly. By major league standards, an average player must run from home plate to first base in no more than 4.3 seconds. Pete Rose best exemplified this quality. He was not the fastest player to ever play baseball. However, Pete possessed 4.3 speed to first base. Many still consider him one of the greatest players in baseball.

Third, a quality baseball player must have a strong arm. By major league standards, a strong arm means a player must be able to throw the baseball 60 feet 6 inches, at least 82 mph by radar gun calibrations. In addition, a player must throw the ball at least 240 feet with less than an 8-foot arch. Players must not only meet these standards, but do so consistently. The best example of such a player is Dave Parker, an outfielder for the Pittsburgh Pirates. He could throw the ball on a line from the 360-foot fence to home plate. Watching him throw the ball from the outfield was like watching a cannon fire a cannon ball. Consequently, he was called the "cannon."

In conclusion, I've personally tried to develop the quality baseball skills revealed by Will Clark, Pete Rose, and Dave Parker. Knowing that a player needs quick hands, average speed, and a strong arm should make me a successful baseball player and, perhaps, others too.

EXAMPLE WRITING TOPICS

The following are some possible topics for an example paragraph or paper. Limit your topic to fit your instructor's requirements. Tell the reader *why* you have chosen your topic, and link your details closely to it.

1. How does a fear of enclosed spaces (or another fear) interfere with a normal life?

2. How have misleading advertisements led you to be disappointed in products or services?

3. How does a bad habit (smoking, speaking frankly) get you into trouble?
4. How did a turning point change your life?
5. How did you learn more from disappointment than from gratification?
6. How has risk-taking (or lack of it) affected your happiness?
7. How has helping others gotten you into trouble?

CHAPTER SIX

Classification

Classification means placing a number of individuals into common groups. It's used to help readers make sense of the parts. For example, a task force may be formed to develop policies to fight drugs in the workplace, especially in small businesses. The task force notes that most large organizations have such policies, but that small and midsize businesses, which employ 80 percent of workers, do not. The task force, through their analysis, has classified a number of businesses into separate types or kinds. Their groupings or classification would look like this:

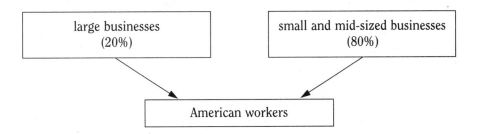

When writing a classification paper, tell your reader at the very beginning how you plan to classify your topic. Then develop each body paragraph by treating each part or aspect in order. To classify effectively, use the following guidelines.

LINK CLASSIFYING TO YOUR PURPOSE

Tell your readers why they should care about your paper. Don't just say "People volunteer for five causes in this rank order: children, cultural, religious, political, and animals," or that "The U.S. Postal Service dominates the overseas bulk mail business with 70 percent of the market." Write your thesis statements like this:

B y knowing that volunteers prefer serving children, cultural, and religious causes, civic and nonprofit charities can direct their appeals to these interests.

Whether your nose is long, the bridge or tip is too wide or drooping, or if you are just dissatisfied with the appearance of your nose, cosmetic surgery will easily correct it.

States eager to sell custom license plates place motorists in three groups: the "hot dogs" who like to design their own, "inner-directed" drivers who will pay more for a sports team or organization tag, and those who won't pay extra for anything.

Decide on your purpose, and tell your readers what it is.

USE A SINGLE GUIDING PRINCIPLE FOR CLASSIFYING

If you were labeling the contents of a file cabinet, you might include *bills, important papers, warranty cards, instruction booklets,* but you wouldn't include *an attractive lamp on top.* If you did, you'd be mixing up the list with an unrelated item (the "lamp on top"). Similarly, if you are classifying shirts by type, don't throw in the kind of fiber: polo, dress, pullover, and *cotton.* Decide on the type of classification, and then follow it throughout your paragraph or essay.

INCLUDE ALL THE PARTS IN YOUR CLASSIFICATION

If you are classifying fuels used in different types of car engines, don't list gasoline and diesel without including electric. If your labels become confusing, limit your groupings. For instance, you might not be able to include all the predators in nature. However, you could deal with the most important ones in your area. Moreover, the impossible job of discussing all the tools needed for home repair could be limited to those used for cutting and fastening. No matter how you focus your classification, include all the parts.

READINGS

As Chapter 1 pointed out, **topic sentences** sum up a paragraph's main idea. Once you have written your topic sentence, develop it with examples or details. These specifics will make your summary statement clearer, more vivid to your reader. The following paragraph groups its details clearly within its general category:

Lists *American* R&B "who's"

Divides category—rhythm and blues—into two groups, American and British

Lists *British* R&B "who's"

Contrasts styles

> Rhythm and blues, like rock 'n' roll, was born and raised in America, with such influential exponents as Aretha Franklin, Marvin Gaye, and Prince. *Now Britain is giving rise to what might be called alternative R & B.* Performers such as Tricky, Portishead, singer Carleen Anderson, Seal, and others have enlivened the accepted, sometimes constraining formats of R & B songs with offbeat rhythms and the kind of enigmatic lyrics one would usually expect from alternative rock. Says Des'ree: "I think British soul tends to be less conventional. American soul music seems to be going through a phase now where most of the songs are quite similar. They've found a formula that works. I don't know if they've exhausted it, but they're employing it quite a bit."

Chapter 2 showed how a **thesis** sums up the main idea for an entire writing; it serves an **essay** as a **topic sentence** serves a **paragraph.** Sometimes, a writer begins an essay with an example, following it with a **thesis:**

Lead-in compares pets to clothing fashions

Thesis divides group—pets—into three

First subgroup: ferrets

Second subgroup: hedgehogs

> As with fashion, pet styles come and go. Dogs and cats may be the mainstays—like classic winter coats or A-line skirts—but pets have gone designer.
> The '90s pet is no-fuss chic, from ferrets to hedgehogs to iguanas.
> When Brandy Moore of Lawrenceville graduated from high school two years ago, she refused her parents' offer of a cruise. She wanted a ferret instead.
> Moore, 20, a hearing aid inspector at Starky Southeastern Labs, carried her baby ferret, Ferris, in a basket and bottle-fed him. He now uses a cat-litter box, barks, and comes when he's called.
> Ferris romps on the Moores' waterbed, plays with David Moore's two Dobermans, and swims in the bathtub. And Ferris steals jewelry, bras—anything that fascinates him.
> Many people are intrigued by hedgehogs, those prickly little fellows that doubled as croquet balls in *Alice in Wonderland.* Georgia authorities say it's one pet trend they hope won't stick around for long.
> It is illegal to sell or breed hedgehogs in Georgia. They can carry a virus that is deadly to livestock.
> Hedgehogs sleep all day, eat insects, roll up in a spiny ball when disturbed, and have a tendency to drool.

Hedgehog owner Rocky Putter wonders if he made a $225 mistake when he bought his hedgehog two years ago.

"He's just something that sits in a cage," says Putter, manager of Love for Sale pet shop in Stone Mountain. "Now that I've had him, I realize some animals . . . are probably better left in the wild."

Third subgroup: reptiles ➤ Atlanta pet shop owners say the real hot pet these days are cold-blooded reptiles: snakes, turtles, lizards, and iguanas. Reptiles are perfect for the '90s: small, undemanding, and low-maintenance.

"It's indicative of what I call the 'scratch 'n' sniff' society," says Perry Buffington, a pop psychologist who appears as Dr. Buff on WXIA/Channel 11 and WPCH-FM (94.9). "People want to be instantly gratified, but don't want to put out any effort."

Iguanas are "easy," says Robin Griffith, manager of Jungle Pets in Gwinnett County. And iguanas are cheap: Babies sell for $14.99. "[They don't] poop in the center of the floor or chew up your sneakers or have to be walked," he says.

Other reptiles are also appealing because of their offbeat nature.

"As people struggle to find who they are and what they stand for," Buffington says, "they'll pick an unusual pet because that makes them stand out."

Draws conclusion: because people buy on impulse, pet fashions change ➤ But designer pets, many times bought on impulse, often become throwaways.

Pot-bellied pigs, so hot a few years ago, have outgrown their cuteness. As people overfeed the pigs, pets guaranteed to weigh 40 to 50 pounds balloon to 300 pounds.

"We buy a significant number of pre-owned pets," Griffith says. "We probably get two or three calls a day from people trying to sell iguanas because their kids have outgrown them."

Conclusion ends by predicting the future ➤ So what's on the horizon? Industry insiders predict rabbits. They're small, they're cuddly, and they breed like, well, rabbits.

"Beauty in the Beast,"
Martha Woodham,
The Atlanta Journal/Constitution

The examples you cite will often prove a point, convincing your readers to share your views. As in the preceding selection, your thesis may be novel or somewhat controversial. Choose details or facts that are vivid and convincing. As they read your writing, readers should be able to visualize your examples. When a man's boss quit smoking, the man asked if he felt better after he'd stopped. The boss replied, "Definitely. I feel better now when I feel bad than I used to feel when I felt good."

In addition, both you and your reader should find your examples interesting and concrete. They not only add variety to your topic, they also extend its range, sometimes for several paragraphs. The following essay is a proposal for a half-hour television show about prisoners on death row. Each topic sentence is re-stated with reasons:

Title serves as thesis, sug-
gesting that the following
essay will provide answers to
its question

Why Will America Tune in to Death Row: True Stories?

Topic sentence: one-sentence
paragraph

It's timely!

Topic sentence

Every day, the death penalty is a topic in newspapers, magazines, TV talk shows, novels, and movies. Witness best-selling novelist John Grisham's latest novel, *The*

Gives reasons why

Chamber—about death row. Or Sharon Stone's next movie, *Last Dance*—about a woman on death row.

Topic sentence

It's provocative!

Topic sentence

Do you know anyone who doesn't have an opinion on

Gives reason why

the death penalty? No matter which side they're on, it's something people are passionate about.

It looks great!

Every episode will be made with the care and quality

Gives reason why

demonstrated in our pilot, "Special Edition: Women on Death Row."

Martin Milner's a great host!

Gives reason why

Audiences remember Milner fondly from *Adam 12* and *Route 66.*

It's focused!

Topic sentence

From the name of the show alone, audiences know just what they're going to get.

Topic sentence

It's life or death!

Unlike those cop shows that deal with all kinds of cases, our shows are linked by the ultimate penalty for a crime—death!

"The Executioner's Docudrama,"
Harper's Magazine

To get ready to meet every distant relative in America, Bill Tonelli, the author of the following selection, surveyed all those listed in a reference book. He reports his findings—some of them surprising—about his fellow descendants of Italian immigrants.

Words to Define

vagrant: wandering, nomadic

questionnaire: survey including a set of questions

ancestry: parentage, those from whom a person is descended

fluently: easily, using many words from the language

Prereading

1. If you put together a survey asking your classmates about their ancestry, what questions would you ask? What would you expect to discover?

2. What is your own ancestry? How are you like or different from these people?

THE UNITED STATES OF TONELLI

Bill Tonelli

Gives reason why ⟶ A vagrant urge seized me: to drive around the country and shake the hand of every Tonelli in America. Before I

Topic sentence: one-sentence paragraph ⟶ went on the road, I sent a four-page questionnaire to all the Tonellis in the book, *The Amazing Story of the Tonellis in America,* and got back about 200 answers. I discovered that only a little more than half (53.3 percent) of the Tonelli Nation have (or had) both parents of Italian ancestry. Most (52.3 percent) are the grandchildren of immigrants. The majority (57.4 percent) did not marry someone of Italian ancestry. Forty percent speak a

Last reason serves as conclusion ⟶ few words of Italian, while 16.6 percent speak it fluently. When Tonellis serve tomato sauce, 67.3 percent make it themselves, 27.6 percent open a jar, and 4.5 percent do it both ways.

Queries for Understanding

1. How long is Bill Tonelli's questionnaire, with how many replies?

2. How many of Tonelli's respondents had both parents of Italian ancestry? were grandchildren of immigrants? did *not* marry someone of Italian ancestry?

3. How many of Tonelli's respondents speak some Italian? speak it fluently?

4. How many of the Tonellis make their own tomato sauce; how many open a jar?

Queries on the Writer's Techniques

1. In his opening statement, Bill Tonelli mentions a chain of causes and effects. What are they?

2. Into which groups does he place the Tonellis?

3. Into which subgroups does Bill Tonelli further divide the Tonellis?

4. Why does Bill Tonelli mention his tomato sauce grouping last in the paragraph? Is it more or less important, more or less interesting than his other data?

Writing Topics

1. To what extent are people defined by their ancestry, as reflected in their names?

2. Consider popular stereotypes that link national origins with habits, belongings, or preferred foods: what are they, and how accurate are they?

The following selection effectively uses classification. Although the groups into which the Scholastic Aptitude Test is divided are rather technical, would-be college students study them for one reason: scores on the SAT affect the kind of college that will admit them.

Words to Define

completions: choices among word groups to make sense of the sentence

comprehension: grasping, understanding meaning

analogies: comparisons or similarities often linked by *like* or *as*

digits: numbers

grid: a pattern of lines crossing one another at right angles

percentile: group into which one falls based on the percentage of those doing better or worse

Prereading

1. Is it fair to use a test like the SAT to determine which colleges will accept which students? Why or why not?

2. What tests of your ability have you taken (without limiting yourself to verbal or mathematical tests)? Where would you rank yourself?

How to Ace the College Entrance Exams

Edwin Kiester, Jr., and Sally Valente Kiester

The Scholastic Aptitude Test has 138 questions, divided into verbal and math sections. There are five 30-minute sections and two 15-minute sections. The SAT's verbal section consists of 19 sentence completions, 19 analogies dealing with word meanings, and 40 reading-comprehension questions. (Each type of question is included in each of the three subsections.) The math portion includes 60 questions on arithmetic, algebra, and geometry. Fifty are multiple-choice; ten are "grid-in" questions that require the student to volunteer his own answer by marking digits on a grid.

SAT verbal and math sections are scored separately on a scale of 200 to 800. Currently a combined score higher than 1200 is sought by the nation's 300 most selective colleges. Fewer than ten percent of students score about 1300, and last year only 17 individuals earned a perfect 1600. In April 1995 a new scoring scale added points to most students' scores without affecting their percentiles. (The College Board says this won't affect the test's difficulty or fairness.)

Queries for Understanding

1. Into what two sections is the SAT divided?
2. Into how many sections is the verbal part of the SAT divided? Which skill is most important?
3. What skills are assessed by the math portion of the SAT? How many of them are multiple choice?
4. How many of the nation's colleges are considered the "most selective?"
5. What scores do these colleges demand?
6. What percentage of students score above 1300? How many earned a perfect 1600 last year?

Queries on the Writer's Techniques

1. Why does the selection deal with the parts of the SAT before explaining how the test is scored?
2. Why does the selection indicate the range of possible SAT scores before telling how well test-takers do on the test?
3. Why do you suppose the test-makers added points to the possible scores—without affecting students' percentiles or rankings on the test?

Writing Topics

1. In what ways is success linked with test scores such as the SAT or IQ?

2. What people have you known or heard about who succeeded in spite of poor performances in their youth? Have failed in spite of good grades in school?

In the following selection, the writer describes how American men, becoming more concerned with the ravages of aging, are getting nips and tucks.

Words to Define

preen: take pride in one's looks

transplants: human tissue that has been surgically moved from one place to another

cosmetic: beautifying, skin-deep

project: present, create in others' minds

procedure: operation

Prereading

1. If you could improve your physical appearance in some way, what change would be most important to you, and why?

2. Argue for or against the view that society places too much importance on people's appearance.

IMAGE ENHANCEMENT

Amanda Husted

If society held a mirror to itself, a lot of Americans would stop to preen. Some of them would be wearing new hair. Men make up 25 percent of cosmetic surgery patients—up 11 percent in four years—the American Academy for Cosmetic Surgery says. Most of them—20 percent—get hair transplants. Another 9.4 percent underwent nose surgery this year, 7.4 percent had eyelid surgery, 6 percent got liposuction (a fat reduction procedure), and 4.7 percent had chemical face peels.

The increase in male cosmetic surgery can be traced to aging—and perhaps sagging—baby boomers. Male patients cite the need to project an image of an alert, aggressive, productive employee, the academy says.

Women still outnumber men 3-to-1 in the pursuit of youth and/or beauty. They most often get liposuction (9.3 percent), eyelid surgery (8.7 percent), nose surgery (7.5 percent), chemical face peels (7.2 percent), and face lifts (3.7 percent). Breast augmentation surgery using silicone gel breast implants has declined 48 percent since 1990, but breast enlargement still accounts for 3 percent of all female cosmetic surgery.

The academy, which surveyed its 1,100 member surgeons, said liposuction has replaced eyelifts as the most common cosmetic surgery, with almost 104,000 patients undergoing the procedure each year. The number of liposuctions has increased 45 percent since 1990.

This year, some 1.2 million cosmetic surgeries will be performed.

Atlanta Journal/Constitution

Queries for Understanding

1. What proportion of Americans having plastic surgery is now men? What kind of plastic surgery is most popular among men, making up what percentage?
2. For what two reasons are American men—especially aging baby boomers—getting plastic surgery?
3. By how much do women outnumber men in getting plastic surgery? What kind is most popular among women?
4. How many people are now getting liposuction each year? How many women are getting plastic surgery of all kinds each year?

Queries on the Writer's Techniques

1. Why does the writer take up plastic surgery for men first in the selection?
2. What are the most significant changes in the types of plastic surgery taking place among women over the last several years?
3. Why does the selection include the total of plastic surgeries each year last?

Writing Topics

1. Agree or disagree with this proposition: people who look attractive are more likely to succeed than those who do not.
2. Agree or disagree: federal law should/should not forbid discrimination against unattractive people?

The following selection describes capoeira, a Brazilian form of self-defense, which offers an aerobic workout—and a philosophy of life.

Words to Define

martial: warlike, combative

staples: basic, most useful parts

simulated: pretended, imitated

incorporates: makes part of itself, takes inside

regional: identifiable part of a larger whole, such as an area of a country

fluid: flowing, quickly moving

Prereading

1. Describe a sport that combines parts or aspects of other sports.

2. If you had a chance to learn a set of athletic skills, what would you choose, and why?

MARTIAL ARTS WITH A BACKBEAT

Diane Cardwell

More than 400 years old, the Afro-Brazilian martial art capoeira (pronounced cop-WEAR-a), combines gymnastic staples like hand and headstands, backbends, cartwheels, and backflips with the roundhouse, front, and back kicks of karate. Set to a pounding Afro-Brazilian beat that controls the speed of the simulated fight, capoeira incorporates fluid, circular motions and steps similar to those in jazz dance. It was developed in Bahia, Brazil, by West African slaves who had to disguise the deadly technique as a playful dance to keep their wealthy landowning masters in the dark.

After slavery ended, capoeira grew as a street-fighting form among the underclass. It was considered the province of hooligans until the 1930s, when the first formal capoeira academy was established by Manoel Machado. He is credited with inventing the faster, more acrobatic regional form that's become increasingly popular in Brazil during the last few years. The traditional form, capoeira Angola, is played slower and closer to the ground. Either way, it is a fluid and demanding sport that builds strength, agility, and discipline.

Swing

Queries for Understanding

1. What two groups of athletic moves does capoeira combine?

2. How is capoeira like both a fight and jazz dancing?

3. How and where was capoeira developed, and in what way?

4. What happened to capoeira after slavery ended in Brazil?

5. What is the main difference between Machado's type of capoeira and the traditional form?

Queries on the Writer's Techniques

1. On what basis does the paragraph group its aspects of capoeira?

2. How did Machado's academy change the acceptability of capoeira?

3. How does the paragraph's conclusion account for the growing popularity of capoeira?

Writing Topics

1. Agree or disagree: self-defense should be offered as a course in the public schools.

2. Agree or disagree: violence on TV, involving karate, kick-boxing, or other forms of attack and self-defense influences the behavior of children.

In the following selection, the writer suggests that while America has neglected the station wagon, Europe has rediscovered it in a new guise.

Words to Define

suburban: areas near cities where people live and drive to and from work

utes: a slang term for "utility vehicles"

suburbia: a noun form of the adjective *suburban*

pride: a family herd or bunch (usually applied to lions)

gaggle: a family herd or bunch (usually applied to geese)

torque: literally "twisting power," used here to indicate horsepower or acceleration

shuttle: transport, carrying people from place to place

commute: driving between work and home

Prereading

1. Describe your dream car. How does it differ from a car your parents might have preferred?

2. If you agree with the feelings expressed in this paragraph, tell why. If not, why not?

THE SCANDINAVIAN SUPERWAGON

Phil Patton

Gone are the Vista Cruisers that once plied America's inland seas, gone the Nomads and Country Squires. Only a handful of full-size station wagons survive—a Caprice here, a Roadmaster there, their simulated wood grain fading in the suburban sunlight. In their place, we drive minivans and sport utes—family haulers. But prides of Subarus and gaggles of Tauruses keep the wagon alive. And all across suburbia, there are signs of a slowly mounting hunger for something more: for sporty wagons, vehicles that bring torque and handling to the weekend kiddie shuttle and the weekday commute.

Esquire

Queries for Understanding

1. According to the paragraph, what kind of car, represented by what popular brands, has disappeared from America's roads?
2. What station wagon brands, marked by what decoration, have barely survived?
3. What three types of vehicles have replaced station wagons, used for what purposes?
4. What new kind of car seems to be replacing "family haulers"?

Queries on the Writer's Techniques

1. What type of car does the paragraph divide into smaller groups?
2. On what basis does the paragraph organize its discussion of these groups?
3. How does the last sentence get ready for a further subdivision of this group?

Writing Topics

1. How has the preference of Americans for cars influenced other parts of our culture, such as restaurants, banks, and so on?
2. How will the replacement of gasoline-driven cars by electric ones affect Americans' driving and living habits?

In the following selection, a black single parent finds both sorrows and joys in the most memorable, poignant turning points of her life.

Words to Define

tumultuous: turbulent, emotionally difficult

designated: specified, pointed out

possessive: taking ownership of

exacted: dictated, ordered

Prereading

1. What person from another generation—younger or older—has deeply influenced you?

TURNING POINTS

Student Essay (Tonya)

I'm a black female, the single parent of two children. In my lifetime I have withstood some tumultuous moments. I've gone from joyous laughter at wedding receptions, through the magical feelings of giving life, to the unspeakable pain accompanying the death of my father. My experiences have given me the ability to fix the things I can, ignore the things I can't, and the wisdom to know the difference.

Both my marriages were short-lived mistakes. The first, in adolescence, resulted from my attempts to escape my parents' constant monitoring. Not until I was well into marriage did I realize I'd exchanged a life of paradise for one of pure hell. I went from my parents' "Turn the music down!" to my husband's "Turn the music off!" My duties changed from designated jobs I shared with my brothers to doing *everything all* the time. After three years of virtual imprisonment by a possessive man, I ended the marriage, escaping with only the child conceived by the union.

Twelve years later, affection victimized me for a second time. Confusing kindness for love, I mistook a strong man for my knight in shining armor. However, I immediately realized I'd made another mistake. Shortly after the birth of my second child, I was aching for freedom. As the price of this freedom, my husband exacted an unnecessary, costly courtroom battle, where only the lawyers won. After a year of airing dirty laundry, the divorce legally ended my marriage. Once again, I walked away with nothing but a child.

Yet the birth of my children was something magical, an unexplainable miracle. In an instant, my feelings changed from throbbing intense pain to delightful tears of joy. My first child transformed me from a girl to a woman in a split second. Despite my unsureness about what lay ahead, she endowed me with responsibility: I knew that I was the sole provider for this baby. My second child changed me from a woman to an experienced mother. She gave me my chance to prove I had the situation under control, and I went on to show the world how to do it.

Most recently, the most devastating event in my life was my father's death. Always a jokester, he laughed the night he called from New York to tell me the results of some medical tests: "Well, Baby, your daddy has the big C." I screamed, I cried, I couldn't believe what I was hearing. After assuring me he'd be all right, we hung up. For the next few weeks, I avoided calling him because I didn't want to hear bad news again.

Later, however, Daddy canceled his reservation for our annual family reunion, saying he was too skinny to go. I immediately went to New York to talk to his doctors, to convince them they'd made a terrible mistake. I had to make Daddy change his mind about dying. When I walked into his hospital room, he was sick, thin, and suffering so much pain he didn't recognize me. I was his only little girl and he didn't know me. That night I begged God to take this pain away from my father: "Please, God, don't let him hurt like that." Finally, a month later my daddy left me. To this very day, I still cry; I feel alone, like something that can never be replaced is missing. I wasn't ready, Lord knows; I just wasn't ready.

In conclusion, I've learned how to be a better judge of people, partly by taking my time getting to know them. I've also realized that once you have accepted the responsibility of having children, your life is no longer your own. Finally, I've learned to prepare myself for the unexpected, to leave space in my life for the element of surprise.

Queries for Understanding

1. What motivated the writer to marry for the first and second times?
2. What outcome opposed to her expectations did the writer's first marriage bring?
3. What outcome opposed to her expectations did the writer's second marriage bring?
4. How does the writer feel about the birth of her children?
5. How did the writer react to her father's illness and death?

Queries on the Writer's Techniques

1. Into what groups does the writer divide, and then subdivide, the defining experiences of her life?
2. How are the writer's feelings about the birth of her children ironic—contrary to her feelings about marriage, for example?
3. How are the writer's gains from experiences both positive and negative?

Writing Topics

1. In what ways do Americans tend to ignore or deny the reality of death?
2. What are the best ways to deal with the death of a loved one?

In the following selection, the writer suggests that retailers are betting that shoppers this year, after several practical Christmases, will buy more luxurious—or at least more fanciful—gifts.

Words to Define

robust: strong, vigorous

precarious: unsure, uncertain

gourmet: unusual, especially fine

apparel: clothing

mohair: heavy, woolly fabric made of Angora goat hair

velour: a velvet-like fabric

bordeaux: red

whimsical: playful, fanciful

beveled: with edges cut at an angle

Prereading

1. If price were no object, what three gifts would you most like to receive?
2. From which group in the following selection would you like to receive gifts, and why?

Velvet Sneakers and Satellite Dishes: Retailers' Picks for the Year's Hot Gifts

In stocking their shelves with velvet sneakers, $140 toothbrushes, and $899 digital satellite systems, merchants took a big gamble. Consumers have been spending carefully all year, but retailers planned for a more robust economy, higher consumer confidence levels, and pent-up demand to spark purchases of expensive products. And, as always, gut instinct played a big role.

"People want quality, not moderate-priced cookware," says a confident Joel Kaplan, a director for Dayton Hudson Corp.'s department stores. Calphalon, gourmet cookware that costs up to $145 for a pot, is selling especially well, he adds.

Guessing shoppers' whims before the holidays is always precarious. And because as much as 80% of all Christmas merchandise has been ordered by mid-November, retailers have little choice but to plug the gifts they've already stocked upon. Here are some of their picks:

Clothing

Apparel, after several slow seasons, is back on many merchants' hot-gift lists. Last year's fleecy, oversized tops and knit pull-on pants are now available in velvet, mohair, and silver fabrics. Early hits from Spiegel Inc.'s holiday catalog: a $59 black velour apron dress and $19.90 velvet Converse sneakers.

At Ann Taylor Stores Corp., Chief Executive Officer Sally Frame Kasaks says women are going beyond 1993's basic silk shirts to buy "layering pieces," such as embroidered vests, bodysuits, and jackets, in colors like bordeaux or peach.

To top things off: J. Crew is betting on a Dr. Seuss-inspired striped stocking cap—in red and white or green and white—for $28.

The company says it expects to sell 10,000 of the whimsical hats this Christmas.

Home Goods

Shoppers will give upscale accessories like brass table lamps for up to $400 and decorative beveled mirrors, according to home-improvement chain Lowe's. Sears, Roebuck & Co. is pushing the $59.99 Ryobi Detail Sander that reaches awkward places and Craftsman cordless screwdrivers and drills for up to $154.99.

Marshall Field stores are featuring a $140 Sensonic toothbrush that vibrates. Dayton Hudson's Mr. Kaplan says another early hit is a $44 Braun "supervolume" hair dryer, whose "fingers" make hair look bigger. But such gadgets have short life spans, he warns. High demand a couple years ago for juicers lasted only one season, leaving Dayton Hudson with lots of the machines on hand.

Electronics

How's this for a problem: Retailers are already worried about meeting demand for 18-inch satellite systems priced from $699 to $899. The size of a large pizza, the dishes receive more than 175 channels. "They're in short supply nationwide," frets a spokesman for Circuit City Stores Inc., Richmond, Va.

Franklin Karp, vice president of merchandising at Harvey Electronics Inc., Secaucus, N.J., said home theater products will drive sales at his high-end consumer electronics chain. This year's hot television: a 40-inch Mitsubishi for $3,000.

Wall Street Journal

Queries for Understanding

1. What economic conditions lead shoppers to buy expensive Christmas gifts?
2. By what time in the year have 80 percent of Christmas gifts been ordered by stores?
3. Among the clothing stocked by retailers, what is the cheapest gift, for how much?
4. What early big seller among home goods is viewed as a risky offering by retailers, and why?
5. What problem regarding which electronics item faces retailers?

Queries on the Writer's Techniques

1. Why does the selection include the piece of Calphalon cookware in the first paragraph?
2. Why is clothing the first group taken up by the selection?
3. What do the home goods mentioned in the second group have in common?
4. What do all the items mentioned in the electronics group have in common?

Writing Topics

1. If a disaster drove you from your house or apartment and you could save only three of your most prized possessions, what would they be, and why?
2. What gifts or objects bought or owned by others seem completely useless or unnecessary, and why?

As a young girl working in a white woman's kitchen, the author of the following selection received an education in human relations.

Words to Define
liberal: progressive, tolerant (usually of other races and ideas)
debutante: young woman with high social status

ludicrous: laughable, ridiculous

extensive: broad, extended

irrelevant: not related to the matter at hand

tatting: making lace with a small shuttle

sacheted: perfumed

perpetually: for ever, without end

impudent: bold, flippant

embalmed: preserving a corpse after death

pouty: protruding the lips to show displeasure

barrenness: inability to have children

ballad: a traditional form of poetry or music

essence: sum and substance

construed: to place a certain meaning on

dilemma: a problem posing two bad choices

preceded: came before

Prereading

1. Consider a turning point in your life that taught you a lasting lesson. What did you learn, and how do you feel about it now?

FINISHING SCHOOL

Maya Angelou

Recently a white woman from Texas, who would quickly describe herself as a liberal, asked me about my hometown. When I told her that in Stamps my grandmother had owned the only Negro general merchandise store since the turn of the century, she exclaimed, "Why, you were a debutante." Ridiculous and even ludicrous. But Negro girls in small Southern towns, whether poverty-stricken or just munching along on a few of life's necessities, were given as extensive and ir-relevant preparations for adulthood as rich white girls shown in magazines. Ad-mittedly the training was not the same. While white girls learned to waltz and sit gracefully with a tea cup balanced on their knees, we were lagging behind, learn-ing the mid-Victorian values with very little money to indulge them. . ..

We were required to embroider, and I had trunkfuls of colorful dish-towels, pillowcases, runners, and handkerchiefs to my credit. I mastered the art of cro-cheting and tatting, and there was a life-time's supply of dainty doilies that would never be used in sacheted dresser drawers. It went without saying that all girls could iron and wash, but the finer touches around the home, like setting a table with real silver, baking roasts, and cooking vegetables without meat, had to be learned elsewhere. Usually at the source of those habits. During my tenth year, a white woman's kitchen became my finishing school.

Mrs. Viola Cullinan was a plump woman who lived in a three-bedroom house somewhere behind the post office. She was singularly unattractive until she smiled, and then the lines around her eyes and mouth which made her look perpetually dirty disappeared, and her face looked like the mask of an impish elf. She usually rested her smile until late afternoon when her women friends dropped in and Miss Glory, the cook, served them cold drinks on the closed-in porch.

The exactness of her house was inhuman. This glass went here and only here. That cup had its place, and it was an act of impudent rebellion to place it anywhere else. At twelve o'clock the table was set. At 12:15 Mrs. Cullinan sat down to dinner (whether her husband had arrived or not). At 12:16 Miss Glory brought out the food.

It took me a week to learn the difference between a salad plate, a bread plate, and a dessert plate.

Mrs. Cullinan kept up the tradition of her wealthy parents. She was from Virginia. Miss Glory, who was a descendant of slaves that had worked for the Cullinans, told me her history. She had married beneath her (according to Miss Glory). Her husband's family hadn't had their money very long and what they had "didn't 'mount to much."

As ugly as she was, I thought privately, she was lucky to get a husband above or beneath her station. But Miss Glory wouldn't let me say a thing against her mistress. She was very patient with me, however, over the housework. She explained the dishware, silverware, and servants' bells. The large round bowl in which soup was served wasn't a soup bowl, it was a tureen. There were goblets, sherbet glasses, ice-cream glasses, wine glasses, green glass coffee cups with matching saucers, and water glasses. I had a glass to drink from, and it sat with Miss Glory's on a separate shelf from the others. Soup spoons, gravy boat, butter knives, salad forks, and carving platter were additions to my vocabulary and in fact almost represented a new language. I was fascinated with the novelty, with the fluttering Mrs. Cullinan and her Alice-in-Wonderland house.

Her husband remains, in my memory, undefined. I lumped him with all the other white men that I had ever seen and tried not to see.

On our way home one evening, Miss Glory told me that Mrs. Cullinan couldn't have children. She said that she was too delicate-boned. It was hard to imagine bones at all under those layers of fat. Miss Glory went on to say that the doctor had taken out all her lady organs. I reasoned that a pig's organs included the lungs, heart, and liver, so if Mrs. Cullinan was walking around without those essentials, it explained why she drank alcohol out of unmarked bottles. She was keeping herself embalmed.

When I spoke to Bailey about it, he agreed that I was right, but she also informed me that Mr. Cullinan had two daughters by a colored lady and that I knew them very well. He added that the girls were the spitting image of their father. I was unable to remember what he looked like, although I had just left him a few hours before, but I thought of the Coleman girls. They were very light-skinned and certainly didn't look very much like their mother (no one ever mentioned Mr. Coleman).

My pity for Mrs. Cullinan preceded me the next morning like the Cheshire cat's smile. Those girls, who could have been her daughters, were beautiful. They didn't have to straighten their hair. Even when they were caught in the rain, their braids still hung down straight like tamed snakes. Their mouths were pouty little cupid's bows. Mrs. Cullinan didn't know what she missed. Or maybe she did. Poor Mrs. Cullinan.

For weeks after, I arrived early, left late, and tried very hard to make up for her barrenness. If she had her own children, she wouldn't have had to ask me to run a thousand errands from the back door to the back door of her friends. Poor old Mrs. Cullinan.

Then one evening Miss Glory told me to serve the ladies on the porch. After I set the tray down and turned toward the kitchen, one of the women asked, "What's your name, girl?" It was the speckled-faced one. Mrs. Cullinan said, "She doesn't talk much. Her name's Margaret."

"Is she dumb?'"

"No. As I understand it, she can talk when she wants to, but she's usually quiet as a little mouse. Aren't you, Margaret?"

I smiled at her. Poor thing. No organs and couldn't even pronounce my name correctly.

"She's a sweet little thing, though."

"Well, that may be, but the name's too long. I'd never bother myself. I'd call her Mary if I was you."

I fumed into the kitchen. That horrible woman would never have the chance to call me Mary because if I was starving I'd never work for her. . . .

That evening I decided to write a poem on being white, fat, old, and without children. It was going to be a tragic ballad. I would have to watch her carefully to capture the essence of her loneliness and pain.

The very next day, she called me by the wrong name. Miss Glory and I were washing up the lunch dishes when Mrs. Cullinan came to the doorway. "Mary?"

Miss Glory asked, "Who?"

Mrs. Cullinan, sagging a little, knew and I knew. "I want Mary to go down to Mrs. Randall's and take her some soup. She's not been feeling well for a few days."

Mrs. Glory's face was a wonder to see. "You mean Margaret, ma'am. Her name's Margaret."

"That's too long. She's Mary from now on. Heat that soup from last night and put it in the china tureen and, Mary, I want you to carry it carefully."

Every person I knew had a hellish horror of being "called out of his name." It was a dangerous practice to call a Negro anything that could be loosely construed as insulting because of the centuries of their having been called niggers, jigs, dinges, blackbirds, crows, boots, and spooks.

Miss Glory had a fleeting second of feeling sorry for me. Then as she handed me the hot tureen she said, "Don't mind, don't pay that no mind. Sticks and stones may break your bones, but words. . . . You know, I been working for her for twenty years."

She held the back door open for me. "Twenty years. I wasn't much older than you. My name used to be Hallelujah. That's what Ma named me, but my mistress give me 'Glory,' and it stuck. I likes it better, too."

I was in the little path that ran behind the houses when Miss Glory shouted, "It's shorter, too."

For a few seconds it was a tossup whether I would laugh (imagine being named Hallelujah) or cry (imagine letting some white woman rename you for her convenience). My anger saved me from either outburst. I had to quit the job, but the problem was going to be how to do it. Momma wouldn't allow me to quit for just any reason.

"She's a peach. That woman is a real peach." Mrs. Randall's maid was talking as she took the soup from me, and I wondered what her name used to be and what she answered to now.

For a week I looked into Mrs. Cullinan's face as she called me Mary. She ignored my coming late and leaving early. Miss Glory was a little annoyed because I had begun to leave egg yolk on the dishes and wasn't putting much heart in polishing the silver. I hoped that she would complain to our boss, but she didn't.

Then Bailey solved my dilemma. He had me describe the contents of the cupboard and the particular plates she liked best. Her favorite piece was a casserole shaped like a dish and the green glass coffee cups. I kept his instructions in mind, so on the next day when Miss Glory was hanging out clothes and I had again been told to serve the old biddies on the porch, I dropped the empty serving tray. When I heard Mrs. Cullinan scream, "Mary!" I picked up the casserole and two of the green glass cups in readiness. As she rounded the kitchen door I let them fall on the tiled floor.

I could never absolutely describe to Bailey what happened next, because each time I got to the part where she fell on the floor and screwed up her ugly face to cry, we burst out laughing. She actually wobbled around on the floor and picked up shards of the cups and cried, "Oh, Momma. Oh, dear Gawd. It's Momma's china from Virginia. Oh, Momma, I'm sorry."

Miss Glory came running in from the yard and the women from the porch crowded around. Miss Glory was almost as broken up as her mistress. "You mean to say she broke our Virginia dishes? What we gone do?"

Miss Cullinan cried louder, "That clumsy nigger. Clumsy little black nigger."

Old speckled-faced leaned down and asked, "Who did it, Viola? Was it Mary? Who did it?"

Everything was happening so fast I can't remember whether her action preceded her words, but I know that Mrs. Cullinan said, "Her name's Margaret, goddamn it, her name's Margaret." And she threw a wedge of broken plate at me. It could have been the hysteria which put her aim off, but the flying crockery caught Miss Glory right over her ear and she started screaming.

I left the front door wide open so all the neighbors could hear.

Mrs. Cullinan was right about one thing. My name wasn't Mary.

I Know Why the Caged Bird Sings, Random House, 1969

Queries for Understanding

1. What differences does the writer spell out between the experiences of young, middle-class black girls and white girls?

2. What oddities or shortcomings does the writer immediately see in Mrs. Cullinan?

3. What contrast does the writer see about Mrs. Cullinan's pretensions and the realities of her situation?

4. What did Miss Glory teach the writer initially about her behavior and the organization of the Cullinan household?

5. What secrets does the writer learn about Mrs. Cullinan and her husband?

6. What judgments does the writer make about Mr. Cullinan's daughters, with what relevance to Mrs. Cullinan herself?

7. What changes in her treatment lead to the writer's act of rebellion, and why?

8. How does the writer get revenge for Mrs. Cullinan's attempts to change her name?

Queries on the Writer's Techniques

1. What double meanings does the title, "Finishing School," convey? Into what groups and subgroups does the writer divide people and experiences?

2. What is the theme of the essay?

Writing Topics

1. How do people use names and titles to influence the ways in which others react to them (consider degrees, occupational titles, nicknames, even pronunciations)?

2. Is the writer justified or unjustified in feeling so sensitive about what she is called?

THE WRITING PROCESS

After choosing a topic for your paragraph or essay, do the following:

1. Describe your attitude or feelings toward this topic in a few words.

2. Explain why the topic interests you: are you involved personally or in the workplace with the topic? Give one reason for choosing this topic.

3. Why would others be interested in this topic? Describe readers who would find your topic entertaining or informative.

4. In a few words, tell what your readers might think, feel, or do after reading your paragraph or essay. Is this what you intended them to do?

5. Give two or three examples that develop or explain your main idea.

6. What might make it hard for you to write a first draft of this topic? Do you know enough about it to handle it well? Is your topic too broad or too narrow? Explain how you can solve these problems in a few words.

The author of the following selection still had pleasant memories of the years she spent in the military. To narrow her topic, she focused on the things she had learned. Then she wrote an exploratory draft.

CLASSIFICATION: FIRST DRAFT

The military is really great because it teaches you a lot of different things. You learn how to work well with others and this is real rewarding experience to everyone concerned in the whole process. In basic, everybody has to mearch together. This isn't easy because some people can't tell their left from their right and it gets very confusing. We got mad at those who couldn't march and the Sergeant took away our personal time. Another example was whhen we packaed our rucksacks with equipment and walked a long ways. We helped each other. You also get to meet a lot of different people in many different places. The military has an iinteresting and exciting and adventuresome lifestyle where you can learn alot.

REVISING THE FIRST DRAFT

1. What words in the draft make the topic interesting?

2. What is the draft's main idea? Which of the examples support the main idea best?

3. Which part(s) of the essay do you think were hardest to write? Why was that?

4. If the writer had more time to write this essay, what part(s) would or should get the most attention?

Louise's responses to these questions help her mark up the early version of her essay, as follows:

Need an introduction, a lead-in to get readers' interest

The military is really great because it teaches

Sum up what "things" military teaches.

you a lot of different things. You learn how

to work well with others and this is real re-

warding experience to everyone concerned in

the whole process. In basic, everybody has to

Pack in more detail: what people did and said, how they solved the problem →

mearch together. This isn't easy because

Tell what more general skills members learn, why it's important

some people can't tell their left from their

right and it gets very confusing. We got mad

at those who couldn't march and the

Begin new paragraph both linked to earlier one and focused on new topic with topic sentence

Give specific example of how soldiers helped each other, describing in detail →

Sergeant took away our personal time. An-

other example was whhen we packaed our

rucksacks with equipment and walked a long

Begin new paragraph with detailed anecdotes telling how you met new people, learned new facts about people elsewhere

Place conclusion in its own paragraph: invite readers to consider a career in the military →

ways. We helped each other. You also get to

meet a lot of different people in many differ-

ent places. The military has an iinteresting

and exciting and adventuresome lifestyle

where you can learn alot.

Based on her responses to the questions and the markings on the first draft, Louise writes an improved second draft of her classification paper. However, her essay is not yet complete. She needs to proofread it, asking the following questions:

Proofreading Queries

1. Have I corrected grammatical problems such as noun/verb agreement?

2. Have I corrected the spelling, particularly with words that sound alike or look alike but are not spelled alike?

3. Have I corrected the punctuation, separating word groups to clarify meaning?

STUDENT CLASSIFICATION ESSAY: SECOND DRAFT

You're almost through the obstacle course

Fragment: fix by connecting to next word group: lifestyle, no other . . . ———————▶

and you can feel your heart racing as the

adrenaline flows through your body. Because

of its exciting lifestyle. No other occupation

is like that of the service. Therefore, joining

the military is a very rewarding experience.

misspelling: replace with "exhilarating"

Besides being very (exillarating,) the service

offers many other worthwhile benefits. Unlike

misspelling: replace with "profession"

any other (profesion,) the military teaches

you how to become a team player and ex-

misspelling: replace with "variety"

poses you to a (vareity) of other cultures. A

valuable lesson learned while in the service is

Fragment: connect to next word group: together, they . . . ———————▶

how to work well with others. When you

have many service members together. They

quickly learn that tasks run faster and

misspelling: should be "smoother"

(smother) when done together. For instance,

when I was in basic training we had to learn

how to march together. It was so confusing

misspelling: replace with "commands"

to understand the (comands) like left face,

misspelling: replace with "column"

half right face, (colum) left, and to the rear

Fragment: fix by connecting to next word group: left, half . . . ———▶

march. We became so frustrated that when

the Drill Sergeant ordered us to go left. Half

of us went right. Although some of the sol-

diers knew how to follow the commands

given, they weren't any help. The ones who

misspelling: replace with "beginning"

knew how to march were (beging) to get an-

gry. The decent marchers started to curse

and look at the bad marchers as if they could

kill them. This animosity we had for one an-

misspelling: replace with "irritate"

Fragment: fix by connecting to next word group: together, the Drill . . .

other began to (iritate) our Drill Sergeant. To

show us that we needed to start working to-

gether. The Drill Sergeant didn't allow us to

misspellings: should be "personal"

have any (personel) time. Since our (personel)

time is the most valued part of our day, his

tactics worked. We began to assist one an-

other by demonstrating marching move-

misspelling: should be "trouble"

ments to the ones who had (truble.) As a re-

sult of the extra help, we all marched better

the next morning. Another example would be

misspelling: replace with "field"

Fragment: fix by connecting to preceding word group: equipment

when we went to the (feild.) We had to pack

our rucksacks (backpacks) with the necessary

equipment. And then marched five long miles

to the campsite. Every step taken seemed to

misspelling: replace with "increase"

make the weight of the rucksack (incraese)

misspelling: should be "soldier"

by at least ten pounds. One particular (solider)

misspelling: should be "soldier"

began to stray behind. Two other (soliders)

had each taken one arm of the straying

misspellings: replace with "soldier" and "assisted"

(solider) and (asisted) her in finishing the

march. As a result, we had all made it to the

campsite together.

Exercise: Proofreading

Proofread the following paragraph:

Besides encouraging teamwork, the military

also gives you the opportunity to learn about

different poeple and their cultures Because

the military service employs people from all

around the United States, you are sure to

meet many different people. These people can

come anywhere from New York City to Om-

aha, nebraska and all the way down to

Brownsville, Texas. For example, after I ar-

rived at my first duty station (Fort Ord, Cali-

fornia), I was able to asociate with people

from throughout the United States. I'm origi-

nally from Wisconsin and I can recall want-

ing a drink of water. Since I didn't know my

way around work yet. I had asked someone

where the bubbler was. Because the person I

asked was born and raised in Georgia, I received a very unusual look. Of course, I had no idae that people from Georgia refered to a bubbler as a water fountain. Another ilustration would be when I became stationed in Germany. Soon after I arrived in Germany, I was sure to stop by the nearby McDonald's restaurant to get a quick bite to eat. When I arrived at the restaurant I was stunned to see beer on the menu. Apparently, the Germans' produce mass quanities of beer in their country and have it available for each meal. Additionally, Germans' consider dogs to be part of the family. Resulting in the permision of dogs to accompany their owners inside even the finest of restaurants

The military offers you a very interesting, exciting and (adventous) lifestyle. Despite all the cutbacks, the service is still recruiting many people. Unfortunately, its a (disapointing) fact that so many people choose not to enter the service. You still have a chance to learn about yourself and the world,

Misspelling: should be "adventurous"

Punctuation problem: should be it's

misspelling: should be "disappointing"

so why not (as the slogan goes) "Be all that

you can be."

After rethinking her second draft, Louise writes a final version of her division and classification paper:

CLASSIFICATION: FINAL DRAFT
"WHAT THE MILITARY TEACHES"

Imagine: You've nearly completed Basic Training and only the difficult obstacle course remains. As you run through it, dodging, weaving, crawling, running, your heart races and adrenaline flows, producing feelings of confidence, superiority, and happiness. Because it is both exciting and rewarding, joining the military is a good choice for anyone. The military teaches cooperation and caring and, unlike any other profession, exposes individuals to a variety of cultures.

One of the most valuable lessons I learned in the service was how to work with others. When many people have to work together, they quickly learn that cooperation gets a job done faster and easier. For example, in basic training, our unit had to learn to march together. The commands were very confusing: left face, half right face, column left, to the rear march. When the Drill Sergeant ordered us to go left, we were so bewildered and frustrated that half of us went right. Although some of the soldiers knew how to follow the commands, they didn't help the rest of us. Furthermore, they got angry and frustrated too. The ones who knew how to march started to curse the bad marchers and looked as though they'd happily send us to the firing range as targets. For our part, we hated them because they knew what they were doing. The Drill Sergeant began to get irritated with our attitudes. We learned very quickly that no one wanted to have an irritable Drill Sergeant. Ours took away our personal time, the most valuable part of the day for any soldier. His tactics worked. We began helping one another by demonstrating the marching movements to each other. Because of the extra help, we all marched better, soothed our Sergeant, and got back our personal time. We learned not only to help each other, but to care about one another as well.

Going into the field was always a challenging adventure. We had to pack our rucksacks (backpacks) with the required equipment. Then we had to march five long, hot miles to the campsite. Every step we took made the rucksack heavier by ten pounds. One soldier began to stray behind. The combination of heat and weight was rapidly becoming too much to endure. Two other soldiers each took one arm of the straying recruit and helped her finish the march. As a result, we all made it to the campsite together as a unit. Caring about others and helping them was necessary for our success as a group.

Besides encouraging teamwork, the military provides a chance for soldiers to learn about different people and cultures. First, because the service employs people from around the United States, I got to meet people from New York City to Omaha, Nebraska, and all the way down to Brownsville, Texas. When I was stationed at my first duty station, Fort Ord in California, it took me awhile to find my way around. One day I was thirsty and wanted a drink of water. Since I'm from Wisconsin, I asked the first person I saw where the "bubbler" was. She stared at me oddly and had no idea what I was talking about. I discovered that she was born and raised in Georgia where a "bubbler" is called a water fountain.

Being in the service often means being posted overseas. This allows soldiers to learn about different cultures. Soon after I arrived in Germany, I missed American fast food and decided to stop by a local McDonald's. All I wanted was a Big Mac and a coke. I was amazed to see beer listed on the menu right next to Coke, Sprite, and Dr. Pepper. The Germans produce massive quantities of beer and have it available everywhere, anytime. As I carried my order to a nearby table, I nearly tripped over a Dachshund. Obviously he wasn't a seeing-eye dog, the only kind allowed in American restaurants. I discovered that Germans consider dogs to be part of their family and take the canines everywhere, even the finest restaurants. Germany, I discovered, was very different from the United States in many ways.

To sum up, the military offers an interesting, exciting lifestyle. Despite all the cutbacks, the service is still actively recruiting. I would encourage anyone to sign up. Why refuse the chance to learn about teamwork, different people, and different cultures? Why refuse the chance to "Be all that you can be"?

CLASSIFICATION WRITING TOPICS

The following are some possible topics for a classification paragraph or paper. Limit your topic to fit your instructor's requirements. Tell the reader *why* you have chosen your topic, and link your details closely to your topic.

1. Describe the kinds of people who try your patience (dawdlers in supermarkets, bad drivers).

2. Describe athletes and others who play games or sports.

3. Describe people with special interests (such as vegetarians or collectors).

4. Describe types of professionals (such as doctors, dentists, teachers, salespersons).

5. Describe kinds of popular movies or books (such as adventure, romance, travel, animal).

6. Describe friends, relatives, spouses.

7. Describe strong points or drawbacks to a particular product or process.

CHAPTER SEVEN

Comparison and Contrast

To compare is to see *similarities*, to contrast is to see *differences*. Comparing and contrasting often affect our daily lives. When considering breakfast, you choose among rummaging in the fridge, bringing in breakfast, or going out for pancakes and coffee. When dressing, you decide whether to pull on jeans or shorts, t-shirt or sweatshirt. You consider whether to see the most recent *Batman Forever*, rent one of the earlier versions, or watch the TV series. When registering for classes, do you sign up for the courses required for your certificate or major, take a fun course, or sign up for a class you can attend with a special friend?

In other words, comparing and contrasting are as natural as breathing. We put two ideas, things, or possibilities side by side. Then, if we can't have both, we choose between them. When you use comparison and contrast to write a paragraph or essay, you base your topic sentence or thesis on your opinion—telling which one of the two you prefer, and why. For example, you might argue that the eight o'clock viewing hour on TV is more child-friendly than later times. You may support this viewpoint by contrasting eight o'clock and later time periods on the basis of strong language, sexy situations, and the moral message. Despite some exceptions, you believe that shows aired during the "family viewing hour" still appeal more to children than shows aired later. A brief paragraph-length contrast would deal with only one of these points. You would need to support your points with examples taken from popular TV shows.

ORGANIZING YOUR ESSAY

Organize your essay either **point-by-point** or **subject-by-subject.** Choose one of these two patterns and then stay with it. Using a point-by-point organization is quite simple. State your **thesis** and **plan,** then see-saw back and forth between each of your points, like this:

1. **Thesis:** The eight o'clock viewing hour on TV is more child-friendly than later times because of milder language, the absence of sexy situations, and stronger moral messages.
2. **First Point:** Language
   a. Eight o'clock programs
   b. Later programs
3. **Second Point:** Sexy situations
   a. Eight o'clock programs
   b. Later programs
4. **Third Point:** Moral messages
   a. Eight o'clock programs
   b. Later programs

If you follow this approach, be sure to move smoothly from one point to the next. Use transitions or sum up a preceding point. In each section, follow the same order: for example, eight o'clock programs first, then later ones.

The second pattern, **subject-by-subject,** covers all three points about one time slot. Then it takes the same approach to the other time slot(s). State your **thesis** and **plan,** and then see-saw back and forth between each of your points, like this:

1. **Thesis:** The eight o'clock viewing hour on TV is more child-friendly than later times because of milder language, the absence of sexy situations, and stronger moral messages.
2. **Subject 1.** The eight o'clock time slot
   a. Milder language
   b. Fewer sexy situations
   c. Stronger moral messages
3. **Subject 2.** Later time slots
   a. Stronger language
   b. More sexy situations
   c. Weak or missing moral messages

If you use the **subject-by-subject** pattern, avoid breaking your essay into unrelated mini-essays. Tie the parts together by using these techniques:

- **Follow the same order throughout the essay.** A rough outline will help you here, giving you a clear order to refer to as you write. Thus, in both sections, you will deal with language, sexy situations, and moral messages in the same order.

- **Tie each section of your paper to your earlier discussion.** For instance, you may say something like this in the second part of your paper: "Unlike squeaky-clean shows like 'The Cosby Show' and 'The Waltons,' NBC's 'Wings' offers plenty of sexual remarks." Making these kinds of links will help you keep your readers' attention and interest.

To compare and contrast well, use the following guidelines.

TELL WHY YOUR COMPARISON OR CONTRAST MATTERS

It is tempting for beginning writers to choose topics such as the differences between high school and college, or how they compare to a brother, sister, or parent. While these topics provide lots of ready material, they often leave readers cold. "Why should I care?" the reader might ask. Make your point. Then develop it with comparison and contrast. For example, your readers all know that rail-thin fashion models are thinner than the average person. However, to make the topic more widely appealing, give your readers a reason for caring. For example, you may argue that "Although supermodels like Elle Macpherson and Naomi Campbell are superthin, they still like to eat." This approach appeals to readers who may know or care little about modeling, but worry about their weight and eating well.

USE CLEAR, SPECIFIC LANGUAGE

Use lots of specific details and facts to help readers form clear pictures in their minds. In a comparison of models' diets with the average person's junk foods, you might list the contents of Macpherson's fridge: "Yogurt, cheese, bacon, eggs, ham, bread, caviar, tomatoes, onions, peanut butter, jam, wine, Coca-Cola, champagne, beer, and whole milk." These examples help readers visualize the point you're making.

LINK YOUR IDEAS

When you move from idea to idea, item to item, link them. Transitions are simple and easy, but easily forgotten. Some transitions signal comparisons or similarities:

similarly	again	also
then	second	equally
moreover	too	furthermore

Other transitions show contrast or difference:

by contrast	but	however

yet	still	on the contrary
nevertheless	on the other hand	

For other ways to connect your points, repeat or sum up with the same or similar words. For instance, you may be comparing and contrasting "theme" restaurants. To compare one with others, you might say, "**Like other theme restaurants**, the Fashion Cafe relies as much on providing a show as a meal." The words *theme restaurants* refer back to a previous list of eateries. You can also use pronouns, such as *they* or *it*.

READINGS

As Chapter 1 pointed out, **topic sentences** sum up a paragraph's main idea. You will use **examples** to make this general concept clearer, more vivid to your reader. By filling out this general idea, your paragraph will draw word pictures in your reader's mind. The topic sentence of the following paragraph not only makes a point readers will care about, but the paragraph develops the topic sentence with specific details:

Topic sentence compares old ("classic") American cars with new, yellow Fords ———▶

Packed with details: used for decades, cheap, stuffed with people ———▶

More details: unsafe, block ——▶ traffic, pollute air, break down ———▶

The Association of Istanbul Drivers and Taxi Owners is trying to phase out the classic American cars used as taxis around the city. They'll replace them with new, canary-yellow Fords. The old taxis, called **dolmuses,** have been used for decades. They're cheap alternatives to regular yellow cabs for short jaunts around the city. Eight passengers typically jam into a dolmus—which means *stuffed* in Turkish. Two sit in front, three in the back, and three in a special middle seat put into the vehicles, which have been "stretched" 16 inches. The taxis won't move until every seat is taken. This is unless a passenger volunteers to pay for any empty spot. But the dolmus (pronounced *dole-moosh*) is no longer considered safe. According to Suleyman Ersal, head of the drivers association. "If we keep those cars, they'll block traffic and pollute the air," he says. "And they break down."

> "Hailing a 1955 Chevy in Istanbul Is
> Going to Get Harder and Harder,"
> *Wall Street Journal*

Chapter 2 showed how a **thesis** sums up the main idea for an entire writing; it serves an essay as a **topic sentence** serves a paragraph.

There Will Be a Brief Recess While We Check Our Wardrobes

Andrea Higbie

Thesis contrasts not only dressing "right" and "wrong" ways but also men's and women's dress ➤

The legal profession has a dress code all its own, though its rules go unspoken. "Clothes can undo the lawyer," said Vivian Berger, the vice dean of Columbia Law School. "Dressing the wrong way will always weaken her chances." On the other hand, dressing the right way can make the case. Image consultants and well-heeled—and coifed and suited—lawyers agree that profession-wide their wardrobe brief is the same: go for low-key and re-fined and brand names that connote those qualities. For men, that means navy or gray suits, white shirts with french cuffs and distinctive though subtle cuff links, Hermès or Countess Mara neckties, and Tag-Heuer watches.

For women, the dress drill is Ferragamo pumps, tai-lored suits, and pearls, and hairstyling and makeup that take their cues from the Isabella Rossellini Lancôme ad-vertisements: short, soft, sophisticated.

Details of "right" 1990s women's dress contrasted to 1980s ➤

"The suit for the '90s is softer than the suit of the '80s, which was about big, padded shoulders and aggres-siveness," said Donna Karan, the designer who is known for "real clothes for real people." For both men and

women's suits ➤

women practicing law, Ms. Karan said, "the '90s suit is in navy or gray chalk stripes, with straighter shoulders; it's soft, but it shouldn't be slouchy."

More contrasts: 1980s and 1990s briefcases

Lawyers today should carry soft leather briefcases (hard ones say, "It's the go-go '80s") and Mont Blanc pens (which announce, "I'm a winner, and *so* refined").

From this sartorial foundation spring dialects as dis-tinct from one another as a final summation in a triple-homicide case is from a real estate closing on a subur-ban split-level. Criminal defense lawyers, for example, can cut a wider swath through the field of fashion than, say, corporate lawyers; lawyers in tax court do not grandstand.

Contrasts legal fashions: criminal vs. corporate and tax court. Explains details of contrasting legal fashions ➤

"Lawyers are far more conservative in their dress than any other professional group because what they do is about brains, not flash," said Camille Lavington, a corpo-rate image consultant based in New York who has helped many practitioners improve their appearance. "Of all lawyers, though, those in criminal defense have the lati-tude to be the most flamboyant because they deal more with emotions."

But flash works against a lawyer when it leaves a residue of slick. Jack S. Hoffinger, a criminal lawyer in Manhattan, said, "If the unstated accusation is that your client is a rich pig, do you as a lawyer want to come in and look like a rich lawyer representing a rich client?"

John Nicholas Iannuzzi, a criminal defense lawyer known for his Borsalino fedoras outside the courtroom, has turned heads inside the courtroom with his double-breasted Kilgore suits—raspberry, sky blue, and white linen in the summer, colored shirts with white collars and cuffs, pocket handkerchiefs (in his jacket and overcoat) and wide Windsor-knot neckties. For Mr. Iannuzzi, who said he tones down his look "a tad" when handling civil cases, the theory of courtroom dress comes down to this: "Juries don't want lawyers to look like them; they want somebody to look up to."

So, slip on those Ferragamos, starch that collar, and wield that Mont Blanc. "In the courtroom, you always want to put your best foot forward," Ms. Berger said, "and your best foot should have the same color sock as your other foot."

Details of dress for criminal lawyer

Final paragraph sums up what and why

The New York Times

This essay contrasts styles of well-dressed lawyers, both men and women, of three types: criminal defense, corporate, and tax court attorneys. In the process, it vividly describes the interest of the well-dressed attorney in up-to-date designer labels.

EXAMPLES:

The following selections are well-written examples of comparison and contrast writing, both paragraph-length and short essays. Your responses to the questions we raise will help you write versions of your own.

According to the author of the following selection, if you carried your suitcase on your head and walked like a Kenyan woman, you'd save a lot of energy.

Words to Define

concentration: close attention, focused thought

energetically: in terms of energy used

pendulums: swinging devices that store energy

Prereading

1. What skill are you especially good at, contrasting it with others?

2. Contrast ways of carrying heavy loads, either as an individual or as part of a group.

No Skycaps Needed
Carl Zimmer

One of the most startling sights on a first trip to Africa is a common one: women carrying things on their heads. Try to carry a suitcase on your head, and you'll probably bite your tongue in concentration and wave your arms madly for balance. But African women walk for miles with heavy jugs of water or pots of food as if they weren't carrying anything. Energetically speaking, they aren't: researchers have found that the women can carry enormous loads without using any extra energy. They aren't defying any laws of physics, though: they're being good pendulums. When they move, they store energy, which carries over into the next step. People who carry things for a living, from Kenyans to Sherpas, tend to use their heads. It's just amateurs that use suitcases and backpacks.

Queries for Understanding

1. What startling sight is common in Africa?
2. What items do African women carry? how and for how far?
3. How effectively do African women carry things?
4. What other people also carry things for a living?

Queries on the Writer's Techniques

1. What contrasts (differences) does the paragraph mention?
2. What comparisons (likenesses) does the paragraph mention?

Writing Topics

1. If you arrived newly in America with no knowledge of American culture, what sights and sounds would strike you as odd or unusual?
2. What differences between men and women in America are most striking?

According to the author of the next selection, in the next decade, waterjet-propelled cargo ships could speed cargo across the Atlantic, unhampered by storms.

Words to Define
aeronautical: dealing with flying, with aircraft

waterjet-propelled: pushed through the water by jets of water

newfangled: modern, up-to-date

knot: a measurement of speed equaling 1.15 miles per hour

Prereading

1. What goods could better be shipped by waterjet-propelled cargo ships than by present-day oceangoing freighters?

2. What sorts of goods or communications would you like to see move faster? What goods or communications should move more slowly—or not at all?

THE OCEAN EXPRESS
Suzanne Kantra Kirschner

"Welcome to the jet age of cargo shipping," brags aeronautical engineer David Giles. Giles is not talking about jet aircraft, however, but cargo ships—waterjet-propelled cargo ships. The company he helped found, Fastship Atlantic, Inc., of Alexandria, Va., intends to build a small fleet of such vessels by the end of the decade. Powered by giant gas turbines, the waterjets will propel 800-foot ships across the Atlantic at 35 to 40 knots—more than twice as fast as any ocean-going freighter today, reducing crossing times from eight to three-and-a-half days. Even storms won't slow these newfangled freighters: They will sail full-speed ahead through waves as high as 50 feet.

Popular Science

Queries for Understanding

1. How soon does who want to build what kind of vessels?
2. How big will Fastship's ships be, powered how, traveling how fast?
3. How much will time to cross the Atlantic be reduced by the new ships?
4. What other advantages aside from speed will the new ships have?

Queries on the Writer's Techniques

1. What contrasts (differences) does the paragraph mention?
2. What comparisons (likenesses) does the paragraph mention?

Writing Topics

1. Predict the future: what significant changes in the everyday routines and occupations of the typical American family are likely to take place in ten years?

2. In contrast to the selection, name some activities that should move more slowly or not happen at all.

According to the author of the following selection, contrary to many reports, taste is the best guide to quality.

Words to Define

slathered: covered thickly

treadmill: an endlessly moving, sloping belt to be walked on for exercise

tango: a Latin American ballroom dance

Prereading

1. What dull-tasting foods are probably good for you, but don't make their eaters happy?

3. What good-tasting foods are probably bad for you—but make people happy?

IF SOMETHING TASTES GOOD
Mike Royko

If something tastes good, it is probably bad. If something tastes really dull, it is probably good. Consider breakfast. On one side of the table: oatmeal with a dash of skim milk and a light sprinkle of sugar. Dull, but good for you. On the other side? A mound of sizzling corned-beef hash topped with fried eggs and slathered in hot sauce. Wonderful, but bad for you. Look into the eyes of the man eating oatmeal, however, and you see the expression of a man on a treadmill. In contrast, the man eating hash looks like a guy doing the tango.

Chicago Tribune

Queries for Understanding

1. What breakfast foods are dull-tasting? How does the eater look?

2. What breakfast foods taste "wonderful"? How does the eater look?

Queries on the Writer's Techniques

1. In the first two sentences, the writer swings back and forth, between one and then the other, with examples. How does he treat the rest of the paragraph?

2. The writer compares the eating of both types of food—dull and wonderful-tasting—to types of exercise: how do these comparisons affect the reader?

3. How do the writer's descriptive words (like *dash* or *mound*) increase the impact of his judgments?

Writing Topics

1. If science could perfect foods that tasted delicious but burned fat, keeping everyone thin, how would Americans be better off? Worse off in any ways?
2. Consider foods that look better than they taste, either on the package or in actuality. How do you account for this difference?

In the following selection, of all the men who courted her mother, the writer remembers her father best.

Words to Define

beaus: boyfriends, male sweethearts

sanctioned: approved, endorsed

amorous: loving, extremely affectionate

embarrassingly: disturbing, distressing

substitute: alternate, fill-in, replacement

annals: historical records

pretext: excuse, pretense

Prereading

1. If you have indirect or direct memories of your parents' courtships, compare and contrast the ones they married with those they didn't.
2. How did religious values influence—or fail to influence—your parents' choice of a lifetime partner? How would they influence your choice?

OUR PARENTS' KEEPERS
Mary Gordon

Every time I got a good report card (and I always did) she would drive to the next town to a bar and grill called the Brick Cafe. It was owned by a man named Charlie, an ex-prizefighter who had briefly been one of my mother's beaus. It's rather unusual that my mother had one beau who was a prizefighter and another who was a rodeo cowboy. These are the only two she ever spoke of, but I think they were the only ones. Except for John Gallagher, a widower, an undertaker. John wanted to marry her. The cowboy and the prizefighter, I think, did not. My father, a writer and Jewish convert, must have had the slightly illegal appeal that the prizefighter and the cowboy did, but he was sanctioned by the priests she worshipped. And he did, remarkably, want to marry her. People who knew them when they were courting say they were publicly, almost embarrassingly amorous. They kissed on the subway. And he wrote her poetry. He would buy her greeting cards, then cut or rip out the printed verse on the inside and substitute one of his own. In 1945, her birthday message included the words: "Never in all the annals of recorded time / existed such sweet pretext for a rhyme."

Queries for Understanding

1. In the writer's view, what unusual jobs did her mother's suitors have?
2. How was the writer's father like and unlike her mother's other suitors?
3. What examples does the writer present of her father's loving treatment of her mother?

Queries on the Writer's Techniques

1. What does the mother's reward of the writer when she got good grades reveal about her character?
2. Why does the writer call the appeal of some of her mother's suitors "slightly illegal"?
3. What relationship to her mother divides her mother's suitors into two groups?

Writing Topics

1. Place those people you or one of your parents dated before marriage in groups, comparing and contrasting them.
2. What patterns of courtship are typical in American society?

In the following selection, the author describes how a small Oregon company run by young adults has a new idea: keeping plastic out of landfills by bringing it into our homes.

Words to Define

ecologically: in terms of links between organisms and their environments

conscious: aware, taking account of

aerosol: a suspension of fine particles that may be sprayed from a pressurized can

metamorphosis: a marked change in appearance or form

post-consumer: used, throw-away

recycling: reusing or getting useful materials from

polyethylene: a plastic used for packaging or containers

extrude: to shape by forcing through a die or mold

Prereading

1. What kinds of trash need recycling to keep them out of landfills?

2. Explain why you would like working in a company like meta morf, or why not?

TAKE THAT PLASTIC AND SIT ON IT
Daniel Pinchbeck

In the ecologically conscious '90s, saying you work in plastics is kind of like saying you still use aerosol deodorant. But meta morf, a small Portland, Oregon, furniture design and manufacturing company run by people in their 20s, is keeping plastic out of our landfills by bringing it into our living rooms. "We use mainly post-consumer plastics, empty shampoo bottles, and the like," says Colin Reedy, the company's 28-year-old designer. "At the recycling plant they grind high-density polyethylene into flakes and then extrude it into what looks like lumber." The resulting plastic wood has distinct advantages over the real thing, according to Reedy: "It is much easier to bend this material or warp it. We don't add any toxic substances, and we can suck up all the chips and scraps and take them back to the factory to make more planks."

Swing

Queries for Understanding

1. Where does the company, meta morf, get its name?

2. What kinds of materials does the company, meta morf, recycle?

3. What process does meta morf use to recycle materials?

Queries on the Writer's Techniques

1. How does meta morf's work with plastics both compare and contrast with the use of aerosol deodorant?

2. Why is the plastic wood resulting from recycling better than lumber (a contrast)?

3. How does meta morf's recycling process protect the environment (a contrast)?

Writing Topics

1. Consider types of waste that are usually discarded by a company you work (or have worked) for: what steps should be taken to keep them out of landfills?

2. In what parts of your work or personal life have artificial substances replaced the real thing: are you better or worse off?

According to the author of the following selection, this year's "leaner" Wienermobile has a lot of beef under the hood.

Words to Define
debut: coming out, presentation

classic: respected, easily recognized shape or quality

aficionados: experts, those who pride themselves on particular knowledge

aerodynamic: moving through the air with little resistance

predecessor: one who comes before, paving the way

Prereading
1. How have products that you have owned improved recently?
2. Tell why you would or would not like to own a Wienermobile.

THE REDESIGNED WIENERMOBILE
Oscar Suris

At the Chicago Auto Show, the biggest new model won't be a Chevy, a Ford, or a Dodge. It will be a Wiener.

Making its world debut today is the redesigned-for-1995 Oscar Mayer Wiener-
mobile. Oscar Mayer calls the 27-foot fiberglass hot dog on wheels a "leaner, keener wiener." In fact, the new Wienermobile, powered by a General Motors engine, is actually 4 feet longer and weighs about two tons more than the '88 classic model—hardly the "lite" Wiener many had hoped for.

The new Wienermobile, which seats six, is larded up with new features. Au-
tomotive aficionados will find a 12-way, electronically adjustable seat for the dri-
ver, a state-of-the-art video system, and a big-screen TV. To parallel park, drivers can count on video cameras at the front and the rear to guide them. A bigger windshield improves the dog's aerodynamics. A look beneath the bun reveals a beefy V-8 engine, compared with a V-6 in the previous model. However, don't expect to see Wienermobiles drag racing: the 10,000 pound vehicle has been clocked going 90 miles per hour, but it takes 24 seconds to go from 0 to 60 mph.

Says Russ Whitacre, who will manage this year: "It's more than a minivan and less than a space shuttle."

But the feature drivers will appreciate even more than the hot-dog-shaped dashboard or the hot-dog-embroidered interior is the Wienermobile's powerful air conditioner. Neither the '88 model nor its '67 predecessor came with adequate air conditioners, and as the Oscar Mayer punsters might say, were never very "chili" on summer days.

Unfortunately for visitors to the auto show, however, Wienermobiles—which would cost more than $75,000—aren't for sale to the public.

The Wall Street Journal

Queries for Understanding

1. How does the size of the new Wienermobile compare with its earlier version?
2. How many earlier versions were there?
3. What new features are included in the new Wienermobile?
4. What are the new Wienermobile's speed and acceleration, compared to its weight?
5. With what other two vehicles does Whitacre compare the new Wienermobile, and how?
6. What is the Wienermobile's most appreciated new feature?
7. What is the cost of the new Wienermobile?

Queries on the Writer's Techniques

1. What contrast does the article draw between Oscar Mayer's claims for the new Wienermobile and the reality?
2. Why does the article discuss the new vehicle's electronics before describing its engine?
3. Why does the article mention the new vehicle's air conditioning as the last of its features?

Writing Topics

1. What buildings can you think of that have been designed to look like the product that is made or sold inside?
2. Consider toys or other objects made to appear like something else (Batman, Spiderwoman, and so on). What features were changed, and how?

In the following selection, a foreign-born woman examines Korean and American culture, finding much in both to admire.

ADAPTING TO THE NEW WORLD
Student Essay (Kim)

Originally, I was born in South Korea and lived there all my life until I married and moved to America. While living in America for five years now, I have tried to adapt to the rapid pace of change in my life. Although I felt apprehensive at first, I doubted that I would find many differences between our two countries. After all, we are much alike even though we speak different languages, and have different traditions and cultures. People in both countries wear blue jeans, love children, and seek freedom. Despite these similarities, I found it difficult to adjust, for so much was alien to me.

Most difficult for me was learning a new language. I discovered that American English combines the influence of many other languages, mostly European but many of them global. The language is basically English, of course, for the English, who came over on the Mayflower, settled here early, and in the largest numbers. On the other hand, the Korean language was heavily influenced by Chinese until about 400 years ago. For Korean learners of English, the different uses of noun and verb are hard to grasp, at first. For example, an English speaker would ask a question by reversing the noun and verb, and often separating the verb, as in "Where are you going?" However, in Korean, one would ask, "You go where?" Learning a new language was hard for me, but an essential part of beginning life in this wondrous land.

Next, I needed to adjust to American food, which is relatively mild, with the exception of Cajun dishes. Generally, Korean food is very spicy, like Kimchi, which covers many types of pickled cabbage and other vegetables; Koreans cannot live without it, and often make their own from old family recipes. In addition, Koreans enjoy low fat, mostly vegetarian diets. The American diet, on the other hand, consists of high-fat, very salty items, like the fast food and instant TV dinners which are so popular. These foods may account for the high rates of heart attacks and strokes, cholesterol-clogged veins, and obesity among Americans.

Finally, Koreans and Americans treat marriage very differently. Even though we have almost entered the twenty-first century, many Korean marriages are arranged by match makers hired by parents. Or, parents of marriageable children will get together and arrange their marriages. Of course, some marriages come about through dating just as in America—young people meet, fall in love, and decide to marry. Yet, despite or because of arranged marriages, the Korean divorce rate is very low compared with American divorces. This may be due largely to the strong family bonds in Korea.

On the other hand, young people in America are allowed the greatest freedom in choosing their partners; they base marriages almost entirely on love, never through match makers. And a very strong trend, nowadays, is for two persons to live together for awhile before getting married, though many never formally marry.

Despite these differences between our cultures, I've realized that Koreans and Americans have much in common. We tend to seek freedom, share the same excitement at a new birth, and want to make good friends. Also, we place a high value on hard work, often spending long hours at our own businesses in order to send our children to good colleges; we want to give them opportunities earlier generations could only dream of. If we can learn to accept cultural differences as unique values, the world may be more peaceful. We need to put aside our often-unfounded attitudes of superiority and prejudice against other cultures.

Queries for Understanding

1. What differences does Kim see between the Korean and American languages?
2. What differences does Kim see between Korean and American foods and eating habits?
3. What differences does Kim see between Korean and American marriage customs?
4. What similarities does Kim draw between Korean and American cultures?

Queries on the Writer's Techniques

1. Why does Kim list the differences between Korean and American culture in the order she does?
2. What lesson does Kim draw about her comparisons of the two cultures?

Writing Topics

1. List some differences and similarities between two ethnic, racial, or nation groups. What can each group learn from the other?
2. Consider the Korean custom of arranged marriages: if you were to arrange a marriage for your present or future children, how would you do it?

In the following selection, a Native American chief facing the loss of his tribe's lands presents a Native American vision of man's relationship to the land, nature, the air, and wild animals.

Prereading

1. Consider a time in the past when you left a way of life behind: how did you react?

LETTER TO PRESIDENT PIERCE, 1855
Chief Seattle

We know that the white man does not understand our ways. One portion of the land is the same to him as the next, for he is a stranger who comes in the night and takes from the land whatever he needs. The earth is not his brother, but his enemy, and when he has conquered it, he moves on. He leaves his fathers' graves, and his children's birthright is forgotten. The sight of your cities pains the eyes of the red man. But perhaps it is because the red man is a savage and does not understand.

There is no quiet place in the white man's cities. No place to hear the leaves of spring or the rustle of insect's wings. But perhaps because I am a savage and do not understand, the clatter only seems to insult the ears. The Indian prefers the soft sound of the wind darting over the face of the pond, the smell of the wind itself cleansed by a mid-day rain, or scented with the piñon pine. The air is precious to the red man. For all things share the same breath—the beasts, the trees, the man. Like a man dying for many days, he is numb to the stench.

What is man without the beasts? If all the beasts were gone, men would die from great loneliness of spirit, for whatever happens to the beasts also happens to man. All things are connected. Whatever befalls the earth befalls the sons of the earth.

It matters little where we pass the rest of our days; they are not many. A few more hours, a few more winters, and none of the children of the great tribes that once lived on this earth, or that roamed in small bands in the woods, will be left to mourn the graves of a people once as powerful and hopeful as yours.

The whites, too, shall pass—perhaps sooner than other tribes. Continue to contaminate your bed, and you will one night suffocate in your own waste. When the buffalo are all slaughtered, the wild horses all tamed, the secret corners of the forest heavy with the scent of many men, and the view of the ripe hills blotted by talking wires [the telegraph], where is the thicket? Gone. Where is the eagle? Gone. And what is it to say goodby to the swift and the hunt, the end of living and the beginning of survival? We might understand if we knew what it was that the white man dreams, what he describes to his children on the long winter nights, what visions he burns into their minds, so they will wish for tomorrow. But we are savages. The white man's dreams are hidden from us.

Peter Nabokov (ed.), *Native American Testimony:*
An Anthology of Indian and White Relations (Viking 1977)

Queries for Understanding

1. What aspects of "white" culture does Chief Seattle criticize, and why?

2. What values of Native American culture does Chief Seattle contrast to "white" culture?

3. What prediction does Chief Seattle make about the future?

Queries on the Writer's Techniques

1. What imagery—language appealing to the senses—does Chief Seattle use to portray his vision of nature?

2. What evidence of humility, of efforts to soften his criticism, does Chief Seattle reveal?

3. Is Chief Seattle's letter balanced, treating both sides of the argument

with equal respect, or is he firmly committed to his own vision? How do you know?

Writing Topics

1. Choose two areas in nature, not widely separated, one relatively untouched by humans and the other revealing human influence, and compare and contrast them.

2. If Americans living today tried to live as Chief Seattle's people did, what would they lose, and what would they gain?

THE WRITING PROCESS

In the following selection, Lateisha, the author, chose dating as the topic of her comparison and contrast essay. Since her grandmother had often expressed her opinions on this topic, Lateisha stresses the differences between dating in her day and in her grandmother's.

STUDENT COMPARISON AND CONTRAST ESSAY: FIRST DRAFT

My idea of a perfect date is really different from my grandmother's. She thinks the ideal date is a perfect gentleman. I'd call him a dork. He's suppose to pick me up on time, my mother gives him some dorky food which he eats and then when I'm ready to go my mom is suppose to see if I look okay. My dad is suppose to tell us to get home early. We go see a really bad movie and I'm suppose to be home by ten pm. I think a perfect date starts when a cool guy blows the horn in the driveway. If I don't come right out, he goes up and rings the bell until my dad opens it. My date would have long hair. i would wear a cool outfit. We go to a great party, drink too much and I get home at dawn. I like my kind of date better than my grandmother's.

REVISING THE FIRST DRAFT

After writing an exploratory draft of her comparison and contrast paper, Lateisha needs to respond to some questions about its quality before revising it:

1. What are the draft's main points of contrast? Which of the examples support the main contrast best?

2. What sentences are well written? What words make the topic interesting?

3. Which part(s) of the essay do you think were hardest to write? Why?

4. When the writer rewrites this essay, what part(s) would or should get the most attention?

Lateisha's responses to these questions help her mark up the early version of her essay, as follows:

Sum up differences in views in terms of dress, transportation, activities ——→

My idea of a perfect date is really different

from my grandmother's. She thinks the ideal

Describe grandmother's background: where she grew up

date is a perfect gentleman. I'd call him a

Focus first paragraph on grandmother's view of date's arrival: pack with specific details of dress and behavior

dork. He's suppose to pick me up on time,

my mother gives him some dorky food which

he eats and then when I'm ready to go my

Focus second paragraph on writer's view of date's arrival: pack in details of loud arrival, pickup, girl's departure ——

mom is suppose to see if I look okay. My dad

is suppose to tell us to get home early. We go

see a really bad movie and I'm suppose to be

home by ten pm. I think a perfect date starts

when a cool guy blows the horn in the drive-

Focus next two paragraphs on contrasting views of date's and girl's dress: pack in detailed descriptions

In final two paragraphs: contrast views of evening's activities: movie and early return vs. wild party, drinking and late return ——

way. If I don't come right out, he goes up

and rings the bell until my dad opens it. My

date would have long hair. i would wear a

cool outfit. We go to a great party, drink too

much and I get home at dawn. I like my kind

In conclusion, sum up writer's reaction to differences in opinions

of date better than my grandmother's.

Based on her responses to the questions and her markings on the first draft, Lateisha writes an improved second draft of her comparison and contrast paper. However, her essay is not yet complete. She needs to proofread it, asking the following questions:

Proofreading Queries

1. Have I corrected grammatical problems such as noun/verb agreement?
2. Have I corrected the spelling, particularly with words that sound alike or look alike but are not spelled alike?
3. Have I corrected the punctuation, separating word groups to clarify meaning?

Fragment: fix by connecting to next word group: no, one . . . ——▶

GRANDMOTHERS VS TEENAGERS

Although teenagers expect grandmothers to

say yes whenever mothers say no. One

misspelling: replace with "exception"

(acception) exists. Teenagers and grand-

punctuation problem: should be "don't"

mothers (dont) agree on the facts of dating.

possessive problem: should be "Grandmother's"

(Grandmothers) idea of a date starts with a

perfect gentleman greeting the girl at the

misspelling: replace with "extremely"

door, taking her to an (extremly) boring

movie, and returning her home by 10:00. The

possessive error: replace with "teenager's"

(teenagers) idea of the same date starts with a

fine guy blowing the horn in the driveway,

misspelling: replace with "going"

(ging) to a wild party, and arriving home at

the crack of dawn. Modern dating is very

misspelling: replace with "different"   possessive problem: should be "Grandmother's"

(diffent) from fifty years ago. (Grandmothers')

theories of the ideal date begin with a gentle-

◀———————————————— *Fragment: fix by connecting to preceding word group: gentleman arriving . . .*

man. Arriving at the door about 7:30. The

possessive problem: should be "lady's"

young (ladies) parents warmly welcome him.

They sit in the living room yapping about the

misspelling: replace with "intelligent"

7:00 news. The boy has to act very (inteligent)

and agree with everything the girls father

posessive problem: should be "girl's"

says. The (girls) mother brings cookies and

milk for him to munch on. He can't turn

misspelling: replace with "because"

them down (becuase) she might consider him

rude. He can only eat about three of the

Misspelling: replace with "fifteen" ———▶

punctuation problem: should be "doesn't"

fifeen so he (doesnt) look like an animal. Af-

ter about thirty minutes of pure hell, the girl

Fragment: fix by connecting to preceding word group: "inspection" ———

comes bouncing down the stairs. Her mother

has to check her over to make sure she

passes inspection. Before she leaves the

misspelling: relace with "strict"

house. Her father gives her date (stict)

instructions to obey speed limits and to ar-

misspelling: replace by "finally"

rive home before 9:30. They (finaly) make it

to the car and creep out the driveway.

To the Student:

Proofread the following paragraph:

On the other hand, the teenager's idea of the

same greeting begins with the boy runing ten

minutes late. He squeals into the driveway on

two wheels, slams the car in park, and ob-

noxusly blows the horn. The girl doesn't ime-

diately come out the boy goes in to hurry her

up. He doesn't even use the walkway. He

would prefer too jump over the flowers. He

constantly rings the doorbell until her father

opens it. The man glares at the boy as if he

could kill him, the boy doesn't let that bother

him. As the boy slings his hair to one side to

show his earring. He demands his date to

hurry. She comes running toward him and

gives him a big, slopy kiss. She informs her

parents that she will return home whever she

feels like it. They run to the car and speed

away intoo the night.

Not only do they disagree on the greet- ◀─── Comma splice: fix by adding a coordinating conjunction: greeting, but . . .

ing, they also disagree on manners of dress.

Grandmother's opinion of the ideal outfit

misspelling: should be "loose"

Run-on: fix by adding coordinating conjunction: up, and her . . .

would include a (lose-)fitting blouse with an

hyphenate double modifier: "ankle-length"

(ankle length) skirt. The girl would (ware) ◀─── Misspelling: should be "wear"

only a touch of make up her hair would be

long and flowing. Her date would wear a

misspelling: replace with "acceptable-looking"

plain, but (exceptable) looking shirt with

misspelling: replace with "trimmed"

matching slacks and tie. His neatly (trimed)

Fragment: replace by connecting to preceding word group: cologne, but only . . .

hair would be washed and combed. He would

misspelling: replace with "too"

have on (to much) cologne. But only to im- ◀───

press the lady.The teen would feel more com-

misspelling: should be "body suit"

fortable in a black spandex (bodysute) with a

gaudy silver belt. A pair of spike heels and

misspelling: should be "earrings"

(earerings) large enough to wear as a necklace

misspelling: should be "finishing"

will add more (finshing) touches. She would

wear tons of eye shadow and lipstick. Her

misspelling: should be "off"

hair would stand up so high (of) her head, it

would almost reach the ceiling. Her date

would be dressed in black leather from head

to toe. He would have on black leather pants

word missing: "t-shirt"

and jacket with a black underneath. He (wuld)

misspelling: should be "would"

have a key chain hanging off his belt loop.

misspelling: should be "shoulder-length"

His (shoulder lenth) hair would be slicked

back with 10 ounces of baby oil. His aroma

misspelling: should be "reek"

would not (reak) of cologne but the awful

smell of beer and cigarettes.The final discrep-

misspelling: should be "where"

ancy is about (were) they will go on their

misspelling: should be "see"

date. Grandmother's opinion is to go (sea)

Gone with the Wind at the movie theater.

They should leave around 6:30 or 7:00 and

misspelling: should be "dinner"

have (diner) at the local restaurant, then at-

misspelling: should be "return"

tend the movie. They should (retrun) home

around 9:30, no later than 10:00. They would

have (two) go back the next night and (sea)
misspelling: should be "to"   misspelling: should be "see"

the end of the movie because it lasted so
                              punctuation problem: should be "doesn't"

long.The teenager's date (doesnt) pick her up
                                    misspelling: should be "while"

until ten o'clock. They ride around for a (wile)

and have a few drinks. Then they go pick up

three or four friends and go to the
misspellings: should be "wildest party"   Misspelling: should be "really"

(widest part) of the year. They get (rely) drunk

and pass out for a while on the couch. Some-

one will wake them up about six o'clock the
                                              — Run-on: fix by
                                              joining word groups
next morning they can go home. They get   morning so they . . .

home, climb into bed, and sleep until about
punctuation problem: should be "o'clock"

        three (oclock) that afternoon. The contrast is
misspelling: replace with "measurable"

(measurble,) obvious and inevitable. Grand-

mothers will no longer see the perfect date.

After rethinking her second draft, Lateisha writes a final version of her comparison and contrast paper:

STUDENT COMPARISON AND CONTRAST ESSAY: FINAL DRAFT
IDEAS OF DATES DIFFER

My grandmother grew up in Ohio and met and married my grandfather there. I grew up in North Georgia, in "red-neck country." She and I are very close, but I see a great deal of difference in some of our ideas. Grandmothers and teenagers do not agree about dating. Grandmothers think that a girl's date should be a perfect gentleman who is prompt and polite. The couple should be neatly dressed and have a quiet, respectable evening. A teenager, on the other hand, wants a date with a good-looking guy who can arrive late, dresses more like a biker than a gentleman, and has an invitation to a wild party. Modern dating is very different from my grandmother's day.

My grandmother's ideal date begins with the gentleman arriving at the door promptly at 7:30. He knocks politely, and the girl's parents welcome him warmly. He is invited into the living room and offered milk and cookies. Of course, he accepts because to refuse would be impolite. On the other hand, he can't eat all the cookies because that would make him look like a pig. He chats intelligently with the girl's parents for about thirty minutes until the girl comes bouncing happily down the stairs. Her mother makes sure she passes inspection before leaving the house. Her makeup, clothes, and hair must be both neat and acceptable. Her father gives the date strict instructions about obeying speed limits and arriving home early. The couple drive sedately out of the driveway in the brown station wagon belonging to the boy's father.

On the other hand, a teenager's usual date begins about ten minutes later than expected and two-and-a-half hours later than Grandmothers expect. The boy always runs late. He squeals into the drive on two wheels of his rusting Chevy pickup, slams the truck in park, and obnoxiously blows the horn. If the girl doesn't come right out, he runs across the lawn, jumps over the flowers, and rings the doorbell repeatedly until the girl's father opens the door. Ignoring the man's glare, the boy slings his hair to one side to reveal his new earring and demands to see his date. The girl comes running down the stairs into his arms, giving him a big, sloppy kiss. She tells her parents that she will return when she feels like it, and they run to the car. The pickup squeals out of the drive and speeds into the night.

Not only do grandmothers and teenagers disagree on the type of young man suitable for dating, but they also disagree on appropriate dating wear. To the older generation, the ideal outfit for a girl would include a loose-fitting blouse worn with an ankle-length skirt. She could wear a touch of make-up, and her hair should be long, carefully brushed, and neat. The boy should wear a plain but clean shirt with tan or blue slacks and a conservative tie. His neatly trimmed hair should be washed and combed. He might wear a moderate amount of cologne to impress his date.

The teens, however, would prefer an entirely different set of outfits. The girl should wear a black spandex bodysuit with a gaudy silver belt, spike heels, and earrings long enough to provide perches for passing birds. She should wear bright, metallic eyeshadow and dark-red lipstick. Her hair should stand up so high that she has to be careful passing under ceiling fans. Her date should wear black leather pants and jacket with a black t-shirt underneath. He should have a chain hanging off his belt loop which is attached to his wallet. His shoulder-length hair should be slicked back with 10 ounces of baby oil, and he should definitely not smell of cologne—beer and cigarettes are more likely.

Finally, grandmothers and teens disagree about where to go on a date. Grandmother prefers a movie like *Gone With the Wind*. She thinks a couple should leave the girl's home between 6:30 and 7:00 p.m., have dinner at a local restaurant, and then attend the movie. They should return home no later than 10:00. Of course, if we followed her ideas, we'd have to go back the next night to see the end of the movie because we'd have to leave when it was half over.

On the other hand, a teenager's date doesn't even pick her up until 10:00 p.m. The couple rides around for awhile and enjoys a few beers. Then they pick up three or four friends and go to the wildest party of the year. They get really drunk and pass out for awhile on the couch. Finally, someone wakes them up about six in the morning so they can go home. The girl gets dropped off at her house as her father leaves for work. She climbs into bed and sleeps until the middle of the afternoon.

Grandmothers and teenagers simply do not agree on the rules of dating. The contrast is measurable, obvious, and inevitable. Each believes her ideas are the only right ones. I discovered that it's a good idea to avoid the topic of dating with my grandmother. That keeps us all a lot happier.

COMPARISON AND CONTRAST WRITING TOPICS

The following are some possible topics for a comparison and contrast paragraph or paper. Limit your topic to fit your instructor's requirements. Tell the reader *why* you have chosen your topic, and link your details closely to your topic.

1. Compare and contrast the first opinion you formed of a person or place and a later opinion.
2. Compare and contrast two towns or locations where you've lived or spent time.
3. Compare and contrast a popular activity today and at a time in the past
4. Compare and contrast two machines or tools you've owned or used.
5. Compare and contrast two jobs or supervisors you've had.
6. Compare and contrast two vacation spots you've visited, describing good or bad experiences.
7. Compare or contrast two books or movies you've experienced.

CHAPTER EIGHT

Process

In a process essay, tell your reader what process you are describing and how it was done. You may either give directions, leading the reader through the process step-by-step, or you may tell the reader how something was put together or done.

If you take the **directional** approach to describing a process, tell the reader **what** to do and **how** to do it, in the right **order.** You have often followed directions yourself: they may have involved preparing a recipe, taking a new or unfamiliar route to a home or airport, or putting together a toy or other project.

If you take an **instructional** approach—telling how something has been done or works, you won't expect your readers to follow your directions literally. Instead, you will describe how something has been done or made in the past. Some examples might include ways in which an emergency room surgeon reattaches a severed finger, how an inspiring classroom teacher asks students to invent an improved paper clip, how a steamboat retraces historic journeys on the Ohio and Mississippi Rivers. Readers aren't expected to actually do these processes. However, they will still be interested in following the way steps are presented or described.

Whichever approach you take, you'll follow the same pattern used in narratives: steps will follow one another in time—in other words, chronologically. To write a readable process paragraph or paper, use the following guidelines.

CHOOSE A TOPIC YOU FIND INTERESTING

If you feel enthusiastic about a topic, you probably also understand the process well. This enables you to communicate your positive feelings to your reader. However, avoid topics that are too complicated to shoehorn into a 400- to 600-word paper. Although a liver transplant recently saved the life of a sports celebrity (temporarily), the operation may be too complicated to cover in a brief essay. On the other hand, avoid something as mindless as "opening your favorite beverage with a hand-operated tool."

DESCRIBE THE PROCESS WHILE DEFINING UNFAMILIAR TERMS

Sometimes you will include a list of ingredients at the very beginning of your essay. Recipes and sets of toy-making directions do this. In other papers, mention tools or define terms as you go along. You might define a term like *deferred maintenance* as "cracked driveways and peeling paint." Sometimes, to make an object more vivid, you will say that "a stereo boombox is a portable 'party machine.' "

START AT THE BEGINNING AND PUT THE STEPS IN TIME ORDER

If you are giving directions, your readers need to know *all* the steps, in logical order. Leave nothing out, even small steps. For instance, when changing your car's oil for the first time, you'd need to know to run your engine first. However, the directions should caution you to be careful when you remove the drain plug, because if that caution came too late in the directions, you could be burned by hot oil.

DESCRIBE EACH STEP FULLY

When giving directions or describing a process, assume that your reader knows nothing about it. Then pack each step with specific, easy-to-visualize details. As you complete the description of each step, let your readers know. Show them what the subject looks, feels, or sounds like at this point in the process. Tell they **why** they should carry out each step ("Although it is resistant to water, don't allow repeated or prolonged exposure to water").

GROUP YOUR STEPS

To avoid making your process paper simply a list, group your steps into paragraph-length units. For example, a maker has created a light bulb that automatically turns on at the desired time and off after six hours. To program the bulb to come on at the same time each day, you simply turn the bulb on at a wanted time. To deprogram it, you simply turn the light off and then on again. These two steps belong together in the directions.

For a longer essay, list your steps in chronological order. Then think how to group them in larger units that can become paragraphs. For example, in an essay "How to Become a Tournament Water Skier," the writer groups the list of individual steps into several larger units; then she will include them in a body paragraph:

List of Steps

Get a Master Craft ski boat

Get tournament ski rope

Get name-brand slalom ski

Get ski gloves

Get wet suit for winter practice

Push with both feet to keep more of ski in water

Learn to use leverage

Keep legs bent

Work out to achieve good physical condition

Find a good place to ski (private pond)

Avoid rough water

Choose pond with vegetation at water's edge (keeps shore from backwashing)

Grouping of Steps

Equipment

    Master Craft ski boat

    Tournament ski rope

    Name-brand slalom ski

    Ski gloves

    Wet suit (winter practice)

Skills

    Push with both feet

    Learn to use leverage

    Keep legs bent

    Work out

Practice Area

    Choose private pond

    Avoid rough water

    Need vegetation at water's edge

    Practice in warm climate

LINK YOUR POINTS WITH TRANSITIONS

Link your points, both between and within paragraphs, with transitions. Here are some of the most useful:

Transitions Showing Sequence

first, . . . second, . . . third	moreover
also	in addition
next	then
after	furthermore

Transitions Showing Results

consequently	as a result
therefore	thus

It's also a good idea to connect your ideas by using pronouns or by repeating words.

READINGS

As Chapter 1 pointed out, **topic sentences** sum up a paragraph's main idea. Use examples to make this general concept clearer, more vivid to your reader. By filling out this general idea, your paragraph will draw word pictures in your reader's mind. The topic sentence of the following paragraph makes a point readers will care about. The paragraph then develops the topic sentence with specific details:

Topic sentence: paragraph will describe process ——▶

Details about line of clothes ——▶

Describes process: (a) application ——▶

(b) division of pay ——▶

It's the old bad-boy look, with a twist. These boys don't just *look* bad. They're all convicted criminals in the Oregon prison system. **And the clothes they're wearing are made by inmates** for the Prison Blues clothing label, created in 1991. So far, 400 American stores carry this line of jeans, shirts, and jackets, as do about 100 in Europe. A mail-order catalogue (featuring some of the felons) is produced by a private marketing company called Big House. Inmates must apply for the garment jobs and are paid what workers on the outside would get. Eighty percent of their pay goes to victim restitution, taxes, and room and board. They keep the rest, but are allowed to spend only a maximum of $30 a week. The rest goes into savings. If Prison Blues are not available at your local Army-Navy-Penitentiary store, try 1-800-497-7472.

The New York Times Magazine

Chapter 2 showed how a **thesis** sums up the main idea for an entire writing. It serves an essay as a **topic sentence** serves a paragraph: to sum up the main idea and tell the writer's viewpoint toward it.

Thesis: main idea of essay, describing how a process was carried out ——————▶

Last summer, a 77-year-old widower posted a large sign outside his elegant home that read: "Wanted: a WIFE! Picture & Performance to Joseph Mullan—Apply Within."

Details of process: effects of ad.
(1) Women respond ——————▶

(2) Mullan finds no replacement ——————▶

(3) Mullan takes down sign ——————▶

(4) Mullan might change his mind ——————▶

The sign generated international publicity, including a front-page story in *The Baltimore Sun*, and attracted nearly 200 applicants from at least three countries. But as aspiring women sent letters with photographs and lined up at his front door, Mullan gradually realized that the one woman he truly wanted—his deceased wife— would never turn up on his doorstep.

"After a while I took the sign down and went to bed," said the frail, silver-haired Mullan. "And now they're all gone." Nevertheless, Mullan says, he had fun, so much fun that he's considering putting the sign back up today. "Why not?" he says.

(1) Missed wife, and
(2) Is eccentric. ——————▶

Mullan is retired. Getty, his wife of nearly 51 years, died of cancer three years ago. "I just missed her," Mullan says. "I really thought I could find somebody." Peggy Greenman, the oldest of his nine children, described him as eccentric. "He's always been a character," she said.

Sign display is both **effect** (of loneliness) and **cause** (of global publicity)——————▶

For the nearly four months that Mullan displayed the 6-foot-square sign, he delighted in the flood of global attention. A friend in Poland spotted his photograph in *Stars and Stripes*, the military newspaper distributed around the world. Another friend saw it in the *London Times*. Mullan and his wife-wanted sign appeared in newspapers and on TV screens throughout the United States.

Further results of ad: women responded ——————▶

As a result, Mullan says, he received about 100 letters from women in this country, Canada, and England. And, he says, about 90 women appeared at his home. Greenman says the women were all ages, some even in their 20s and 30s. Others were old friends who saw the story in *The Sun* or on TV and stopped by to visit. Still others were merely curious, but many were serious.

Mullan draws conclusions from process ——————▶

"I learned there were a lot of women who wanted to get married," Mullan says, laughing. "They were here so much the maids got sick and tired of answering the door."

The Baltimore Sun

DEALING WITH MODERN-DAY VAMPIRES EVOKES A SENSE OF "ONCE BITTEN TWICE SHY"

Student Essay (Denise)

A thick fog falls upon the cold room and the silence becomes deafening. Suddenly, the door opens and the patient freezes. Donating blood can be stressful and traumatic, terrifying many donors. Most people are afraid to give blood. They may have heard old war stories from previous donors or had a bad experience themselves. As a result, the pain too often overshadows the needs of injured patients for blood. To prevent a bad experience donating blood, medical personnel need to relax their donors, distract their attention from the process, and insert the needle only once.

To begin with, blood is drawn for many reasons. For one, blood transfusions during surgery sometimes require several pints of donated blood. In addition, blood tests often detect many diseases, including diabetes, hepatitis, HIV, AIDS, and many birth defects. Early detection of diabetes, for example, can avoid serious disablement or even death. In addition, early diagnosis of birth defects can lead to early treatment to lessen the worst effects of the problem.

Knowing the reasoning behind blood testing can help reduce the tension felt by donors. As I learned from personal experience, relaxation is the key. When I had blood drawn the first time, at the age of thirteen, I expected to have my finger pricked. However, when the phlebotomist (literally, one who draws blood) pulled out the needles and tubes from my arm, I lost every shred of dignity. Because I was so tense, the experience was as bad as I expected. It left a permanent memory. Moreover, it was traumatic because I was so tense.

As a phlebotomist (pr. flee-BOT-uh-mist) myself, I have given blood many times. Through personal experience, I have learned how to lessen the pain of blood donation. Often my patients sweat, shake, and feel faint while sitting in my chair, waiting to give blood. It helps to focus their attention on something else: I tell them to look away and pay no attention to what I am doing. While talking to my patient and watching him or her relax, I wait until they least expect it. Then I stick them. Since their attention was elsewhere, they don't mind the pain. As a result, patients often say I don't hurt them; in fact, they would be glad to have me take their blood again.

Along with avoiding pain, relaxation averts the need for a second try. The reasons for this are simple. Watching the needle actually going into the arm increases patients' stress level. Stress increases the heart rate, which interferes with circulation of the blood. Under stress, the body usually takes the blood away from the arms and directs it to the internal organs. When this happens, the veins lose some of their pressure. Then, when they are stuck, the veins sometimes roll: the needle may miss, requiring another stick to draw blood. Personally, since I don't like to be stuck more than once, I try to relax when giving blood.

Knowing that blood tests and donations save lives will give patients confidence. Therefore, if patients must be stuck only once to draw blood, they will feel more comfortable having blood taken later. They should also realize that phlebotomists share their concerns: they don't hurt patients on purpose. The people who stick you also get stuck.

To sum up, these helpful hints will help patients avoid pain when donating blood:

- Look away when the phlebotomist gets his/her equipment ready;
- Don't watch the process of taking blood;
- Imagine yourself somewhere else;
- Finally, take deep breaths and relax.

Queries for Understanding

1. For what reasons is blood drawn?
2. What personal interest(s) does the writer have in the topic of the essay?
3. Why is it important for blood donors to relax?
4. What advice does the writer give blood donors to avoid pain?

Queries on the Writer's Techniques

1. Where and what are the thesis (the main idea) and the plan (the separate points) of the essay?
2. Why should the writer and the reader care about the writer's choice of topic?
3. What specific examples does the writer use to support her main points?
4. How does the writer link paragraphs together?
5. How does the conclusion of the paper sum up effectively?

Writing Topics

1. Describe the best way to calm a person before beginning a difficult process.
2. What is the best way to conduct an experiment?

In the following selection, the author tells us that storms and hurricanes don't leave off where the atmosphere ends.

Words to Define

monitor: watch closely, especially for problems

hydroelectric: creation of electric power from water-driven generators

complex: complicated, uncontrollable

megawatts: measure of power output: million (mega) + unit of power (watt)

cascade: resembling a series of small waterfalls

negligence: careless act

geomagnetic: having to do with the earth's magnetic field

auroras: streamers of light visible in northern skies

phantom: ghost, vision detached from reality

fluctuations: irregular changes

rogue: a deviation from the expected

conductor: something that allows electricity to flow along it

igneous: rocks once molten

induced: led to action, started

Prereading

1. Describe a turning point in a process you carried out, one that surprised you or spoiled the process. What did you learn from it?
2. Describe the crucial impact of weather or time of day on a process you were carrying out or observing.

SPACE WEATHER

Eric J. Lerner

On March 13, 1989, in the early morning hours, technicians at the Hydro-Quebec power company in Montreal were in their control room as usual. They were watching the maplike "mimic board" that allows them to monitor the condition of their power grid. That grid supplies electricity not only to Montreal but to all of Quebec Province, to a total of 6 million people. At 2:44 A.M. a light started flashing on the mimic board: there was trouble up north. A voltage regulator had shut down on one of the main lines that run from the LaGrande hydroelectric complex in northern Quebec to Montreal and other cities in the south. As the next sixty seconds ticked away, six more lights started flashing. Voltage levels in the grid became dangerously complex. Then a circuit breaker tripped one of the five lines coming out of LaGrande: within a second the other four had gone as well. LaGrande and its 9,500 megawatts were now completely isolated from the grid. As the startled technicians looked on helplessly, a cascade of broken circuits rippled around the province, cutting off the rest of Hydro-Quebec's generators. In all, it had taken less than 90 seconds for power to collapse in the entire grid.

The blackout cost Hydro-Quebec more than $10 million, and it cost the power company's customers tens if not hundreds of millions. The blackout had not been caused by a design flaw, nor by operator negligence, nor indeed by any human error at all. The source of the problem had been the sun.

Every now and then the sun ejects a huge blob of hot, electrically charged gas, or plasma. The blobs travel hundreds of millions of miles out into the solar system, and they carry part of the sun's magnetic field with them. Several times a year, one of the blobs happens to hit Earth. The result is called a geomagnetic storm. As the plasma plows into Earth's magnetic field, it squashes the field violently, setting compass needles aflutter; charged particles pour into the space around Earth and zing down the magnetic field lines toward the poles; the northern and southern auroras spread their crazy glowing curtains across the sky. People who operate satellites go crazy, too. Geomagnetic storms often disable expensive satellites by triggering phantom commands in their fragile electronics; in 1994, for instance, a storm knocked out a quarter-billion-dollar Canadian communications satellite for nearly six months before engineers got it back under control.

But the most worrisome threat is to power grids. The fluctuations in Earth's magnetic field during a geomagnetic storm induce rogue electric currents in Earth's surface. In regions where the ground doesn't happen to be a good conductor—such as Quebec, which sits on a shield of igneous rock—the currents gladly surge through power lines instead. The longer the lines—LaGrande is 600 miles from Montreal—the greater the voltage difference induced by the magnetic fluctuations and the stronger the currents.

Discover

Queries for Understanding

1. Explain the who, what, where, when, and why of the above essay, as presented in the first five sentences.
2. What exactly isolated LaGrande and its 9,500 megawatts from the grid?
3. What were the costs of the power shutdown, for whom?
4. What *didn't* cause the problem? What did?

5. Why do fluctuations in Earth's magnetic field during a geomagnetic storm damage power grids?

Queries on the Writer's Techniques

1. Where and what are the thesis (the main idea) and the plan (the separate points) of the essay?
2. Why should the writer and the reader care about the writer's choice of topic?
3. What specific examples does the writer use to support his main points?
4. How does the writer link paragraphs together?
5. How does the conclusion of the paper sum up effectively?

Writing Topics

1. Describe a process involving technology: taking a picture, for example, or creating a costume.
2. Describe ways of carrying out some process in nature, like hunting, fishing, or bird-watching.

In the following selection, the author describes how a new invention lets cows milk themselves, but not without some cost to their owners in money and irritation.

Words to Define

bovine: cow-like

identification: to place or separate into a group

ultrasonic: frequencies too high for the human ear

sensors: devices that receive and respond to a signal

promoting: leading to the growth of

longevity: long life

pulsating: to get bigger and smaller in a rhythmic way

vacuum: the absence of air pressure

conventional: accepted, traditional

technological: application of science to industry

glitches: flaws, shortcomings

Prereading

1. What processes could be improved, in your view, by making them fully automatic?
2. If you could automate more parts of your life, which parts would you put at the top of your list?

BARNYARD BREAKTHROUGH: COW MILKS HERSELF

Dana Milbank

It wouldn't be accurate to say that Frank Miezenbeek's cows possess above-average intelligence. But his Holsteins have a talent shared by few of their breed: They can milk themselves. As Mr. Miezenbeek watches proudly on a farm in Vijfuizen, the Netherlands, the cows line up like so many customers in a post office. One at a time, Trijnte, Catie, Janke, Zoeki, and others march into the milking parlor without so much as a moo, deposit their milk, and return to the herd.

The technological revolution has come to the barnyard. Thanks to the work of Dutch scientists, cows can milk themselves with the help of a computer. The high-tech bovine, wearing a computer chip in her collar for identification, approaches the machine whenever she feels the urge for a milking. A robot equipped with ultrasonic sensors does the rest. The farmer is alerted by beeper if anything goes wrong. "It's a little impersonal, but the cows tend to like it," says Wim Wygteren, an executive of robot manufacturer Prolion Development. So do farmers, who no longer have to get up with the cows.

The robot saves them about four hours a day and reduces labor costs. Round-the-clock robotic milking allows cows to relieve their udders three times a day instead of the usual two, promoting an increase in milk production of 15%. It is also said by Prolion to reduce udder disease to boost cow longevity. Though the machine can't handle the high volume of industrial farms, it could change the life of the family-farmer with a herd of under 100 cows.

A cow enters the milking stall, usually encouraged by a sweet snack released if the computer (reading her ID chip) decides it is time for a milking. Once she's inside, gates close around the cow as the robotic milkmaid slides underneath, its sensors spinning like a ship's radar. It finds the "reference teat" first, then hooks to all four with a rubber pulsating vacuum.

The milking device washes the teats, checks for problems with the udders, and milks, all within a few minutes. The robot will try five times to hook the machine to the cow; if it fails, the cow is sent into a separate chamber, and the farmer is alerted. Cows seem to learn the system after being pushed in two or three times. If they forget, some farms remind them with a moving electric fence.

But farmers will feel squeezed to justify the machine's cost. The robotic three-stall milker sells for about $250,000, double the price of conventional milking machines, which are attached to the cow by hand.

"It's a very expensive machine, and I can't see how my boss will earn it back," says Mr. Miezenbeek, the farm manager. "I can't see the advantage that much." His new system is plagued by technological glitches. Mr. Miezenbeek's beeper goes off about 10 times a day, as early as 3:30 a.m. and often because of false alarms. "Socially, it's a disaster," he says. As he talks, his beeper sounds twice.

Queries for Understanding

1. How are Frank Miezenbeek's cows different from other cows, and why?

2. What advantages are cited in the second paragraph for the new milking system?

3. How many steps are there in the automatic milking system, and what are they?

4. What built-in error-detecting steps exist?

5. What shortcomings in the new system still need to be worked out?

Queries on the Writer's Techniques

1. Where and what are the thesis (the main idea) and the plan (the separate points) of the essay?

2. Why should the writer and reader care about the writer's choice of topic?

3. What specific examples does the writer use to support the main points?

4. How does the writer link paragraphs together?

5. How does the conclusion of the paper sum up effectively?

Writing Topics

1. Describe a process in which technology has created new, unforeseen problems.

2. Deal humorously with some process: how to fail a course, or how to make a boring task exciting.

THE WRITING PROCESS

Wayne, the author of the following selection, chose water skiing as the topic of his essay for two reasons: he enjoyed the sport, and he knew how professionals developed their skills.

FIRST DRAFT: STUDENT PROCESS ESSAY

I've always wanted to be a water skiier, like the ones on television but that isn't real easy. A water skiier needs a lot of things in order to be good. Like some good skiis and a boat. They also need to be able to keep their legs bent right, and be in good physical condition. Other things needed for water skiing are water and weather. The water needs to be a good pond and the weather needs to be nice. And, its expensive too. But, I bet that if I had all of this I could be a good skiier like on TV. Then I'd be famous and everybody would know me because I was on TV. I'd like to known as a real good athlete. Maybe I could even compete in the Olympics if I was a good water skiier that would be fun.

REVISING THE FIRST DRAFT

To revise his first trial draft, Wayne looks most closely at its organization. He'll ask the following questions and write in notes on his first draft:

1. Is the thesis of the process paper clear to the reader at the beginning of the paper? Is it clear to the reader why the writer's viewpoint matters?
2. Do the sentences in the draft grow out of the thesis, in the right order? Are the sentences carefully linked together, with helpful transitions, pronouns, and repeated words or synonyms?
3. Has the writer used enough specific, concrete details? Do the details effectively support the paper's main idea?
4. Does the paper's conclusion grow clearly out of the essay?

After answering these questions on organization, Wayne marks up his draft, like this:

Sum up and add specific details: since when, watching who, on what channel ——▶

I've always wanted to be a water skiier, like

the ones on television but that isn't real easy.

Sum up and add details: type of boat, ski rope, brand-name, ski, clothing, friend to drive boat ——▶

A water skiier needs a lot of things in order

↓ Begin new paragraph here

to be good. Like some good skiis and a boat.

◀—— List groupings here: equipment, skills, practice place

They also need to be able to keep their legs

Sum up and add details: muscles work together, push evenly with feet, use ——▶

bent right, and be in good physical condition.

Begin new ——▶ paragraph here

Other things needed for water skiing are wa-

ter and weather. The water needs to be a

Sum up and add ——▶ details: pond secluded and surrounded by trees and vegetation, warm climate

good pond and the weather needs to be nice.

↓ begin conclusion here: new paragraph

And, its expen-sive too. But, I bet that if I

had all of this I could be a good skiier like on

Shift emphasis in conclusion: sum ——▶ up expensive equipment, complicated athletic skills, hard-to-find good location. But challenge worth it.

TV. Then I'd be famous and everybody would

know me because I was on TV. I'd like to

known as a real good athlete. Maybe I could

even compete in the Olympics if I was a good

water skiier that would be fun.

Based on his responses to the questions and his markings on the first draft, Wayne writes an improved second draft of his process paper. However, his essay is not yet complete. He needs to proofread it, asking the following questions:

Proofreading Queries

1. Have I corrected grammatical problems such as noun/verb agreement?
2. Have I corrected the spelling, particularly with words that sound alike or look alike but are not spelled alike?
3. Have I corrected the punctuation, separating word groups to clarify meaning?

REVISED VERSION: STUDENT PROCESS ESSAY

I have been water skiing, since I was twelve.

Comma after skiing to set off introductory subordinate clause

contraction: wasn't

When I (wasnt) skiing I'd spend my time

watching the pros on ESPN. I still envy their

Run-on sentence: put period after abilities. Then capitalize However and set comma

skills and abilities however to become a tour-

nament (waterskier) an athlete needs reliable

equipment, athletic skills and a suitable place

to practice. First to become a tournament

competitor a skier needs the right

Need a comma after competitor to clarify meaning

misspelling: omit e

(equipement). To begin with, nobody can wa-

ter ski without a boat. The Master Craft ski

no 'e' in "towing"

boat is designed for (toweing) water(skiers.)

Confusion of it's/its: spell contraction. "It's" for it is.

Its necessary to have a friend drive the boat

make infinitives parallel: "to be" keeps consistent present tense

and ~~being~~ there if something ~~went~~ wrong ~~is~~

~~helpful.~~ Of course, you will need a (tournemnt)

wordy: take out "is helpful"   *typo here: should be "tournament"*

ski rope and a name brand slalom ski. Brands

like O'Brien, H.O., or E.P. are the best be-

cause they are the most reliable and are used

typo here: should be "skier"

by most of the pros. A (skiier) needs proper

typo and word confusion: should be "clothing too"

(lothing to.) Ski gloves help avoid callouses

wordy: replace with "practicing"

and a wet suit will allow ~~you to practice~~ in

the winter. Assembling all the proper equip-

ment expensive and time consuming. Next, a   *Sentence lacking: a verb is a fragment: add the verb is*

noun/verb agreement error: should be "needs"

good skier (need) to develop adequate skiing

misspelling: should be "muscles"

skills. His (museles) need to work together in

Set off transition with comma

perfect unison. For example a skier needs to

push evenly with both feet to keep more of

the ski in the water. He also needs to learn

misspelling: should be "leverage"

how to use (levage) instead of trying to out-

Set off transition "Next" with comma

power the boat. Next he needs to keep his

misspelling: should be "accelerate"

legs bent so he can (acellerate) while being

Fragment is missing both subject and verb: Fix by adding A skier needs . . .

pulled and decelerate in a turn. To work out

daily because he relies on his back, arm, and

misspelling: should be "muscles"

To the student: proofread the following paragraph

leg (musles.) Finally, a skier a suitable prac-

tice area. I like a private secluded pond be-

cuase at public lakes other boats make alot

of waves. Also, a pond usually is surrounded

by trees which stop the wind. This cuts down

misspelling: should be "It's"

on "natural" waves. (Its) difficult to practice

typo: should be "rough"

for tournament skiing in (rought) water. A

pond also needs to have vegetation around

Run-on here: put period after " climate." Then capitalize "Even

the water's edge to keep the shore from back

washing. Finally, try to find a pond in a

warm climate even with a wet suit, skiing in

cold weather can be very unpleasant. A cor-

Fragment is missing add verb can make after area

rectly chosen practice area the difference be-

Comma splice: correct by inserting and after comma or changing comma to period

tween an adequate skier and a tournament

skier. Water skiing is not easy. The equip-

ment is expensive, the athletic skills are com-

plicated. Even finding a good location is

misspelling: should be "difficult"

(dificult.) But, the challenge is worth it. Win-

misspelling: should be "tournament"

ning a (turnament) is a thrill few skiers ever

experience.

After solving his problems with organization and proofreading, Wayne writes a final version of his process paper:

FINAL VERSION: STUDENT PROCESS ESSAY "LEARNING TO WATER SKI"

I have been waterskiing since I was twelve. When I wasn't skiing, I'd spend my time watching the pros on ESPN. I still envy their skills and abilities. However, to become a tournament water-skier, an athlete needs reliable equipment, athletic skills, and a suitable place to practice.

First, to become a tournament competitor, a skier needs the right equipment. To begin with, nobody can water ski without a boat. The Master Craft ski boat is designed for towing water skiers. It's necessary to have a friend to drive the boat and to be there if something goes wrong. Of course, you will need a tournament ski rope and a name-brand slalom ski. Brands like O'Brien, H.O., or E.P. are the best because they are the most reliable and are used by most of the pros. A skier needs proper clothing, too. Ski gloves help avoid calluses, and a wet suit will allow practicing in the winter. Assembling all the proper equipment is expensive and time consuming.

Next, a good skier needs to develop adequate skiing skills. His muscles need to work together in perfect unison. For example, a skier needs to push evenly with both feet to keep more of the skis in the water. He also needs to learn how to use leverage instead of trying to outpower the boat. Next, he needs to keep his legs bent so he can accelerate while being pulled and decelerate in a turn. A skier needs to work out daily because he relies on his back, arm, and leg muscles.

Finally, a skier needs a suitable practice area. I like a private, secluded pond because at public lakes other boats make a lot of waves. Also, a pond usually is surrounded by trees which stop the wind. This cuts down on "natural" waves. It's difficult to practice for tournament skiing in rough water. A pond also needs to have vegetation around the water's edge to keep the shore from backwashing. Finally, try to find a pond in a warm climate. Even with a wet suit, skiing in cold weather can be very unpleasant. A correctly chosen practice area can make the difference between an adequate skier and a tournament skier.

Waterskiing is not easy. The equipment is expensive, and the athletic skills are complicated. Even finding a good location is difficult. But the challenge is worth it. Winning a tournament is a thrill few skiers ever experience.

PROCESS WRITING TOPICS

The following are some possible topics for a process paragraph or paper. Limit your topic to fit your instructor's requirements. Tell the reader *why* you have chosen your topic, and link your details closely to your topic.

1. Describe how to learn or improve a skill.
2. Describe how to collect something or develop a hobby.
3. Describe how to buy a recreational product, computer, VCR, or other electronic gadget.
4. Describe how to overcome shyness, make friends, or meet a future spouse.
5. Describe how to choose a new or used car, place to live, or roommate.
6. Describe how to put together or renovate some item.
7. Describe how to plan a party, wedding, or birthday.
8. Describe how to carry out a vacation successfully and cheaply.

CHAPTER NINE

Cause and Effect

Showing the links between cause and effect means showing that an effect not only *follows* a cause, but that something *made it happen*. You may handle the links between cause and effect in several ways.

LIST SEVERAL CAUSES THAT RESULT IN A SINGLE EFFECT

You may list several causes that result in a single effect, as in the saying, "Hot words make a real cool friendship." For example, engineers were asked to design an extremely lightweight, four-cycle, gasoline engine. The **result** of their efforts stemmed from several **causes:**

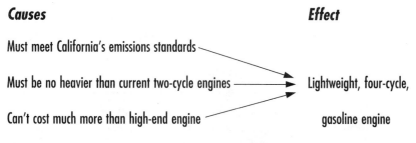

Causes

Must meet California's emissions standards

Must be no heavier than current two-cycle engines

Can't cost much more than high-end engine

Effect

Lightweight, four-cycle, gasoline engine

The **causes** are listed in their order of importance.

LINK ONE CAUSE TO SEVERAL EFFECTS OR RESULTS

You may choose to link only one cause to several effects or results. The following example links job burnout (a cause) to several effects:

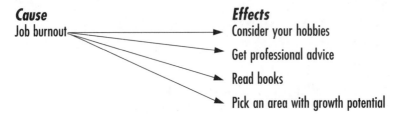

Cause
Job burnout

Effects
Consider your hobbies

Get professional advice

Read books

Pick an area with growth potential

TREAT CAUSES AND EFFECTS EQUALLY

Treat causes and effects equally, dealing with several of each. This approach can be used to describe an activity like bargaining, which involves various causes leading to a number of results. This pattern looks like the following:

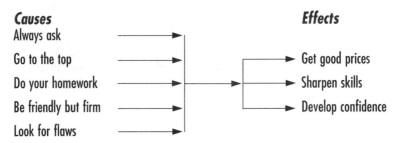

Causes
Always ask

Go to the top

Do your homework

Be friendly but firm

Look for flaws

Effects
Get good prices

Sharpen skills

Develop confidence

TRACE A CAUSE-AND-EFFECT CHAIN

Trace a cause-and-effect chain to show how one cause has an effect, which in turn causes another effect, which may lead to another effect, and so on. The first incident is the original cause. The following incidents are both effect and cause. They each result from the one before and cause the one after it. For example, 22,000 people are infected by cat-scratch disease every year. The disease moves in stages from infection to cure, as in this diagram:

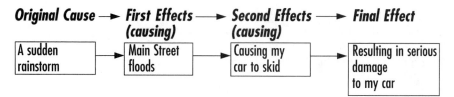

To handle cause-and-effect relationships well, follow these guidelines:

- **Treat only the most important, most timely causes and effects.** Many cause-and-effect relationships include minor as well as major factors. Leave out trivial factors, identifying the ones you do mention as important. An accident report should mention weather conditions, traffic, the speed of cars involved, and darkness. It should leave out arrangements for handling participants' luggage or sympathetic comments by bystanders.

- **Organize your writing clearly.** Choose one of the patterns described earlier before beginning a draft or when beginning to revise. List causes and effects in order of time or importance.

- **Use linking words or transitions** such as the following to reveal **sequence** or **results**:

first, second, third	also	in addition	finally
moreover	after	furthermore	next
then	consequently	as a result	therefore
thus			

Chapter 1 showed how **topic sentences** sum up a paragraph's main idea. In cause-and-effect paragraphs, you will gain your readers' attention by citing specific causes and effects. This approach will help your readers visualize your meaning. The following example cites several causes leading to a single effect. In the process, the paragraph brings in interesting, memorable details:

Cause: sums up ⟶ Judy Epstein was talking with a man in the steam room of her 50th Street gym. The fellow was complaining that
Restates cause ⟶ the equipment was always broken. That day it was the
Details (causes) ⟶ whirlpool and the shower.
Further details (causes) ⟶ *He*: I'm fed up with this gym. There's always something in need of repair. If it's not the sauna, it's the whirlpool. If it's not the shower, it's the steam room. That's why I
Sums up effect ⟶ joined the 32d Street branch.
She: So, what are you doing here?
Final detail (cause) ⟶ *He*: The pool's broken at 32d Street.

Ron Alexander, "Metropolitan Diary"

Chapter 2 showed how a **thesis** sums up the main idea for an entire writing; it serves an **essay** in the same way as a **topic sentence** serves a **paragraph.** In the following example of a cause-and-effect essay, the title looks ahead to the thesis. After a brief narrative of the crucial incident, the essay restates the thesis.

"No More Fowl Play: Worker Who Attacked "Rooster" Wins Lawsuit"

Narrative sums up:
Cause: rooster surprise
Effect: Lineberry throttles rooster

It was a tradition at the truck plant: An employee would dress up as a rooster, sneak up behind tardy workers, and surprise them with a flap of feathers and a loud crow.

Funny? Not to Marshall Lineberry.

Grumpy from back pain, the 50-year-old assembly line worker responded to the buffoonery by throttling the "rooster."

Thesis of essay ——►

A judge ruled that the bird had it coming.

"It certainly should not have been unexpected," Pulaski Circuit Judge Colin Gibb said.

Initial cause ——►

It all began 15 months ago, when Lineberry showed up late for his 6 a.m. shift at Volvo GM Heavy Truck Corp.

Cause-and-effect chain: three incidents ——►

The rooster sneaked up behind him and let out his "cock-a-doodle-do!" Lineberry turned around, jumped on top of the rooster, and began choking it. According to a Virginia Employment Commission report, he had to be pulled off by two people.

Further cause-and-effect chain: four more incidents ——►

Volvo GM suspended Lineberry for three months for violating Shop Rule No. J9S, which prohibits fighting on the floor, a foul apparently applicable to fowl. Lineberry, an 18-year employee of the plan who made more than $15 an hour, applied for unemployment benefits. The employment commission denied his claim. Lineberry sued.

Final result: judge rules against company

Last month, Gibb told the commission to eat crow and pay up. The judge ruled that the rooster's act amounted to provocation sanctioned by the employer and that the bird itself violated several company rules.

Lineberry said he is owed $1,600 to $1,800.

After the attack, the unidentified rooster voluntarily quit the prank, which Volvo GM Human Resources Manager Steve Plastek said was "well-accepted" around the factory.

But Lineberry called the act "a time bomb getting ready to go off."

He said he was told that if he hadn't taken out the rooster, someone else would have.

Associated Press, *Atlanta Journal/Constitution*

This essay clearly traces a cause-and-effect chain. It moves from the original incident, Lineberry's late arrival at work, to its final result, a court ruling in his favor. The essay first provides a brief summary of the original incident, Lineberry's startling by the rooster and the judge's ruling. The essay then takes the readers from cause to effect, this one causing another effect, and so on. The details of the case are vivid, even comic, arranged in time order by the writer.

To develop ideas for your own treatment of cause and effect, freewrite sentences for five or ten minutes. Develop one or more cause-and-effect incidents by linking concrete, specific details together. Or make lists of incidents you can recall. Later on, you can use these resources in more carefully organized sentences and paragraphs.

TEACH YOUR CHILD TO WONDER

Mary Budd Rowe

It was a strange sight: a man standing before a fountain, watching the falling water and tilting his head from side to side. Drawing closer, I saw he was rapidly moving the fingers of his right hand up and down in front of his face.

I was in seventh grade, visiting Princeton University with my science class, and the man at the fountain was Albert Einstein. For several minutes, he continued silently flicking his fingers. Then he turned and asked, "Can you do it? Can you see the individual drops?"

Copying him, I spread my fingers and moving them up and down before my eyes. Suddenly the fountain's stream seemed to freeze into individual droplets. For some time, the two of us stood there perfecting our strobe technique. Then, as the professor turned to leave, he looked me in the eye and said, "Never forget that science is just that kind of exploring and fun."

Nearly half a century later, I've spent an entire career trying to impart Einstein's words to adults and children all over the world: science *is* exploring, and exploring is fun.

Sadly, far too few schools make the subject appealing. Science courses introduce more new vocabulary than foreign-language classes do. Textbooks are as dull as dictionaries. As a result, too many children think that science is only for people as smart as Einstein.

Reader's Digest

Queries for Understanding

1. What technique was Einstein using to see the individual drops in a fountain?
2. What criticism does the writer make of science education as it's usually presented in the schools?

Queries on the Writer's Techniques

1. What is the main idea in the selection? Is it summed up in a single sentence, or does the reader need to put it together?
2. How does the writer use both narrative and examples to develop her main idea?
3. Why does the writer mention Einstein in her last sentence?
4. What causes and effects does the writer treat in the selection?

Writing Topics

1. Think of a particularly interesting, exciting, or stimulating learning experience in or outside of a formal classroom. What **caused** this experience to happen? What **results** did this experience have?

THE POWER OF FORGIVENESS

Student Essay (Lewis)

It was 12:37 a.m. as the bus pulled from the terminal at Bowling Green, Kentucky. The streets were silent and the night was cool. I'd gotten my sister on her way to Ft. Knox after a weekend visit. At this time, I wanted nothing more than to go back to the dorm and get some rest. I never thought that a trip to the bus station could be so dramatic, that I would face death because of others' prejudice. Later on, I would need to overcome the effects of that prejudice.

After giving my sister spending money, I couldn't afford to take a cab back to the dorm. So I decided to get a little exercise and run to the dorm, about four miles away. When I had gone about two blocks, I noticed a truck slowly following me. When I turned around to see who it was, the driver sped up, went to the next block, and turned right. After I'd run another couple blocks, I noticed the truck in front of me. A guy on the passenger side started yelling at me, "Hey, bootlip, rug head, nigger." However, I continued running, pretending to ignore them.

The guys took the next left as I continued jogging up the hill to the campus. Three blocks further on, they appeared again. This time, the driver had three other guys sitting in the back of the truck. "Nigger, we're going to kill you," they yelled as they threw cans and bottles at me. Trying not to show any fear, I continued my uphill journey to Western Kentucky University. By this time, I feared for my life and started praying silently to God. I knew that each step would bring me closer to a safe haven.

When the guys in the pickup took the next left, I passed them by, and I didn't see or hear from them for three more blocks. However, as I approached the corner of the fourth block, they surprised me. Five white guys jumped from the corner and surrounded me. One guy wearing a University of Louisville baseball cap said to me, "Where ya' goin', Niggah?" and pushed me into a guy behind me. "Where'd ya steal that sweat suit?" Petrified beyond response, I bounced from one guy to another. Then the guy wearing the U of L hat hit me in the stomach. As I folded over, another guy kicked me in the side. Immediately after that blow, another kicked me hard in the rear, and then blows came from everywhere.

As I fell to the sidewalk, I felt a stick break on my back. There were more kicks to my face and ribs and then, I felt nothing.

When I awakened, my mother was sitting beside my bed. When she saw me move my head, she simply said, "Thank God." It took me three weeks to get out of the hospital, and seven more to recover from four broken ribs, a broken collar bone and arm, fractured skull, and severely beaten face. Physically, I did recover.

As people came to see me, I felt the tension between the blacks and whites. Coincidentally, the police reported that I was "assaulted by five unknown assailants" and left it at that. They failed to investigate either the vehicle or the license plate number that a witness reported.

When I got better, I purchased a .38 caliber handgun and walked the street every night for at least a month. I didn't speak to, eat with, or associate with white people in any form or fashion. One night, as I was walking away from the bus stop, I saw the pickup. As I waited for the driver to come out of the convenience store, the anger and hatred rose within me. All the malice I've ever felt transferred to the index finger of my right hand on the trigger of my .38.

When the guy came out of the store, I grabbed him from behind and jammed the gun in his side. I dragged him behind the building and put the gun to his throat. "Do you remember me?" I asked. "Uh . . . yeah," he answered. "Before I blow your brains out, I want to know why you all did that to me that night." When this man started to cry and plead for his life, I felt immensely powerful. However, he said, "I really am sorry and I came to see you in the hospital. I'm the one who sent the card. Don't hate the whole white race for the mistakes of the few . . . I wrote that."

I remembered the card. As I looked at that man again, I saw the pain he had been carrying for four months. As I let up on the trigger, I looked at him and said, "I forgive you," and walked away. Then I took the bullets out of the gun and threw them to the ground.

As I walked up the hill to Western Kentucky University, each step gave me a new freedom. When I got to the top of the hill, I was a brand new man. I was not only free of malice and prejudice; I had become a man who could forgive the prejudice of others. I had decided that night to walk in a new power: the power of forgiveness.

Queries for Understanding

1. What initial action leads to the writer's situation, jogging on the streets at night?

2. What leads the writer's tormentors to shout threats and racial epithets at the writer?

3. What actions seriously injure the writer, putting him in the hospital?

4. What leads the writer to find and threaten one of his antagonists with death?

5. Why does the writer exchange hopes of revenge for forgiveness?

Queries on the Writer's Techniques

1. What is the impact on the reader of the writer's direct quotes of his threateners?

2. What is the effect of the list of injuries suffered by the writer?

3. What is the effect of quoting the writer's antagonist when the writer traps and threatens him?

4. What is the theme of the selection?

Writing Topics

1. Consider an incident when you yourself were victimized by someone who unfairly attacked your race, gender, appearance, or other trait: how did you react, and why?

2. Describe a radical change in motivation or action resulting from a sudden insight, either in yourself, someone you know, or someone you have heard about.

In the following selection, the author describes how a chance accident that dumped thousands of plastic toys into the North Pacific has helped scientists study the movement of ocean currents and winds.

Words to Define

boon: stroke of luck or good fortune

susceptible: exposed or open to

intentionally: as the result of purpose or design

deteriorate: to fall apart or decline

ultimately: in the end or at last

oceanographers: scientists who study the ocean

Prereading

1. What toy-like or household items can be used to study or teach science (consider items such as balloons, toothpicks, cooking oil, and so on)?

2. How have you used simple materials to make toys for yourself or others?

AFTER 3 YEARS, PLASTIC DUCKS TELL TALE OF TIDES

A storm that washed 29,000 plastic ducks and other bathtub toys into the North Pacific nearly three years ago has proved to be a boon to scientists studying ocean currents.

In what a Seattle oceanographer, James Ingraham, called "the quack heard 'round the world,' " a cargo container filled with the toys washed overboard in a storm near the international date line in January 1992.

About 10 months later, the first of the toys—yellow ducks, blue turtles, red beavers, and green frogs—began showing up on beaches in Sitka, in southeast Alaska.

Over the next 10 months 400 toys were reported found along a 530-mile stretch of coast along the Gulf of Alaska, according to an article in the weekly *Transactions of the American Geophysical Union.*

Mr. Ingraham, an employee of the National Marine Fisheries Service who is the co-author of the article, said the accident that dumped toys was the greatest boon for research on North Pacific patterns since 61,000 Nike athletic shoes were spilled in the same area two years earlier.

"We never had anything like the ducks," said Mr. Ingraham, noting that the toys bob almost completely above the surface, leaving them susceptible to wind as well as ocean currents. The toys, no more than five inches long, were being shipped to Tacoma, Wash., from Hong Kong.

Other items that have been studied—the shoes, bottles that were intentionally dropped in the 1950s and 60s, and more modern drift devices traced by satellite—are unaffected by winds.

As a result of the reports on the toys, which struck land about six months earlier than researchers predicted, Mr. Ingraham adjusted his computer model of the North Pacific tides to include the effect of the wind.

While none of the toys has been sighted outside the North Pacific, Mr. Ingraham and his fellow author, Curtis Ebbesmeyer, also a Seattle oceanographer, received word last month of a duck found near Ocean Shores, Washington, about 3,000 miles from where they went into the ocean.

Mr. Ingraham said the report had not yet been confirmed but it appears the toy made a complete loop of the Gulf of Alaska and then sailed south. Ultimately, some of the plastic toys are likely to pass through the Bering Strait, make their way in ice packs across the Arctic Ocean and end up in the North Atlantic, the oceanographers said.

"Plastic takes a long time to deteriorate," Mr. Ingraham said.

The two authors say that the ducks, along with some of the shoes, could end up looping back across the Pacific and reach land in Asia.

"We're still hoping somebody will pick up a Nike shoe in the Orient, back where they came from," Mr. Ingraham said.

Queries for Understanding

1. Sum up the facts about the dumping of the plastic toys: **how many, what, when, where,** and **how?**

2. What did the drifting patterns of the toys show researchers that other drift devices had not, and why?

3. How far had one of the toys drifted, and to where?

4. According to researchers, how far will some of the plastic toys eventually drift?

Queries on the Writer's Techniques

1. What is the main idea in the essay? Is it summed up in a single sentence, or does the reader need to put it together?

2. What other drift devices have scientists used to study ocean currents, and how do they contrast with the plastic toys?

3. How does the writer use **facts, quotations,** and **comparison and contrast** to support the main points of the essay?

4. What transitions does the writer use to link the ideas in the paragraph?

5. What causes and effects does the writer treat in the selection?

Writing Topics

1. What unintended actions have you or one of your acquaintances performed that had unforeseen results, either good or bad? What did you learn from these experiences?

2. How has playfulness affected your ability to learn new techniques or your outlook on your personal or professional life?

In the following selection, a young woman charts the ways in which a new baby changed her appearance and behavior.

How Motherhood Changed My Appearance

Student Essay (Kelli)

I once spent a great deal of time working on my appearance. My long hair often took thirty minutes or more to get just right. Then, I often spent another fifteen minutes on make-up. My clothes were always picture perfect and very stylish. After I became a mother, lack of time and physical demands led to more practical ideas about my appearance. To achieve this practicality, I cut my hair, began putting on less make-up faster, and started wearing more sensible clothing.

Before my son Taylor was born, my hair was long and difficult to fix. When he was two months old, I was leaning over him, changing his diaper. Suddenly, he reached up and grabbed a big handful of hair with what felt like the strength of a full-grown man. Hearing me yipe, my mother said, "Kelli, you are going to have to cut off all that hair. The older he gets, the harder he's going to pull it." The next morning, planning to take Taylor to visit my grandmother, I took a shower. When I began to fix my hair, Taylor started to cry. He wouldn't quiet down long enough for me to finish my hair. Exasperated, I decided to cut my hair short, in a simple style. This decision kept my hair out of Taylor's reach and let me fix it in less than five minutes.

I also used to enjoy making up my face. However, lack of time and physical demands cut short my make-up time along with my hair. First of all, I couldn't keep my baby quiet long enough for me to completely make up my face. If by some stroke of luck I did finish it, my make-up would be completely gone within a couple of hours. Taylor, you see, is a very big child, a hefty fifteen pounds at five months. Even in the winter, lifting and carrying a baby that heavy made me break out in a sweat. In a matter of hours, the make-up I had worked so hard to put on would be gone. So, I began wearing only the basic necessities: powder, mascara, and chapstick. This let me apply my make-up in less than two minutes and keep it on all day.

I also began wearing comfortable, inexpensive clothing to help me handle the physical demands of motherhood. I needed comfortable clothes which let me get down on the floor and play with Taylor at any given moment. Since my clothes got dirty quickly, they needed to be cheap and washable. I realized this, too, when Taylor spit up on my shirt the first time. As he got older, his messes just got bigger. When he started eating baby food, he would spit back food he didn't like. Most of his foods stain clothing, especially carrots. As a result, I began wearing old, comfortable clothes which didn't show dirt or stains.

Last week, I ran into a high school friend who hadn't seen me since graduation. When I said "Hello," she didn't even recognize me. "I can't believe how different you look," she remarked. I sighed, "Becoming a mother greatly reduces the time you can spend on yourself." She didn't seem convinced. One day, when she becomes a mother herself, she will understand.

Queries for Understanding

1. What kinds of attention needed by the baby are new to the writer?

2. What actions, specifically, by the writer's baby affect her appearance?

Queries on the Writer's Techniques

1. What is the main idea in the essay? Is it summed up in a single sentence, or does the reader need to put it together?

2. How does the writer use transitions, pronouns, and repeated words to make connections between the topics of her body paragraphs?

3. How does the writer of the essay support its points with the use of the following: **facts, quotations, comparison and contrast?**

Writing Topics

1. How have changes in your life such as marriage, divorce, children, or a move affected your actions and behavior? What did you learn from these experiences?

2. How have family members, friends, and acquaintances reacted to changes in your life? Must people actually experience changes in their own lives to fully understand them in others?

In the following selection, a young Hispanic student discovers that America's unity owes much to its multicultural diversity.

Words to Define

contraption: device, gadget

barrio: a mostly Spanish-speaking community in a U.S. city

maneuvered: moved with a plan in mind

formidable: large, impressive

superstructure: structure built on top of something (as used here, upper body)

mobilized: to put into operation

obnoxious: disagreeable, unpleasant

gringo: Northerner, Yankee

idiocies: foolish or stupid utterances

anchorage: place of safety

recitations: act of reciting memorized materials publicly

persistently: doggedly, stubbornly

assortment: mixed grouping

barbaric: uncivilized

demonstration: presentation, showing

collage: combination of different materials (from art)

resonant: vibrant, booming

benchmark: milestone, landmark

SCHOOL DAYS

Ernesto Galarza

In Tucson, when I asked my mother again if the Americans were having a revolution, the answer was: "No, but they have good schools, and you are going to one of them." We were by now settled at 418 L Street, in Sacramento, California, and the time had come for me to exchange a revolution for an American education.

We walked south on Fifth Street one morning to the center of Q Street and turned right. Half of the block was occupied by the Lincoln School. It was a three-story wooden building, with two wings that gave it the shape of a double-T connected by a central hall. It was a new building, painted yellow, with a shingled roof that was not like the red tile of the school in Mazatlán. I noticed other differences, none of them very reassuring.

We walked up the wide staircase hand in hand and through the door, which closed by itself. A mechanical contraption screwed to the top shut it behind us quietly.

Up to this point the adventure of enrolling me in the school had been carefully rehearsed. Mrs. Dodson, our neighbor, had told us how to find it and we had circled it several times on our walks. Friends in the *barrio* explained that the director was called a principal, and that it was a lady and not a man. They assured us that there was always a person at the school who could speak Spanish.

Exactly as we had been told, there was a sign on the door in both Spanish and English: "Principal." We crossed the hall and entered the office of Miss Nettie Hopley.

Miss Hopley was at a roll-top desk to one side, sitting in a swivel chair that moved on wheels. There was a sofa against the opposite wall, flanked by two windows and a door that opened on a small balcony. Chairs were set around a table and framed pictures hung on the walls of a man with long white hair and another with a sad face and a black beard.

The principal half-turned in the swivel chair to look at us over the pinch glasses crossed on the ridge of her nose. To do this she had to duck her head slightly as if she were about to step through a low doorway.

What Miss Hopley said to us we did not know but we saw in her eyes a warm welcome and when she took off her glasses and straightened up she smiled wholeheartedly. We were, of course, saying nothing, only catching the friendliness of her voice and the sparkle in her eyes while she said words we did not understand. She signaled us to the table. Almost tiptoeing across the office, I maneuvered myself to keep my mother between me and the gringo lady. In a matter of seconds I had to decide whether she was a possible friend or a menace. We sat down.

Then Miss Hopley did a formidable thing. She stood up. Had she been standing when we entered she would have seemed tall. But rising from her chair she soared. And what she carried up and up with her was a buxom superstructure, firm shoulders, a straight sharp nose, full cheeks slightly molded by a curved line along the nostrils, thin lips that moved like steel springs, and a high forehead topped by hair gathered in a bun. Miss Hopley was not a giant in body but when she mobilized it to a standing position she seemed a match for giants. I decided I liked her.

She strode to a door in the far corner of the office, opened it and called a name. A boy of about ten years appeared in the doorway. He sat down at one end of the table. He was brown like us, a plump kid with shiny black hair combed straight back, neat, cool, and faintly obnoxious.

Miss Hopley joined us with a large book and some papers in her hand. She, too, sat down and the questions and answers began by way of our interpreter. My name was Ernesto. My mother's name was Henriqueta. My birth certificate was in San Blas. Here was my last report card from the Escuela Municipal Numero 3 para Varones of Mazatlán, and so forth. Miss Hopley put things down in the book and my mother signed a card.

As long as the questions continued, Doña Henriqueta could stay and I was secure. Now that they were over, Miss Hopley saw her to the door, dismissed our interpreter, and without further ado took me by the hand and strode down the hall to Miss Ryan's first grade.

Miss Ryan took me to a seat at the front of the room, into which I shrank— the better to survey her. She was, to skinny, somewhat runty me, of a withering height when she patrolled the class. And when I least expected it, there she was, crouching by my desk, her blond radiant face level with mine, her voice patiently maneuvering me over the awful idiocies of the English language.

During the next few weeks Miss Ryan overcame my fears of tall, energetic teachers as she bent over my desk to help me with a word in the pre-primer. Step by step, she loosened me and my classmates from the safe anchorage of the desks for recitations at the blackboard and consultations at her desk. Frequently she burst into happy announcements to the whole class. "Ito can read a sentence," and small Japanese Ito, squint-eyed and shy, slowly read aloud while the class listened in wonder: "Come, Skipper, come. Come and run." The Korean, Portuguese, Italian, and Polish first graders had similar moments of glory, no less shining than mine the day I conquered "butterfly," which I had been persistently pronouncing in standard Spanish as boo-ter-flee. "Children," Miss Ryan called for attention. "Ernesto has learned how to pronounce *butterfly!*" And I proved it with a perfect imitation of Miss Ryan. From that celebrated success, I was soon able to match Ito's progress as a sentence reader with "Come, butterfly, come fly with me."

Like Ito and several other first graders who did not know English, I received private lessons from Miss Ryan in the closet, a narrow hall off the classroom with a door at each end. Next to one of these doors Miss Ryan placed a large chair for herself and a small one for me. Keeping an eye on the class through the open door she read with me about sheep in the meadow and a frightened chicken going to see the king, coaching me out of my phonetic ruts in words like *pasture*, *bow-wow-wow*, *hay*, and *pretty*, which to my Mexican ear had so many unnecessary sounds and letters. She made me watch her lips and then close my eyes as she repeated words I found hard to read. When we came to know each other better, I tried interrupting to tell Miss Ryan how we said it in Spanish. It didn't work. She only said "oh" and went on with *pasture*, *bow-wow-wow*, and *pretty*. It was as if in that closet we were both discovering together the secrets of the English language and grieving together over the tragedies of Bo-Peep. The main reason I was graduated with honors from the first grade was that I had fallen in love with Miss Ryan. Her radiant, no-nonsense character made us either afraid not to love her or love her so we would not be afraid, I am not sure which. It was not only that we sensed she was with it, but also that she was with us.

Like the first grade, the rest of the Lincoln School was a sampling of the lower part of town where many races made their home. My pals in the second grade were Kazushi, whose parents spoke only Japanese; Matti, a skinny Italian boy; and Manual, a fat Portuguese who would never get into a fight but wrestled you to the ground and just sat on you. Our assortment of nationalities included Koreans, Yugoslavs, Poles, Irish, and home-grown Americans.

Miss Hopley and her teachers never let us forget why we were at Lincoln: for those who were alien, to become good Americans; for those who were so born, to accept the rest of us. Off the school grounds we traded the same insults we heard from our elders. On the playground we were sure to be marched up to the principal's office for calling someone a wop, a chink, a dago, or a greaser. The school was not so much a melting pot as a griddle where Miss Hopley and her helpers warmed knowledge into us and roasted racial hatreds out of us.

At Lincoln, making us into Americans did not mean scrubbing away what made us originally foreign. The teachers called us as our parents did, or as close as they could pronounce our names in Spanish or Japanese. No one was ever scolded or punished for speaking in his native tongue on the playground. Matti told the class about his mother's down quilt, which she had made in Italy with the fine feathers of a thousand geese. Encarnación acted out how boys learned to fish in the Philippines. I astounded the third grade with the story of my travels on a stagecoach, which nobody else in the class had seen except in the museum at Sutter's Fort. After a visit to the Crocker Art Gallery and its collection of heroic paintings of the golden age of California, someone showed a silk scroll with a Chinese painting. Miss Hopley herself had a way of expressing wonder over these matters before a class, her eyes wide open until they popped slightly. It was easy for me to feel that becoming a proud American, as she said we should, did not mean feeling ashamed of being a Mexican.

The Americanization of Mexican me was no smooth matter. I had to fight one lout who made fun of my travels on the *diligencia*, and my barbaric translation of the word into "diligence." He doubled up with laughter over the word until I straightened him out with a kick. In class I made points explaining that in Mexico roosters said "qui-qui-ri-qui" and not "cock-a-doodle-doo," but after school I had to put up with the taunts of a big Yugoslav who said Mexican roosters were crazy.

But it was Homer who gave me the most lasting lesson for a future American.

Homer was a chunky Irishman who dressed as if every day was Sunday. He slicked his hair between a crew cut and a pompadour. And Homer was smart, as he clearly showed when he and I ran for president of the third grade.

Everyone understood that this was to be a demonstration of how the American people vote for president. In an election, the teacher explained, the candidates could be generous and vote for each other. We cast our ballots in a shoe box and Homer won by two votes. I polled my supporters and came to the conclusion that I had voted for Homer and so had he. After class he didn't deny it, reminding me of what the teacher had said—we could vote for each other but didn't have to.

The lower part of town was a collage of nationalities in the middle of which Miss Nettie Hopley kept school with discipline and compassion. She called assemblies in the upper hall to introduce celebrities like the police sergeant or the fire chief, to lay down the law of the school, to present awards to our athletic champions, and to make important announcements. One of these was that I had been proposed by my school and accepted as a member of the newly formed Sacramento Boys Band. "Now, isn't that a wonderful thing?" Miss Hopley asked the assembled school, all eyes on me. And everyone answered in a chorus, including myself. "Yes, Miss Hopley."

It was not only the parents who were summoned to her office, and boys and girls who served sentences there who knew that Nettie Hopley meant business. The entire school witnessed her sizzling Americanism in its awful majesty one morning at flag salute.

All the grades, as usual, were lined up in the courtyard between the wings of the building, ready to march to classes after the opening bell. Miss Shand was on the balcony of the second floor off Miss Hopley's office, conducting us in our lusty singing of "My Country tiz-a-thee." Our principal, as always, stood there like us, at attention, her right hand over her heart, joining in the song.

Halfway through the second stanza she stepped forward, held up her arm in a sign of command, and called loud and clear: "Stop the singing." Miss Shand looked flabbergasted. We were frozen with shock.

Miss Hopley was now standing at the rail of the balcony, her eyes sparking, her voice and resonant, the words coming down to us distinctly and loaded with indignation.

"There are two gentlemen walking on the school grounds with their hats on while we are singing," she said, sweeping our ranks with her eyes. "We will re-main silent until the gentlemen come to attention and remove their hats." A minute of awful silence ended when Miss Hopley, her gaze fixed on something be-hind us, signaled Miss Shand and we began once more the familiar hymn. That afternoon, when school was out, the word spread. The two gentlemen were the Superintendent of Schools and an important guest on an inspection.

I came back to the Lincoln School after every summer, moving up through the grades with Miss Campbell, Miss Beakey, Mrs. Wood, Miss Applegate, and Miss Delahunty. I sat in the classroom adjoining the principal's office and had my turn answering the telephone when she was about the building repeating the message to the teacher, who made a note of it. Miss Campbell read to us during the last period of the week about King Arthur, Columbus, Buffalo Bill, and Daniel Boone, who came to life in the reverie of the class through the magic of her voice. And it was Miss Campbell who introduced me to the public library on Eye Street, where I became a regular customer.

All of Lincoln School mourned together when Eddie, the blond boy every-body liked, was killed by a freight train as he crawled across the tracks going home one day. We assembled to say good-bye to Miss Applegate, who was off to Alaska to be married. Now it was my turn to be excused from class to interpret for a par-ent enrolling a new student fresh from Mexico. Graduates from Lincoln came back now and then to tell us about high school. A naturalist entertained us in assem-bly, imitating the calls of the meadowlark, the water ouzel, the oriole, and the killdeer. I decided to become a bird man after I left Lincoln.

In the years we lived in the lower part of town, LaLeenCon, as my family called it, became a benchmark in our lives, like the purple light of the Lyric Theater and the golden dome of the Palacio de Gobierno gleaming above Capi-tol Park.

Barrio Boy, University of Notre Dame Press, 1971

Queries for Understanding

1. How did the writer and his mother prepare for his entrance to Lincoln School?

2. What physical traits persuaded the writer to like Miss Hopley?

3. What facts needed to be established in order to enroll the writer in school?

4. How did Miss Ryan overcome the writer's fears of tall, energetic teachers?

5. What aspects of English did Miss Ryan emphasize in her private lessons for the writer?

6. What nationalities were represented in the writer's first grade?

7. What values did Lincoln School impress on its students?

8. What lesson about Americanization did Homer teach the writer?

9. For what purposes did Miss Hopley call assemblies?

10. What lesson did the writer learn from Miss Hopley's interruption of their singing of "My Country 'Tis of Thee"?

Queries on the Writer's Techniques

1. Why did the writer and his mother rehearse their approach to Lincoln School?

2. Why did the writer describe the appearance of the building, the door closer, and Miss Hopley's swivel chair in such detail?

3. What techniques does Miss Ryan use to encourage her students' learning?

4. What point does the writer make by describing both Homer's physical and mental traits?

5. What motivates Miss Hopley to stop the children's singing of a patriotic song?

6. Why is the writer so impressed by the naturalist who imitates bird songs?

Writing Topics

1. Describe a turning point in your life when you left one stage and entered a new one: what caused the change and how did you feel?

2. What are the traits of an ideal teacher, and how would you rank them in order of importance?

THE WRITING PROCESS

After choosing a topic for your cause-and-effect paragraph or essay, consider the following questions.

1. Describe your attitude or feelings toward this topic in a few words.

2. Explain why the topic interests you: are you involved personally or in the workplace with the topic? Give one reason for choosing this topic.

3. Why would others be interested in this topic? Describe readers who would find your topic entertaining or informative.

4. In a few words, tell what your readers might think, feel, or do after reading your paragraph or essay. Is this what you intended them to do?

5. Give two or three causes or effects that develop or explain your main idea. Are they part of an extended anecdote, or are they rather diverse?

6. What might make it hard for you to write a first draft of this topic? Do you know enough about it to handle it well? Is your topic too broad or too narrow? Explain in a few words how you can solve these problems.

The author of the following student essay, Valancia, a nontraditional student, knows that many other students like her are working while pursuing an education. She thinks she could write a good cause-and-effect paper about her financial struggles while attending school. To get started, she wrote the following first draft.

Student Cause-and-Effect Essay: First Draft
Tough to Save Money

I really have a tough time saving money for a lot of reasons. I like to buy new stuff for my car and this takes nearly everything I make at work. This makes my life miserable. Because I can't save money I have to live with my parents, driving an old car and work at a rotten job.

As if living with my parents wasn't bad enough, I've got to put up with my sisters. All of us have to share the bathroom. And they take my stuff. They always do lots of things that drive me crazy. They appropriate my stuff. If I could save money, I could move out. It would be worth it.

And I have to drive a beat up old Cavalier. It's not only bad looking. It sounds terrible and everybody stares at me. If I could save money, I'd get a new car.

Finally, my job is terrible. The doctors yell at me all the time because they're frustrated with Medicaid patients. It's not my fault they have to do charity work with these people. I don't get Medicaid myself.

Staying at home with three sisters, driving a beat up car and dealing with an undesired job has influenced me greatly in pursuing my college degree.

REVISING THE FIRST DRAFT

After writing her first draft, Valancia begins the revision process by answering the following questions (with a friend to help her, perhaps):

1. What words in the draft make the topic interesting? What sentences are well written?
2. What is the draft's main idea? Which of the examples best support the main idea?
3. Which part(s) of the essay do you think were hardest to write? Why?
4. If the writer had more time to write this essay, what part(s) would or should get the most attention?

After answering these questions on organization, Valancia marks up her draft, like this:

Indicate age, motives, ways of reaching goals. Also replace lot of ⟶ I really have a tough time saving money for a lot of reasons. I like to buy new stuff for my

car and this takes nearly everything I make

at work. This makes my life miserable. Be-

cause I can't save money I have to live with

my parents, driving an old car and work at a ⟵ *Emphasize motive: to afford college. Then make plan parallel: live . . . drive . . . and . . .*

rotten job.

    As if living with my parents wasn't bad

enough, I've got to put up with my sisters. ⟵ *Develop living with parents into its own paragraph, with detailed support: follow their rules, share with sisters, etc.*

All of us have to share the bathroom. And

they take my stuff. They always do lots of

things that drive me crazy. They appropriate

my stuff. If I could save money, I could move

out. It would be worth it.

Need transition: In addition to dealing with sisters, . . . ⟶ And I have to drive a beat up old Cavalier.

It's not only bad looking. It sounds terrible

and everybody stares at me. If I could save

Pack in specific supporting detail: different paint colors, worn-out brakes and shock absorbers, and squeaking noises.

money, I'd get a new car.

Explain how she copes with job stress: force smile, pray.

Finally, my job is terrible. The doctors

Explain doctors' motives.

yell at me all the time because they're frus-

trated with Medicaid patients. It's not my

fault they have to do charity work with these

In conclusion, emphasize poor quality of present life as well as hopes for change when finishing college.

people. I don't get Medicaid myself.

Staying at home with three sisters, dri-

ving a beat up car and dealing with an unde-

sired job has influenced me greatly in pursu-

ing my college degree.

Based on her responses to the questions and her markings on the first draft, Valancia writes an improved second draft of her cause-and-effect paper. However, her essay is not yet complete. She needs to proofread it, asking the following questions:

Proofreading Queries

1. Have I corrected grammatical problems such as noun/verb agreement?
2. Have I corrected the spelling, particularly with words that sound alike or look alike but are not spelled alike?
3. Have I corrected the punctuation, separating word groups to clarify meaning?

STUDENT CAUSE-AND-EFFECT ESSAY: FIRST REVISION

At the tender age of twenty, I want to be

misspelling: should be "independent"

(independant.) However my worst habit, an in-

Set off appositive— inability ... —with comma

ability to save money has delayed my

Fragment: connect
to next word group:
salary, it's . . .

education. Because my bills exceed my salary.

(Its) impossible for me to save money for col-

punctuation problem: should be "It's"

Run-on:
separate with
colon: ways: I still
live . . .

lege. As a result, my life is suffering in many

ways I still live at home, I drive an old car,

and I have an undesired job.

Lacking a college education, I still dwell at

misspelling: should be "disadvantages"

home, with its many (disavantages.) Worst

no cap: should be "of"

(Of) all, I must share one bathroom with my

punctuation problem: should be "o'clock"

three sisters. If we all have an eight (oclock) ◄—Fragment: connect
with next word
group:
appointment, . . .

appointment. One person showers while the

other brushes their teeth. Lord forbid someone

misspelling: should be "early"

has an (eary) morning call of nature. Not only

do we have inadequate bathroom space and ◄— Comma splice:
connect with
coordinating
conjunction: time,
but

time, there is no sense of ownership. Everyone

misspelling: should be "possessions"

appropriates my (possions.) For instance, one

day I came home from ten long hours of work,

fragment: connect
with preceding word
group: bed,
wearing

and found one of my sisters lying in my bed.

Wearing my new shirt, watching my television,

punctuation problem: should be "that's"

in my bedroom. If (thats) not a high price to

misspelling: should be "education"

pay for my lack of (eduction,) I do not know

what is.

Exercise:

Proofread the following paragraph:

In addition to dealing with three trifling sisters at home. I have to drive a beat up out

dated car. Contrary to my dream of driving a

band new BMW, I drive a nineteen eighty-

four Cavalier. My Cavalier has several discol-

oration's, and squeaks whenever in motion.

When its not embarrassing me with piercing

squeaking noises, its backfiring or stalling in

traffic.

After squeaking half the way, and stalling

misspelling: should be "finally"

Fragment: connect
with preceding word
group: *face and
say . . .*

the other half, I (finaly) arrive at my unde-

sired job. Instantly I force a smile on my

face. And say a silent prayer. Prayer is the

punctuation problem: show possessive as "world's"

method I use to deal with the (worlds)

biggest pains, doctors. The doctors bring all

misspelling: should be "frustrations"

their (fustrations) to my department. They

complain endlessly about Medicaid patients.

They yell at me. Because they are doing   ◄— Fragment: connect
                                                    with preceding word
                                                    group: *me because
                                                    they . . .*

charity work for these people. It does not

matter that I am a working citizen who is

not receiving Medicaid. The doctors gear

misspelling: should be "their"

(there) anger toward me, because I work in a

hyphenate double modifiers: "non-degree"

(non degree) job. After two years of verbal

misspelling: should be "college"

abuse, getting a (collage) degree was the only

thing on my mind.

Fragments: connect
and change singular
to plural verb: *job
have influenced
me...*

Staying at home with three sisters, dri-

ving a beat up car, and dealing with an unde-

sired job. Has influenced me greatly in pur-

suing my college degree.

After closely analyzing her second draft, Valancia writes the final version of her paper.

STUDENT CAUSE-AND-EFFECT ESSAY: FINAL DRAFT
TOUGH TO SAVE MONEY

At the tender age of twenty, I want to be independent. To do this, I must get a college education. However, my worst habit, an inability to save money, has created problems for me. Because my bills exceed my salary, I can't save enough money for college. As a result, I must cut corners to get my degree. To afford college, I must still live at home, drive an old car, and work an undesirable job.

First, going to college takes all my money. Thus, I must live at home, with its many disadvantages. I still have to follow my parents' rules: no weeknight dates, home by midnight on the weekend. Worst of all, I must share one bathroom with my three sisters. If we all have eight o'clock appointments, one person showers while the others brush their teeth. We all hope no one has an early morning call of nature. We not only lack adequate bathroom space and time, but my sisters have no sense of ownership. Everyone blithely helps herself to my possessions. For instance, one day I came home from ten long hours of work. There in my bedroom, I found one of my sisters lying in my bed, wearing my new shirt, watching my television. If I had the money to move out, no one would mess with my belongings but me.

In addition to dealing with three annoying sisters at home, I must drive an old, broken-down car. Instead of a brand new BMW, I must drive a 1984 Cavalier. Three different paint colors adorn the hood. Not only the shock absorbers but the brakes are worn out, so the car squeaks when moving. When it's not embarrassing me with piercing squeaking noises, it's backfiring or stalling in traffic. If I didn't want my education so badly, I'd invest in a beautiful, red BMW. This way, I'd have not only reliable transportation, but an object of pride.

Finally, my job would make a saint burst into tears after only a few hours. When I arrive at work, I force a smile on my face and say a silent prayer. Prayer is my way of dealing with the world's biggest pains, doctors. Because I work in a lowly job in records, they aim their anger at me. As if my job weren't hard enough, they unload all their frustrations on my shoulders, complaining endlessly about Medicaid patients. Forced to do charity work for these people, they unreasonably blame me. The doctors don't realize that, unlike their patients, I deserve none of their abuse. I am a working citizen who is not receiving Medicaid. Thus, I've endured two years of verbal mistreatment just to get a college diploma.

Going to college has affected my life, mostly for the worse. I must live at home with my sisters, drive a broken-down old car, and work at an undesirable job. Therefore, the day I receive my diploma will certainly be one of the happiest in my life.

CAUSE-AND-EFFECT WRITING TOPICS

The following are some possible topics for a cause-and-effect paragraph or paper. Limit your topic to fit your instructor's requirements. Tell the reader *why* you have chosen your topic, and link your details closely to your topic.

1. Describe an unreasonable fear or bad habit.
2. Describe a turning point in your life.
3. Describe the influence on you by a member of an older or younger generation.
4. Describe a success or failure that taught you something.
5. Describe an act of great bravery or cowardice.
6. Describe a family remembrance or ceremony.
7. Describe the reasons for wide popular interest in some sport, fad, hobby, or style.

CHAPTER TEN

Definition

To help others understand us, we define the terms and expressions we use. For example, a college student working in a paint factory may be told that her fellow workers "throw down" with their bodies. Unless the student knows that the expression *throw down* means "they work hard every day," she will be mystified by this phrase. In another example, an article on the great baseball player Babe Ruth comments that "He was colossal, but he also played with panache." If readers don't know that *panache* means "swagger, dash, or verve," the sentence will means little to them. In other words, to be understood in our ordinary, everyday conversation or writing, we need to define the terms we use.

As in the preceding examples, we can often define terms briefly with a synonym or group of words. Mark Twain once explained the difference between the right word and the almost-right word as the difference between lightning and a lightning bug. And David Letterman gave new meaning to the word *sharing* when he took issue with a statement: "People say New Yorkers can't get along. Not true. I saw New Yorkers, complete strangers, sharing a cab. One guy took the tires and the radio; the other guy took the engine."

For writing purposes, however, you will often write a paragraph-length or even essay-length definition. A glance through a magazine or collection of essays will reveal articles that define difficult or controversial terms or ideas such as *Down syndrome, boredom, ethnic cleansing, Marxism,* and *affirmative action.* At times, you will define a term people often misuse or fail to understand. Or the term may be slang or linked to a particular topic or business, for example, *nerd* or *RAM.* You may even take a common term like *the romance novel* or *walleye pike* and present its history, examples, or brief anecdotes. To write clear definition paragraphs or essays, use the guidelines in the following sections.

SPELL OUT YOUR PURPOSE

Make sure you know, and that you tell your reader, why a brief or extended definition is important. For example, as a salesperson, you might need to explain to a buyer how and why a battery is corrosion resistant. You are not only informing your readers, but persuading them.

USE LANGUAGE YOUR READERS UNDERSTAND

Define technical terms using nontechnical language. Defining an environmental wall as a "self-cleaning ecosystem" may not mean much to your readers. However, most readers can grasp the definition "sucks air through porous rock covered with moss and running water." Use your own language, and don't quote from a dictionary or encyclopedia. Above all, use specific, concrete details. A mouse to a computer user is something else to a pest exterminator. A clear definition makes the rest of your document more understandable and usable.

DEFINE YOUR TERMS IN AS MANY WAYS AS YOUR READERS NEED

Defining your terms involves not only using simple language, but giving specific examples. These might include comparing and contrasting the term to other terms, using synonyms, telling what it is *not*, including a description, and placing it in a cause-and-effect chain.

READINGS

As Chapter 1 pointed out, **topic sentences** sum up a paragraph's main idea. You then use examples to make this general concept clearer, more vivid to your reader. By filling out this general idea, your paragraph will draw word pictures in your reader's mind. The topic sentence of the following paragraph defines the phrase, "Japanese war fantasy novels." The paragraph then develops the topic sentence with specific details.

> Fifty years after the end of World War II, the Japanese armed forces are rising again. And this time, Japan is

Topic sentence: names
definition paragraph will
treat ⟶

Detail: how many,
when ⟶

Detail: history rewritten ⟶

Detail: another name for
novels ⟶

winning. **The revival of the Imperial military is taking place in World War II combat novels that have become popular in Japan,** after being nearly taboo for decades. Dozens, if not hundreds, of such war fantasy books have been published in the past few years. In so many of them, history is rewritten so that Japan triumphs in battles it actually lost. The paperbacks, published only in Japanese, are being called war simulation novels because they imagine what would happen if Japan had taken a different course in World War II. There does not appear to have been any significant negative reaction to the novels, inside Japan or from abroad. However, publishing industry officials say there have been some complaints that the books glorify combat or are anti-American.

Chapter 2 showed how a **thesis** sums up the main idea for an entire writing; it serves an essay as a **topic sentence** serves a paragraph. That is, it sums up the main idea and tells the writer's viewpoint toward it. The following student essay won Barnard College's annual writing competition for 11th grade girls in New York City's public high schools. Its title, "A Woman I Admire," is also its thesis. The essay uses several approaches to define the term embodied in its title.

Thesis names topic and
embodies writer's attitude ⟶ # A WOMAN I ADMIRE

It's 10 o'clock, time to wake up Mama. Frustration washes over me because I'm sitting on my bed, covered with books. One by one, I push them aside.

I open my bedroom door into a wall of darkness. I look back into my lighted room with regret and creep into the living room. All the lights are off and the shades are drawn.

Physical detail: first
impression ⟶

On the couch lies Mama. Her hair is standing on all ends and her face is a perfect mask of peace. I give her shoulder a shake, telling her that it's 10 o'clock. Instantly, her eyes pop open and she starts to get up. I turn to go back to my bright room, when she asks me to make her a cup of coffee. I swivel around, and a spark of anger flicks through my eyes. The guilt quickly replaces it. How can I be angry? Every day she gets up and goes to work on four or five, sometimes only two hours of sleep. She even works overtime every chance she gets. I tell her not to push herself, but she says we need the money. And all she's asking me for is a cup of coffee.

Detail: mother's first
actions ⟶

So I go to the kitchen. I leave the lights off, as if light

Detail: though tired, mother rises quickly ———▶

Detail: mother is forgiving, understanding ———▶

Writer sums up mother's virtues, defining both her mother and herself

Draws conclusion ———▶

would be an intrusion on Mama's dark world. I pour a cup of coffee and add milk and sugar just the way Mama likes it. I take it back to her. She's already dressed and sitting up on the couch.

I hand her the cup of coffee and she thanks me. I tell her Dad called and said he wasn't coming to do the work on the porch on Saturday. She simply nods her head as she drinks her coffee.

All too quickly, she has to leave. She hands me my $3.60 for school and kisses me on the cheek. As always, she tells me she loves me. Then she walks out the door and drives off to her job.

I watch from the door in wonder. How does she do it? How does she always remember to give me $3.60 for school? How does she always remember to tell me that she loves me? How does she work all night and do errands all day? How does she raise me and my sisters on her own? She never gives up or says, "I can't go today." She never, ever, doesn't get up, no matter how little sleep she's gotten.

I shut and lock the door. I walk silently through Mama's dark world and go back to my bright room. I replace the books on my lap. Before I begin again, I turn my eyes toward God and silently thank the Lord for Mama.

Amelia H. Chamberlain,
Townsend Harris High School, Queens

In the following selection, a seldom-seen creature of the deep is defined in a series of striking images.

Words to Define

mesmerizing: hypnotizing, catching one's complete attention

prominent: main, outstanding

iris: the round, colored portion of the eye

formidable: large, impressive

tentacles: long, flexible limbs used for grasping

Prereading

1. Define an object from your immediate surroundings using figures of speech, which are often introduced by words such as *like* or *as*.

2. Choose a term from your present field of study and define it in ordinary language.

THE GIANT SQUID

Arthur Fisher

The mesmerizing eyes of the giant squid, with a prominent dark iris, are the largest in the animal kingdom, as big as hubcaps. At the center of the crown of arms is the creature's formidable mouth, with a strong parrotlike beak and a rasping, toothed tongue called the radula, which together make mincemeat of its food. The powerful arms, thick as a man's thigh, bear rows of sharply toothed circular suckers "the shape of a plumber's helper." So do the clublike ends of the far thinner but muscular tentacles, which can clamp down on prey like the jaws of some enormous pliers.

Popular Science

Queries for Understanding

1. How big are the giant squid's eyes?
2. How do the giant squid's mouth and tongue function?
3. What parts make up the giant squid's arms?
4. What are the ends of the giant squid's tentacles designed to do?

Queries on the Writer's Techniques

1. In what order does the writer describe the parts of the squid's body, and why?
2. What comparisons define the squid's eye?
3. What comparisons and traits define the squid's mouth?
4. What comparisons define the squid's arms?
5. What comparisons define the squid's tentacles?

Writing Topics

1. Define a figure from sports or popular entertainment, using comparisons.
2. The giant squid is clearly a success in its surroundings. Define either the term *success* or some example of a successful being in its own surroundings.

According to the author of the following selection, the stories in popular romance novels are the same, but their characters and settings have become much more diverse, including cultures seldom dealt with before.

Words to Define

brawny: strong, muscular

anticipation: feeling or realizing beforehand

protagonists: main characters

libido: sexual desire

synonymous: expressing a similar meaning

compromise: a middle course

potential: ability to come into being

ethnicities: pertaining to a religious, national, racial, or cultural group

essences: the most important parts

magnates: powerful, influential business persons

moguls: rich, powerful persons

religious observances: practice of religious rites or ceremonies

Pinkerton agents: private detectives linked with the Pinkerton Agency

characterize: describe

genre: a type or group of literary works

contemporary: modern, up-to-date

dearth: lack, shortage

Prereading

1. Define what is meant by a "good" movie, novel, or TV series.
2. Define a term from popular entertainment, like *exciting, gripping*, or *emotional*.

THE NEW ROMANCE NOVELS

Traci Grant

A man clutches a woman to his brawny chest. His arms, bulging with muscles, grasp her tiny waist. Her curly locks are flung over her shoulders. The neckline of her blouse plunges down her chest. He looks longingly at her luscious lips. Her eyes are closed in anticipation of what the next searing moment may bring.

The imagery on the cover of *Night Song*, by Beverly Jenkins, is typical of a historical romance novel. The man in his soldier-type pants and the woman in her shirtwaist blouse and flowing skirt suggest an era when men were men, women were ravished, and nobody seemed to mind that. But this particular cover deserves another look. No, make that a triple take.

The man and woman holding each other are black.

"He's still tall, dark, and handsome," says Monica Harris, an editor at Kensington Publishing Corp., which last summer launched Arabesque, a line of black romance novels. "He's heroic in the same way other characters in other romances are. She is just as intelligent and beautiful. The only difference is that they're black."

In the past year [1994], the number of romance novels featuring black characters has surged, with these books now representing up to 5 percent of the romance novel market, at least 10 times the amount published in all previous years, say publishing industry officials. Long a stronghold of wealthy, white protagonists with big houses, fancy cars, and healthy libidos, romance novels—which make up 50 percent of the paperbacks published each year—are increasingly featuring African, African-American, and Caribbean main characters.

"I think it's wonderful that these books are finally being published. Why not? We're just the same. We have the same needs, desires, and interests. We have intelligence and we love, like everyone else. Why not have books that reflect that?" said Dorothy Yancey, a 70-year-old Mashpee, Mass., resident who attended a romance author's book signing at Brown and Clark Booksellers in her hometown recently.

"When I was in school, I loved to read romantic novels, but so seldom were there any by African-Americans," says Gray Foxx, 64, of South Plymouth, Mass. "I'm more interested in these because I have more in common with the writer. I can relate to it. They're talking about me."

Author Mildred Riley scribbled her name on the pages of her steamy new novel, *Journey's End*, for Yancey, Foxx, and other fans. Riley's book is a post–Civil War tale of a buffalo soldier, a young woman who joins his cattle drive to Colorado, and the torrid love affair that involves them.

Riley, who will admit only to being in her 70s, cranked out her first romance novel, *Yamilla*, in the mid-1980s, after retiring from nursing. The writing, she says, was the easy part. She sent her manuscript, about the life and loves of a young female slave in America, to more than 20 publishers. She received more than 20 rejections.

"Sometimes they would send it back without comment," says Riley, who lives in Whitman. "Sometimes they would just tell me it didn't meet their guidelines. I got one rejection letter that simply said, 'We don't publish books for black people because black people just don't read.'"

"I was furious. It was hurtful. And it was just plain wrong."

In 1984, New York romance novelist Sandra Kitt penned the first black novel published by Harlequin Books, a name synonymous worldwide with romance. But after agreeing to publish *Adam and Eva*, Harlequin editors looked askance at her other novels that focused on black characters, she says. "They only wanted the ones with white characters," Kitt says. "I couldn't get them to accept the other black novels. They said they didn't know anything about the market."

Finally, nearly a decade later, Harlequin asked Kitt to write a novel about an interracial romance. "I found it ironic that all those years I couldn't get them to publish another story where the main characters were black, but, all of a sudden, they decided they were interested in interracial couples," she says.

Harlequin's compromise came after careful observation of the market for black readers. It also came after Terry McMillan. In 1992, McMillan's novel

Waiting to Exhale, about four black women searching for love, vaulted onto the *New York Times* and *Publisher's Weekly* best-seller lists and held on to those top spots for weeks. Kitt, Riley, and publishing executives agree that McMillan opened the gate for black writers and black readers and also proved that a crossover audience existed for books about black culture.

"Terry McMillan doesn't write romances, but she has to get the credit here," Kitt says. "Her book was read by everyone, not just blacks. It made publishers sit up and pay attention."

And once they started paying attention, especially since McMillan proved there was the potential for profit, major publishers began to welcome African-American authors and their stories. Readers of all races and ethnicities were clearly interested in romantic tales that reflected portions of society that don't often make their way into the public consciousness: black lawyers, magnates, moguls, photographers, engineers, teachers, journalists; buffalo soldiers, slaves, frontiersmen, Pinkerton agents. Anything that illuminates the existence of black people in history or the present day finds its way onto the pages of these novels.

"We stress the romance part of it," Harris says. "We have to have 'boy meets girl and boy gets girl at the end.' It's really not all that different. The difference is by the virtue of the characters being African-American. Things like expressions, food, and music are affected. All small details, but they are important."

For Kitt, the challenge is to mix the essences of black culture into the layers of a story, into descriptions of the backgrounds of characters, the hairstyles, religious observances, and language. Kitt's characters sometimes wear braids with beads in them or hair extensions. Sometimes they say, "Go on, girl," to someone who gets a big promotion at work. Sometimes they characterize a child as "working their last nerve."

Noelle Maxwell, the main temptress in *Temptation*, by Donna Hill, comes from the New Orleans bayou, has a "copper-toned face" and "honey-colored hair, fashioned after the actress Halle Berry." Studly Jackson Duncan greets someone in Angela Benson's *Bands of Gold* by giving him an Omega (a black fraternity) handshake. These are details that have long been missing from the majority of romance novels and that mean something to black readers; these are touches that fans gush over when they meet Kitt and Riley in person.

"There's no real difference in the genre," Riley says. "The contemporary ones are really the same as [nonblack] novels. But as far as I can tell, a lot of white people don't seem to realize there is a black middle class in America that are as contemporary as they. These novels show them that."

They also offer readers new stories and subjects, whether historical or contemporary. Publishing officials say the novels are doing well with all types of readers because of the wealth of fresh subjects the novels cover.

"These novels do two things," Kitt says. "You're still getting a romance. The women who read them were and still are romance readers. They just have something a little different to read now. And you're getting a love story with positive black characters that has a happy ending."

Harlequin, which publishes 70 new romance titles each month from a corps of about 1,200 writers, admits that the number of novelists of color—African-Americans, Asians, and Latinos—remains low. But those numbers have gotten better, says Katherine Orr, vice president of public relations for Harlequin Books.

"It's not that there weren't African-American women reading the books all along. I just don't think they were writing them. But this [phenomenon] is going to grow," Orr says.

Leticia Peoples is one of many who disagree with the notion that there ever was a dearth of black authors. After studying the romance novel market, Peoples created her own publishing company, Odyssey Books, in 1990 to offer a refuge and an outlet for black writers.

"I discovered most of the main companies were not accepting books with African-American characters," says Peoples, who had no background in publishing at the time. "I had to do something. I felt there was a market. I didn't know how large, but so many women read novels by Judith Krantz and Danielle Steele. I thought African-American writers should also be given consideration."

Queries for Understanding

1. How is the increase in romance novels with black characters measured?
2. What part of all novels published each year is made up by romances?
3. What event led Harlequin books to ask for a romance novel with interracial characters?
4. What portions of society—that don't often make their way into the public consciousness—are reflected in romantic tales?
5. What challenge regarding black culture does Sandra Kitt face in writing her novels?
6. How many novels does Harlequin publish each month, from how many writers?

Queries on the Writer's Techniques

1. What twist does the writer add to her summary of a romance novel plot?
2. How are black romance characters like white romance characters?
3. What are the main differences between the white romance novels and black ones?
4. What do readers attending a book signing by romance authors like about black romances?
5. What details of black culture does Kitt work into her novels?

Writing Topics

1. What groups in American society are poorly represented in popular fiction? What changes would define novels written about these groups?

2. Decide which heroic or admirable qualities would define a particular ethnic group in American society, and tell why and how.

The author of the following selection describes an industry secret that is so secret industry insiders don't know it.

Words to Define

imprecise: general, hard to measure exactly

subliminal: below the level of awareness

mimic: imitate, parody

logo: emblem, trademark

assertion: claim, statement

Prereading

1. Define the effective traits of an advertising or marketing device.

2. Define a fad or style now popular in society.

THE WATCH SECRET

Sara Olkon

It's time to consider a marketing mystery: Why do watches in print advertisements almost always give the time as 10:10?

The answer is, well, somewhat imprecise.

Industry insiders have plenty of theories. "It connotes a warm and enveloping feeling, like a person's arms outstretched. It's 'V' for victory," says Mike Carberry, president of Henry J. Kaufman & Associates, an ad agency in Washington, D.C. Even if consumers don't notice the placement of the hands, it has a subliminal effect on them, he says.

"It's more like a happy face than a sad face," says Missy Faren, a marketing consultant for Gevril, a small watch company in Manhattan. George Rudenauer, advertising account supervisor for TAG Heuer watches, calls the position "upward positive."

But Rory Gevis, a stylist who works on commercial photo shoots, believes 10:10 was the time Abraham Lincoln was shot. (He was actually shot at about 10:15.)

Other watch industry experts say the watch hands mimic the proper position of a driver's hands on the steering wheel of a car . . . or that it's a pleasant time of day—or night—for many people.

"It's easier to read this way," explains Jeff Prine, a senior editor at Accessories Magazine. It's merely an effort by marketers to best display the logo, counters Hans Beck, President of Breguet watches.

Why, then, do digital watches in ads read 10:10?

Robert Nelson, who has been selling watches on the streets of New York for three years, still hasn't figured it out. "It must be an insider secret," says Mr. Nelson, who is far less particular about how his watches are set.

"People used to use 8:20, but it looked like a frown," says Susie Watson, advertising director for Timex. She claims Timex was the first to use 10:10 in print ads, a trend that caught on about two decades ago. (Her assertion is hotly contested by several rivals, however.) Timex, perhaps to set itself apart, now uses 10:09.36.

That doesn't explain why Timex models with a date feature are set for Wednesday, Oct. 14.

"We call it 'Timex Day' around here, but no one knows what that means," Ms. Watson says. Timex employees, by the way, don't get the day off.

The Wall Street Journal

Queries for Understanding

1. How do industry insiders answer the question why, in print advertisements, watches with hands almost always give the time as 10:10?

2. How do industry insiders answer the question why digital watches in print advertisements almost always give the time as 10:10?

3. Why are Timex models with a date feature set for Wednesday, October 14?

Queries on the Writer's Techniques

1. In what order does the writer deal with the time and date shown on watches, and why?

2. In the selection, what kinds of people are considered to be "industry insiders"?

Writing Topics

1. Check out the print or TV ads for a popular product like an automobile, sports shoe, or fast food outlet, and define its success.

2. Collect some slang terms used in ads for popular products, and define them. To organize your paragraph or essay, tell what the terms have in common—their users, places you can hear them, and so on.

In the following selection, the author suggests that it's good to have a mystery fish that refuses to let you figure it out.

Words to Define

walleye: a freshwater game fish with bulging eyes

circa: about (in regard to time)

pristine: pure, unspoiled

antique: especially old

frequent: to spend time at

stripers: a striped bass, a game fish

shad: a food fish related to the herring

loll: to hang around in a relaxed way

foul-hooked: to entangle or twist one's hook, in fishing

Prereading

1. Consider an outdoor area you are familiar with: what traits define it?
2. Make a list of specialized terms regarding a particular sport, and then define them in everyday words.

DELAWARE RIVER WALLEYE ELUDE EXPERTS

Stephen C. Sautner

Sixty years ago, Ray Bergman wrote about Delaware walleye fishing in his classic, *Just Fishing*. Bergman tells about a trip he takes with a secretive walleye expert circa 1911. Trolling sea lamprey larvae at night through unnamed Delaware River pools, they catch plenty of walleye up to five pounds, and hook an unseen monster that straightens the hook.

Reading the story today, it's also easy to picture what Bergman doesn't mention, but must have been there: an undeveloped and pristine Delaware River—no airplanes overhead, no car headlights, and no lights period except for maybe a small oil lantern in the boat. The river's silence broken only by the call of an owl or the creak of oarlocks. Bergman and his friend sipping strong coffee and speaking in whispers or grunts, if at all. These images reminded me of my experiences on the river last April.

I caught two Delaware River walleye. They were both about the same size—maybe 20 inches. I don't expect any more until next year. The fish are there, and I'll fish for them. I just can't catch them.

More so than any other Delaware River fish, the walleye leave anglers scratching their heads. The walleye are a sort of antique of the Delaware. Released in the river sometime last century, the walleye quietly make a living without too many people taking notice, or ever figuring out how to catch them. The striped bass that frequent the lower river are cloaked in mystery for many, but if you spend enough time there, you'll figure out the secret. All you need is high water in May or June and a good herring run, and the stripers will move up from tidewater to blast anything that moves. End of mystery.

But you never know when a walleye will show up. More times than not you'll hear fishermen say that they catch walleye "by accident," usually while shad fishing. In fact, the first walleye I ever saw hit my friend's shad dart. He set the hook and we saw a bronzed, big-eyed fish loll on the surface. A second later the fish was gone.

My three biggest walleye, all around six pounds, came over a two-day period in late May seven years ago. And, true to form, I wasn't fishing for them. One was caught while casting an eight-inch swimming plug for striped bass. I cranked the fish in, thinking I had foul-hooked one of the sawbellies that were spawning by the thousands in the pool I was working. The other two came the next day while herring fishing. Casting a tiny gold spoon on four-pound test line, I hooked what felt like a catfish. But it was another huge walleye. Two casts later, I caught another. I went the next two years without even seeing a walleye caught. I've since learned very little else about this fish, other than that most of them die of old age in the Delaware. I've seen plenty of walleye in the upper river that come very close to 13 pounds. You can see one, too. Just drop a canoe in around Hancock, N.Y., and look in the deeper pools as you float down the river. Look for the walleye's eyes, which show up white, or the white slash on the bottom of the tail. Sometimes that's all you'll see in the deep water.

Most of the fish are smaller—up to four pounds or so. But every so often those white eyes will be placed a good eight inches apart, and the white of the tail will be as long as your hand. The submarine-size walleye hide in the shade of a boulder. You can try casting for these fish, but you'll have more of a chance trying to get a carp to rise to a dry fly, or a trout to hit a spinnerbait. But those huge walleye must eat, right?

As luck would have it, I usually catch about one walleye a year. The annual walleye has become as much a rite of spring as seeing the first migrating osprey. Come April, just before the shad run begins, when the Delaware gets high and off-color from snowpack up north, I'll wander down to the Lambertville, N.J., Wingdam with a fresh supply of lead-head jigs in various colors.

More times than not, I won't catch anything, see anything, or do much more than snag the bottom a lot. But inevitably on one of these springtime walleye trips, I'll set the hook into one more rock, but this time it actually pulls back. After a fight that ranks somewhere around hooking a fair-size stick, I'll be holding a walleye that's as shocked to see me as I am it. The annual walleye.

It's good to have a mystery fish, a fish that refuses to let you figure it out. The walleye have not changed for me; I still can't catch them. I know what conditions to look for: low pressure, showers, high temperatures in the 60s; water temperature in the low 40s and rising—that's when walleye go on a pre-spawn feeding binge; a fishing spot below a waterfall, which is a perfect pre-spawn walleye feeding area; a river that's high and off-color, so the walleye, which are light-sensitive, won't sulk in deep water waiting for darkness. And I still don't catch a thing.

The Delaware River walleye remain as they have always been—the antique fish that Ray trolled sea lamprey larvae for in deep, nameless, and secret pools.

The New York Times

Queries for Understanding

1. What qualities made the Delaware River "pristine" in 1911?
2. Why does the writer call the walleye an antique? A mystery fish?
3. What markings distinguish the walleye?
4. For what variety was the author fishing when he caught his three largest walleye?
5. Under what conditions and in what location can walleye best be caught?

Queries on the Writer's Techniques

1. What contrasts does the writer draw between fishing on the Delaware River in 1911 and fishing today?
2. What contrast does the writer draw between the walleye and another mystery fish, the striped bass?
3. Why does the author prefer fishing for walleye rather than other Delaware River fish?

Writing Topics

1. Define a favorite sport in terms of the players' feelings about it. How does it contrast with other similar sports?
2. Define a playing area or locale for some sport in terms of vision, sound, smell, and touch.

In the following searing recollection, a young woman defines an all-too-common sign of our times: spousal abuse.

Words to Define

spousal: marriage partner

infinite: never ending

mayhem: violent turmoil

insomnia: sleeplessness

posttraumatic: after a deeply emotional disturbance

SPOUSAL ABUSE

Student Essay (Linda)

Spousal abuse is a terrible injustice involving emotional, mental, verbal, and physical attacks which destroy its victims' sense of well-being. As a result of abuse, victims suffer low self-esteem and stress long after the relationship ends.

The arguments seemed infinite, but really lasted only a few hours. They usually started with something trivial: I overlooked one of his socks in the wash hamper or wore my hair different. I was always at fault because I forgot to do something or didn't do it right. Quarreling would slowly simmer on a back burner in our minds by late afternoon, as the tension kept building. Waiting until we were in bed, he resumed the arguments. They usually lasted until daylight peered through the window's blinds. During the first few hours, my emotions poured out in tears and pleas in self-defense. When exhaustion took its toll, I surrendered. Finally emotionless, my tear-swollen eyes stared into a bleak future. For days, I tread lightly, afraid to speak, thinking only of keeping peace between us.

Mental abuse went hand-in-hand with verbal torment. He fed on my weakness, using mental torture to tighten his control over every aspect of my life. He told me when to eat, sleep, bathe, cook, and clean. When he decided I should quit smoking, I knew not to touch a cigarette until he granted permission. For long periods, he ruled out contact with my family. When members visited, fear of my husband's fury kept me from opening the door. I sat crouching in a corner, sobbing as I yelled, "Go away! Go away!"

The verbal bashings astonished me because I had never experienced them. My parents never yelled or used abusive language toward any of us. However, my husband raged and yelled for no reason. He made me his verbal punching bag. He criticized my clothing, saying, "You look stupid!" or "You look slutty!" He repeatedly ridiculed my lack of common sense, often in the presence of friends. Using my fear of him as a weapon, he threatened the lives of everyone I loved. He described his plans for mayhem in blood-curdling detail. Though he never threatened to kill me, he promised to drive me to suicide. I fought it every hour of every day. The thought of my darling children living under his authority sent chills through me.

Along with verbal and mental abuse, physical fights broke out without warning. I insulted him during an argument once and soon realized my mistake. When I opened my eyes, panic bolted through me; I had been knocked unconscious. A few weeks later, in a fit of rage he dislocated two of my fingers. In defiance of a direct order, I had lit a cigarette. Far from trying to provoke a physical fight, I was trying to loosen his strangling chains of control. Cuts and bruises never entered my thoughts; I just wanted him to stop. Afterward, I would stand before my mirror in awe, pondering how to conceal the new purple blemish on my cheek. Asked about it, a humiliating lie leapt from my throat.

Determined to tear me down, he wanted to rebuilt a model to his liking. I shudder to think it almost worked. My mind refuses to cease its spinning. Questions, answers, and memories fill my thoughts. If I do sleep, I often wake in sweaty screams, tears hot in my eyes. On nights like these, I pray for insomnia. Like the nights, days are hard. Flashbacks haunt me like gray ghosts. To the average person, a handshake is a friendly gesture. But to me, it may unleash a flood of suppressed images. Even in response to kind gestures, my mind explodes, forcing painfully vivid memories upon me.

I have taken the first step to recovery by leaving an abusive milieu—I am divorced. The mental and physical abuse have stopped. I now attend group support sessions to rebuild my self-esteem and deal with posttraumatic stress. It helps talking with other survivors of abuse. I know I am no longer alone in my struggle for peace and sanity.

Queries for Understanding

1. How did arguments start, and how long did they last?
2. Which of her husband's demands bothered the writer most?
3. What was the most important reason the writer resisted suicide?
4. Why do you think the writer concealed evidence of physical abuse so long?
5. Why did the writer find group support sessions so helpful?

Queries on the Writer's Techniques

1. What is the writer's thesis, and where does it appear?
2. What is her plan, and where does it appear? How closely does she follow it?
3. In what order does the writer place the aspects of her definition—most to least important, or the other way around?
4. What devices—transitions, pronouns, repeated words—does the writer use to link her ideas together?

Writing Topics

1. Consider a difficult time in your life: define it or the kind of person you were at the time.
2. When you faced difficulties in your life, what helped you most: define the quality of that help.

Rachel Carson's book *Silent Spring*, from which the following selection is taken, first sounded the alarm about the damaging effects of chemical pesticides and fertilizers, an alarm whose aftereffects are still being felt today.

Words to Define

viburnum: shrubs or trees with white flowers and black or red berries

abundance: a large quantity

blight: a disease or withering

maladies: sicknesses

moribund: on the verge of death

throbbed: beat or pounded rapidly

pollination: the first stage in the reproduction process of plants

stricken: taken ill

brooded: sat on or hatched eggs

granular: having a grainy texture

counterparts: an opposite number, ones similar to others

substantial: not imaginary, real

specter: a threatening possibility

Prereading

1. Describe how a natural area is defined by changes from place to place, season to season.
2. Describe the relationship among the plants and animals in a natural area familiar to you.

SILENT SPRING: A FABLE FOR OUR TIME

Rachel Carson

There was once a town in the heart of America where all life seemed to live in harmony with its surroundings. The town lay in the midst of a checkerboard of prosperous farms, with fields of grain and hillsides of orchards where, in spring, white clouds of bloom drifted above the green fields. In autumn, oak and maple and birch set up a blaze of color that flamed and flickered across a backdrop of pines. Then foxes barked in the hills and deer silently crossed the fields, half hidden in the mists of the fall mornings.

Along the roads, laurel, viburnum and alder, great ferns, and wildflowers delighted the traveler's eye through much of the year. Even in winter the roadsides were places of beauty, where countless birds came to feed on the berries and on the seed heads of the dried weeds rising above the snow. The countryside was, in fact, famous for the abundance and variety of its bird life, and when the flood of migrants was pouring through in spring and fall people traveled from great distances to observe them. Others came to fish the streams, which flowed clear and cold out of the hills and contained shady pools where trout lay. So it had been from the days many years ago when the first settlers raised their houses, sank their wells, and built their barns.

Then a strange blight crept over the area and everything began to change. Some evil spell had settled on the community: mysterious maladies swept the flocks of chickens; the cattle and sheep sickened and died. Everywhere was a shadow of death. The farmers spoke of much illness among their families. In the town the doctors had become more and more puzzled by new kinds of sickness appearing among their patients. There had been several sudden and unexplained deaths, not only among adults but even among children, who would be stricken suddenly while at play and die within a few hours.

There was a strange stillness. The birds, for example—where had they gone? Many people spoke of them, puzzled and disturbed. The feeding stations in the backyards were deserted. The few birds seen anywhere were moribund; they trembled violently and could not fly. It was a spring without voices. On the mornings that had once throbbed with the dawn chorus of robins, catbirds, doves, jays, wrens, and scores of other bird voices there was now no sound; only silence lay over the fields and woods and marsh.

On the farms the hens brooded, but no chicks hatched. The farmers complained that they were unable to raise any pigs—the litters were small and the young survived only a few days. The apple trees were coming into bloom but no bees droned among the blossoms, so there was no pollination and there would be no fruit.

The roadsides, once so attractive, were now lined with browned and withered vegetation as though swept by fire. These, too, were silent, deserted by all living things. Even the streams were now lifeless. Anglers no longer visited them, for all the fish had died.

In the gutters under the eaves and between the shingles of the roofs, a white granular powder still showed a few patches; some weeks before it had fallen like snow upon the roofs and the lawns, the fields and streams.

No witchcraft, no enemy action had silenced the rebirth of new life in this stricken world. The people had done it themselves.

This town does not actually exist, but it might easily have a thousand counterparts in America or elsewhere in the world. I know of no community that has experienced all the misfortunes I describe. Yet every one of these disasters has actually happened somewhere, and many real communities have already suffered a substantial number of them. A grim specter has crept upon us almost unnoticed, and this imagined tragedy may easily become a stark reality we all shall know.

Silent Spring, Houghton Mifflin, 1962

Queries for Understanding

1. What healthy vegetation flourishes in Carson's ideal community?
2. What healthy animal life flourishes in Carson's community?
3. What human activities took place when nature around the community was healthy?
4. How did the blight affect the wild animals?
5. How did the blight affect farm animals and people?
6. How were the farms, roadsides, and streams affected by the blight?
7. What evidence of the blight's cause appears, and who is to blame?

Queries on the Writer's Techniques

1. What seasons does the first paragraph describe, and how?
2. Why does Carson wait until the end of the second paragraph to mention people?

3. In the third paragraph, in what order does the blight strike living beings?

4. What wildlife dominate the fourth paragraph, with what effect?

5. What contrasts appear on the farms and roadsides?

6. What is a fable? How does Carson's description justify her use of this term in her title?

Writing Topics

1. Describe some place or object that has changed noticeably, from better to worse, or vice versa.

2. Define some disease by describing the victim before, during, and after.

THE WRITING PROCESS

In the following student essay, Helena chose to define her concept of a small town by describing Salley, the town where she grew up. Salley is not only a typical small town, but celebrates its uniqueness with an annual Chitlin' Strut.

STUDENT DEFINITION ESSAY: FIRST DRAFT

I have always liked living in a small town. I live in Salley. One could problay drive right though Salley and not recognize it a town. Salley has a small population. First, in the center of Salley sit our police department in a one room small building, In addition, Salley has only one convience story, the Mini Mart. Salley also has a restarant called Harleys in a big, beautiful, vlue house. Salley, in addition, has a clothing store called the Salley Factory Outlet which is a small bilding on Maine St. Salley also has a small factory called Salley Manufactory Company located on Maine St. Finally, Salley has a Chitlin strut held each year the weekend after Thanksgiving. People from miles arond come to Salley to get a taste of our mouth watering chitlins. Everyone that attends the Strut is happy when they leave because they enjoyed all the events. As a small town, Salley provides little excitement but beautiful memories.

REVISING THE FIRST DRAFT

To revise her first draft, Helena looks most closely at its organization. She'll ask the following questions and write in notes on her first draft:

1. Is the thesis of the definition paper clear to the reader at the beginning of the paper? Is it clear to the reader why the writer's viewpoint matters?

2. Do the sentences in the draft grow out of the thesis, in the right order? Are the sentences carefully linked together, with helpful transitions, pronouns, and repeated words or synonyms?

3. Has the writer used enough specific, concrete details? Do the details effectively support the paper's main idea?

4. Does the paper's conclusion grow clearly out of the essay?

After answering these questions, Helena marks up her draft, like this:

Wordy opener: combine ideas. ——▶

I always liked living in a small town. I live in

Salley. One could problay drive right through

Sum up traits that define town: police station, convenience store, restaurant, clothing store, small factory ——

Salley and not recognize it is a town. Salley

has a small population. It doesn't have a traffic light due to it being small.

wordy: omit

~~First,~~ in the center of Salley sits our police

↓ *occupies*

department in a one room small bilding. It

Wordy: say Surrounded by flowers, nicely decorated, it houses one cop, Keith, who keeps

doesnt really look like a police station because it decorated so nicely. It has flowers

around it that makes it look nice. One cop,

Need more detail: town hasn't had murder in year

Keith, keeps things in order. Keith is a tall,

thin man with a rather large stomach. To

To indicate transition between paragraphs, say Keith's wife, Hilda, works in convenience store, then describe her ——▶

scare people, he walks around with his hand

near his gun. In addition, Salley has only one

convience store, The Mini Mart, a small

square building with lots of products. In fact,

it now sells hotdogs. keith's wife works in the

store. She is a medium height, obese woman.

No new paragraph here, since both places deal with food. However, indicate contrast: Hartley's is "upscale," compared to convenience store ⟶

Her left hand misses a thumb. Despite the condition of her hand, she is a quik worker.

Salley also has a restarant called Hartleys in a big, beautiful, vlud house. The restaurant sells its food in an all you can eat buffet style that consist of numerous mouth watering dishs.

move transition for readability

Salley, (in addition,) ~~has~~ a clothing store

awkward: replace with "occupies . . ."

called the Salley Factory Outlet ~~which is~~ a

Combine ideas: it displays latest styles inside store, painted bright, eye-catching yellow

small bilding on Maine St. It contains all of the latest styles. The styles are revealed in its showcase. Inside of the store is a bright eye

begin sentence with preposition "In . . ."

catching yellow. The dressing room ~~is~~ a

set off by comma

medium sized room filled with mirrors ~~they~~

Tell why workers dress well first: to help sell clothes ⟶

~~enable~~ customers ~~to see themselves com-~~ ~~pletely while trying~~ on cloths. The workers in the Outlet have to dress business like. The

use idea earlier: to tell why

owner feels that (the cloths will sell better) if the workers wear them. The workers, in addition, wear a bright smile which also

use earlier to tell why

(keeps sells) up.

need transition to introduce new paragraph

Awkward: omit ⟶ ~~Salley has a~~ small factory called Salley

use at beginning of sentence to help orient reader

Manufactory Company (located on Maine St.)

wordy: omit ———▶ ~~It contains alot of~~ machines used to make

clothing to be sold in the Factory Outlet. A

replace with "there" to avoid repetition

lot of the towns people work ~~in the factory.~~

In the mornings they go in rested with clean

break up long sentence

Place cause and effect in order: first, mention hard work. Then describe resulting messy clothes ———▶ clothes on when they come out they are tired

as dogs. There cloths look a mess becase of

all the hard work they put into making the

cloths.

Link strut to small-town atmosphere ———▶ Finally, Salley has a Chitlin strut held each

year the weekend after Thanksgiving. People

from miles around come to Salley to get a

define term; tell how served and what side dishes

taste of our mouth watering (chitlins.) The

Tell how chitlins are prepared ———▶ chitlins have the hold town smelling stink

but doesn't stop the chitlin eaters from buy-

ing them. Parking space is limited during the

Chtlin Strut so people park along side the

Indicate that parade is high point of celebration ———▶

rods and walk to the maine events. The

parade starts at 10a.m. Every year the crowd

give details about how crowd reacts

waits to see Mrs. Piggy shack her but as she

Indicate contrast between festivities and rest of year ———▶ walks in the parade down Maine St. Everone

that attends the Strut is happy. As a small

town, Salley provides little excitement but

◀——————————————— *Good definition of a "small town"*

beautiful memories.

Based on her responses to the questions and her markings on the first draft, Helena writes an improved second draft of her definition paper. However, her essay is not yet complete. She needs to proofread it, asking these questions:

Proofreading Queries

1. Have I corrected grammatical problems such as noun/verb agreement?
2. Have I corrected the spelling, particularly with words that sound alike or look alike but are not spelled alike?
3. Have I corrected the punctuation, separating word groups to clarify meaning?

I have always liked living in a small town,

comma splice here: correct by changing "it" to "which"

Salley, ~~it~~ is so small it has no traffic light. In

fact, outsiders could probably drive right

though it without recognizing it as a town.

For the townspeople, it provides a police sta-

misspelling: should be "convenience"   *misspelling: should be "restaurant"*

tion, a (convience) store, a (restarant,) a

clothing store, and a small factory. After

Thanksgiving, it attains a brief moment of

annual fame, when it holds the Chitlin'

capitalize second word of title: "Strut"

(strut.) In the center of Salley, our police de-

partment occupies a one-room, small

misspelling: should be "building"

(bilding.) Surrounded by flowers and nicely-

comma splice (after Keith): change "he" to "who"

decorated, it houses one cop, Keith, (he)

Fragment begins with Although. Put comma after ⟶

keeps things in order. Keith is a tall, thin

man with a large stomach. Although the

should be plural: "years"

town hasn't had a murder in (year,) let alone

a serious crime wave, Keith thinks he'll

(impess) people if he keeps his hand near his

misspelling: "impress"

gun as he walks around.

Keith's wife, Hilda, works in Salley's only

misspelling: should be "convenience"

Fragment: connect
to next sentence by
adding comma
after woman ⟶

(convience) store, the Mini Mart. A medium-

height, obese, jolly woman. She works

misspelling: should be "efficiently"

quickly and (efficitly) even though her left

hand misses a thumb. The store recently

Fragment begins By
adding. Connect to
preceding: by ⟶

caused a stir in town. By adding freshly made

Fragment ends with
experience. Replace
period with
comma ⟶

hot dogs to its stock of products. For those

wanting an "upscale" dining experience. Sal-

ley houses a restaurant called Hartley's in an

misspelling: should be "blue"

imposing, beautiful (vlue) house. Hartley's in-

"dish" should be plural "dishes"

cludes numerous mouth-watering (dish) in

an all-you-can-eat buffet style.

fragment missing a verb: insert "occupies"

In addition, a clothing store called the Sal-

Fragment begins
with *Displaying*. Fix
with comma after
styles, displaying ⟶

ley Factory Outlet a small building on (Maine)

misspelling: should be "Main"

Street. It pretends to offer all the latest

styles. Displaying them inside the store,

which is painted a bright, eye-catching yel-

Fragment missing
subject: fix with
subject
customers ⟶

low. In their dressing room, a medium-sized

chamber lined with mirrors, try on clothes.

To help their offerings sell more quickly, the

clerks wear the most up-to-date fashions.

Fragment begins
with *Prompted*. Fix
by connecting to
next sentence:
owner, they . . .

Prompted by the store's owner. They also

keep sales up by smiling brightly and greet

everyone who enters the store: "Good morn-

ing! Can I help yuh?"

Farther out on Main street is located a

misspelling: should be "factory"

small (factry,) the Salley Manufacturing Com-

wrong verb: use "lining"

pany. The machines (line) its workspace

make clothing sold locally at the Factory

Outlet and at nearby locations. Lots of

misspelling: should be "townspeople"

Fragment begins
with *Wearing*. Fix by
comma after
rested.

(townspoeple) work there. In the mornings,

they go to work rested. Wearing clean

clothes. However, after a day's work, they

Run-on: Need period
after *dogs*, then
capital B for
Because

misspelling: should be "tired"

come home (tried) as dogs because of the

hard work they put in making garments,

misspelling: should be "own"

Fragment: fix
connecting with
preceding sentence:
omit period and
make By lowercase

their (won) clothes are sweaty and rumpled.

misspelling: should be "small"

However, Salley capitalizes on its (smal)

town atmosphere. By putting on a Chitlin'

Strut the weekend after Thanksgiving.

"Chitlins" is a southern term for deep-fried

misspelling: should be "served"

hog intestines, (sevred) with barbecue and

punctuation error. Need comma after "sauces," for series

other sauces slaw, and french fries. Chitlins

misspelling: should be "sound"

Run-on: put period
after *people*. Then
capitalize *They*

don't (sond) very appetizing to most people

and they smell very "distinctive" when

(there) being fried in huge vats. How-

misspelling: should be "they're"

Fragment missing use verb buy after towners ———▶

ever, both the locals and out-of-towners

chitlins by the ton. Since parking space is

set off introductory subordinate clause with comma after limited

Fragment beginning with which. Connect to preceding by replacing period with comma after parade and making Which lowercase ————————▶

limited people park alongside the (rode) and

misspelling: should be "road"

walk to the main events. The high point of

the celebration is the parade. Which starts at

misspelling: should be "laughs"

10:00 a.m. Every year the crowd (laghs) and

claps when Mrs. Piggy struts and sashays

misspelling: should be "parade"

along with the rest of the (prade.)

Exercise: Proofreading

Correct any errors in the following paragraph:

After everyone enjoys the Strut. They go

home. The the town settles back into its

dusty sleepiness. Waiting for the next year's

festivies. As a small town, Salley provides lit-

tle excitement but beautiful memories.

After solving her problems with organization and proofreading, Helena writes a final version of her definition paper.

STUDENT DEFINITION ESSAY: FINAL VERSION LIVING IN A SMALL TOWN

I have always liked living in a small town, Salley, which is so small it has no traffic light. In fact, outsiders could probably drive right through it without recognizing it as a town. For the townspeople, it provides a police station, a convenience store, a restaurant, a clothing store, and a small factory. After Thanksgiving, it attains a brief moment of annual fame, when it holds the Chitlin' Strut.

In the center of Salley, our police department occupies a one-room, small building. Surrounded by flowers and nicely decorated, it houses one cop, Keith, who keeps things in order. Keith is a tall, thin man with a large stomach. Although the town hasn't had a murder in years, let alone a serious crime wave, Keith thinks he'll impress people if he keeps his hand near his gun as he walks around.

Keith's wife, Hilda, works in Salley's only convenience store, the Mini Mart. A medium-height, obese, jolly woman, she works quickly and efficiently even though her left hand misses a thumb. The store recently caused a stir in town by adding freshly made hot dogs to its stock of products. For those wanting an "upscale" dining experience, Salley houses a restaurant called Hartley's in an imposing, beautiful blue house. Hartley's includes numerous mouth-watering dishes in an all-you-can-eat buffet style.

In addition, a clothing store called the Salley Factory Outlet occupies a small building on Main Street. It pretends to offer all the latest styles, displaying them inside the store, which is painted a bright, eye-catching yellow. In their dressing room, a medium-sized chamber lined with mirrors, customers try on clothes. To help their offerings sell more quickly, the clerks wear the most up-to-date fashions; prompted by the store's owner, they also keep sales up by smiling brightly and greeting everyone who enters the store: "Good morning! Can I help yuh?"

Farther out on Main street is located a small factory, the Salley Manufacturing Company. The machines which line its workspace make clothing sold locally at the Factory Outlet and at nearby locations. Lots of townspeople work there. In the mornings, they go to work rested, wearing clean clothes. However, after a day's work, they come home tired as dogs. Because of the hard work they put in making garments, their own clothes are sweaty and rumpled.

However, Salley capitalizes on its small-town atmosphere by putting on a Chitlin' Strut the weekend after Thanksgiving. "Chitlins" is a southern term for deep-fried hog intestines, served with barbecue and other sauces, slaw, and french fries. Chitlins don't sound very appetizing to most people, and they smell very "distinctive" when they're being fried in huge vats. However, both the locals and out-of-towners buy chitlins by the ton. Since parking space is limited, people park alongside the road and walk to the main events. The high point of the celebration is the parade, which starts at 10:00 a.m. Every year the crowd laughs and claps when Mrs. Piggy struts and sashays along with the rest of the parade. After everyone enjoys the Strut, they go home. Then the town settles back into its dusty somnolence, waiting for the next year's festivities. As a small town, Salley provides little excitement but beautiful memories.

DEFINITION WRITING TOPICS

The following are some possible topics for a definition paragraph or paper. Limit your topic to fit your instructor's requirements. Tell the reader **why** you have chosen your topic, and link your details closely to your topic.

1. Describe a defining trait like overconfidence or insincerity.
2. Describe a successful or unsuccessful coach, teacher, salesperson, or executive.
3. Describe some type of music, film, book, or architecture.
4. Describe an up-to-date fad or style in clothing, hairstyles, or cars.
5. Describe someone who "walks to his or her own drummer" or conforms closely to society.
6. Describe a fine or terrible nightspot, class, restaurant, or retail store.
7. Describe a hobby, sport, or type of entertainment.

CHAPTER ELEVEN

Persuasion

Arguments meant to persuade take place every day, whether dealing with a new car design ("The new generation Taurus and Sable push the envelope without tearing it to pieces") or with the character of motorcycle riders ("Bikers once considered terrible and jobless have produced such upstanding citizens as lawyers, doctors, and senators"). People may argue for a number of reasons:

- **They may want to get something done by passing a law:** "Tell your congressperson that citizens should be able to bring relatives to this country."
- **They may hope to persuade someone that they have the best solution to a problem:** "If you spend more on batteries than you did on your portable CD, switch to Runnymede Renewables; they're the only batteries made to be reused 25 times or more."
- **They may want to change someone's point of view on some topic:** "Current theory holds that, with rare exceptions, sharks do not intentionally attack human beings."

To argue persuasively, decide on a purpose for handling some topic. Sum up it clearly as a topic sentence for a paragraph or a thesis for an essay. Then support your point with reasons and evidence. When you write a persuasive paragraph or essay, keep the following guidelines in mind.

DECIDE WHY YOU SUPPORT AN OPINION

You may hold some opinion because your family and friends also hold it. Before you can persuade others, however, you need to understand your own reasons for your opinion. To clarify these reasons in your own mind, try using one of the prewriting devices discussed in Chapter 2, such as listing, clustering, or freewriting. Make a list of your reasons for holding a belief about some issue or idea. Then talk over this list with classmates and friends, especially those who might disagree with you. They might ask, for instance, whether your reasons fit everyone or just a select group. Do you have facts or statistics to support your view? Listing the things that support your view and talking over your view with others will let you know, right from the start, whether your viewpoint is well founded or whether you need to do some research. Perhaps you need to talk to a knowledgeable expert or do some reading on the topic.

CONSIDER OPPOSING ARGUMENTS

Prewriting about your topic and talking it over with others will probably turn up opposing arguments. If your issue is controversial, it will have at least two sides. To make sure you've kept your opponents' views in mind, consider making two lists: one list that supports your point of view and another parallel list of viewpoints that disagree with yours. Making such lists will not only help you clarify your thinking, it will also help you put together a strong topic sentence or thesis. Here's an example of a list of the arguments for and against mandatory motorcycle helmets:

My point of view: against required motorcycle helmets
Bikers are often outstanding citizens, including lawyers, doctors, and senators.

Wearing helmets blocks the senses and obstructs vision.

Most accidents involving bikers could be prevented by safety training courses.

Of the top twelve states with the best motorcycle safety records, only one has a helmet law.

Most accidents involving bikers are the car driver's fault.

My opponents' point of view: for required motorcycle helmets
Fatal accidents went up when Congress did away with sanctions against states failing to require helmets for bikers.

Most medical bills for injured bikers are paid by public funds.

The motorcycle rider is unprotected when cruising down a highway straddling thousands of pounds of force.

Most injuries to bikers involve the head, which can be cheaply protected by helmets.

The public interest should override bikers' interest in personal freedom.

Listing arguments for and against your position will help you decide which of your arguments seem the strongest; you can also tell which of your opponent's arguments you want to challenge. You might also want to combine ideas or weed out some of your weaker points. If your essay is to be a short one, you may need to decide which two or three of your strongest points to emphasize.

DESIGN A CLEAR THESIS AND PLAN

Once you have considered both sides of an issue, design a working thesis. You might find it easiest to shape your thesis by using an **on the one hand this** and **on the other hand that** approach.

On the one hand, those in favor of helmet laws argue that motorcycle riders are especially susceptible to head injuries and that public funds pay most of the injured bikers' medical bills.

On the other hand, states could avoid helmet laws by requiring bikers to take courses in safety training, by enforcing DUI laws more strictly, and by requiring hospitalization insurance for motorcycle driving licenses.

Stating a thesis this way helps you pick out the strongest arguments on both sides. It also helps you give a clear direction to your paragraph or essay before you actually write a draft.

DECIDE HOW TO ORGANIZE YOUR ESSAY

The organization of persuasive essays may follow many different patterns. However, you will find it helpful to create an outline before you write the first draft. Several simple patterns are available. For example, you might want to weaken your opposition's position first, and then leave your points firmly in your readers' minds:

First Pattern
> **Thesis**
>> **First body paragraph:** Disprove the first point with which you disagree.
>>
>> **Second body paragraph:** Disprove the second point with which you disagree.
>>
>> **Third body paragraph:** State and support your most important point.
>>
>> **Fourth body paragraph:** State and support your second point.
>>
>> **Last paragraph:** Sum up.

Another pattern of organizing your paper is to present evidence that supports your views. Then show the flaws or shortcomings in your opposition's point of view:

Second Pattern:
Thesis

First body paragraph: State and support your most important point.

Second body paragraph: State and support your second point.

Third body paragraph: Disprove the first point with which you disagree.

Fourth body paragraph: Disprove the second point with which you disagree.

Last paragraph: Sum up.

A third approach involves using one of your points to undercut an opposing argument. Thus, by following this pattern you would challenge each one of your opposition's points by arguing a main point and supporting it with reasons or facts:

Third Pattern:
Thesis

First body paragraph: State and support your most important point while challenging a claim made by your opposition.

Second body paragraph: State and support your second point while challenging a claim made by your opposition.

Third body paragraph: State and support your third point while challenging a claim made by your opposition.

Last paragraph: Sum up.

Each of these patterns is flexible enough to allow you to test the strengths of your position and probe the weaknesses of the opposition's viewpoint. Once you have chosen an organizational pattern, collect supporting evidence. You may do so by drawing on your own experience, perhaps by using one of the prewriting devices described in Chapter 2. This might involve simple list-making or clustering. You might also gather material by talking over your topic with friends, interviewing an expert, or checking your library's resources.

SUPPORT YOUR POINTS
LOGICALLY AND FACTUALLY

Many of the writing techniques discussed earlier in this book will help you support your arguments. Here are some approaches:

- **Use a narrative or descriptive passage:** "Riding a motorcycle can make one feel free, with the wind blowing through your hair, until suddenly, it all comes to a halt with a crash."
- **Compare and contrast:** "A study done by the Motorcycle Safety Foundation shows that for a 14-year period, 1977–1990, states with mandatory helmet laws had 12.5 percent more accidents and 2.3 percent more fatalities than non-mandatory states."
- **Link causes and effects:** "Both sides agree that highway safety and high medical insurance costs must be addressed."
- **Give examples:** "Bikers across the United States have banded together to form antihelmet organizations to fight for their rights."
- **Define terms:** "All children and teenagers should be required to wear helmets while riding on motorcycles until the age of twenty-one or until they have completed a mandatory safety course."

Remember: you must not only persuade your readers that your opinions are well thought out, with logical and factual support, but you must also persuade them that you are a reasonable, thoughtful person. You are trying hard to accommodate *both* your own supporters and those who disagree with you on a particular issue.

READINGS

At times, your persuasive writing will be brief: a single paragraph. You will also develop longer persuasive essays with body paragraphs, each one handling a part of your thesis. As Chapter 1 pointed out, topic sentences sum up a paragraph's main idea. You then support the topic sentence to make this general concept clearer, more vivid to your reader. By filling out this general idea, your paragraph will help your reader understand, even share, your point of view. The author of the following paragraph tries to show readers a particular way of viewing a problem. To do so, the problem is defined in the paragraph's topic sentence. Then statistics are provided to support the author's position.

WHAT IS POLLUTING OUR BEACHES?

Joe Brancatelli

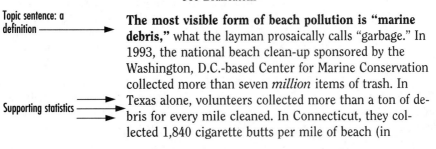

Topic sentence: a definition →

The most visible form of beach pollution is "marine debris," what the layman prosaically calls "garbage." In 1993, the national beach clean-up sponsored by the Washington, D.C.-based Center for Marine Conservation collected more than seven *million* items of trash. In Texas alone, volunteers collected more than a ton of debris for every mile cleaned. In Connecticut, they collected 1,840 cigarette butts per mile of beach (in

Supporting statistics →

Supporting statistics

December, 1994, the Hanuama Bay beach in Honolulu, Hawaii, became the first "no smoking" beach). CMC volunteers also gathered more than 40,000 rubber balloons, 25,000 plastic six-pack holders, 300,000 glass and plastic beverage bottles, and 200,000 metal beverage cans.

Popular Science

Chapter 2 showed how a **thesis** sums up the main idea for an entire writing; it serves an essay as a **topic sentence** serves a paragraph. That is, it sums up the main idea and tells the writer's viewpoint toward it. The title for the next selection looks ahead to its thesis. This essay uses both reasons and examples to support the argument embodied in its title.

Toymakers Drawing Their Ideas from Movies

Example of toymakers' influence on films →

When filmmakers crafted the new Batmobile, they consulted some unusual mechanics: toymakers at Hasbro's Kenner Products, who wanted a longer hood and lower cockpit for the flashy car.

Expands scope of argument to a decade and several toymakers →

Defines key term →

That's just one of many ways toy companies are becoming entwined with Hollywood. In a business that hasn't had an original megahit since Cabbage Patch Kids a decade ago, toymakers have grown increasingly reliant on Power Rangers, Ninja Turtles, or Disney creations for their ideas and sales. There's even a new word for it: entertoyment.

Thesis: expands on preceding ideas →

Addicted to using movie and TV characters, many toymakers have shelved much of their own research and development, and changed the way toys are created. Some parents and psychologists say they're even changing the way children play. Prepackaged characters and well-defined roles can limit youngsters' imaginations and fantasy play, they say.

Example paragraph: takes **both** sides of argument →

"I am torn," says Robert Solomon, chairman of Dakin, a maker of toys tied to the films *Congo* and *Casper*. "As a dad, I wish there was a little more imagination for my kids. As a businessman, I say this is the sign of the times. The days of the Hula-Hoop—like *Leave It to Beaver*—are gone."

Arguments make comparisons with previous toys, sales levels →

Toy manufacturers say Hollywood-related toys sell so well they would be foolish to invest heavily in the risky business of creating the next Frisbee or Etch-A-Sketch.

Sums up with sales ⟶ Last year, nearly half the $17 billion in retail toy sales
Introduces examples ⟶ came from licensed goods based on movies and TV
shows, up from 10 percent a decade ago. Toy companies
expect $300 million in sales tied to Power Rangers this
year, $130 million from Batman gear, and $100 million
from merchandise linked to Disney's *Pocahontas*.

In return for the stiff royalty fees they pay for licensing, toymakers play a bigger role in Hollywood:

- A Disney animator says one scene in *Pocahontas*—when the raccoon
  Meeko briefly braids the star's hair—was created after a suggestion from
  Mattel, which wanted to be able to make Braided Beauty Pocahontas
  dolls.
- For *Batman Forever*, Kenner got Warner Bros. to put the Riddler in
  tights because baggy pants don't look good on toy action figures, says
  Rick Watkins, a former Kenner toy-development manager.

Two specific examples from well-known films

Wall Street Journal

In the following selection, the author takes an unpopular position among others
of her age group: that the state should raise the age for driving permits to 16
rather than 15 as it is now.

Prereading

1. On what issues do teenagers disagree with their parents?
2. On what issues are teenagers themselves divided?

ABOLISHING THE RIGHT TO A BEGINNING DRIVING PERMIT AT THE AGE OF FIFTEEN

Student Essay (Ingrid)

Most teenagers take a driving permit for granted when they turn fifteen, especially since it requires only a commonsense test and a fifteen-day waiting
period. The availability of this permit speeds up the process of getting not only a
license, but a car as well, in some cases. Therefore, I think the state should raise
the age of licensed drivers from fifteen to sixteen. Even then, they should not be
allowed to drive for a year except during the day and with a licensed driver over
the age of twenty-one with them in the car.

I realize that both parents and teenagers are likely to resist any change in the
present licensing law. For their part, parents think their children should begin
driving early to run errands for them or drive themselves to or from after-school
activities. They also want their children to have the things they didn't have as

children. Many parents rush their children into getting a license by saying, "If you get your license, we will buy you a car." These promises increase the desire of teenagers to get their licenses. Moreover, my grandmother thinks that most accidents are caused not by teenagers but by older people whose reflexes have slowed down. If parents raise their children to have responsibility, she thinks, teenagers won't drive carelessly. My friends also think that the law should remain the same because a change would penalize all teenagers, especially those who drive carefully with or without an older person in the car.

However, fifteen-year-olds aren't mature enough to have driving rights. Teenagers with a license often think they also have adult rights like drinking alcohol or partying as late as they please. Moreover, when teenagers rush into getting a license, their inexperience could cause more accidents. I have heard of many deaths because a teenager was driving too fast or driving under the influence because they thought everyone did it. On a personal note, my parents wanted me to hurry and get my permit. However, I didn't feel ready at fifteen. In fact, I wasn't prepared to take the test until I had been driving for six months.

In conclusion, raising the age for drivers' licenses would lower both the accident and fatality rates for both teenage drivers and their victims. Along with a change in the age requirement for licenses, the police should rigorously enforce the laws, not just for the age requirement but for speeding and driving under the influence. Only with these changes can everyone using the roadways feel safe and secure.

Queries for Understanding

1. What requirements must fifteen-year-olds meet in Ingrid's state to be issued a driver's permit?
2. What additional requirements for licensing teenagers would Ingrid add?
3. Why do parents push teenagers into getting their driving permits, according to Ingrid?
4. What arguments in favor of early driving permits are presented by Ingrid's grandmother? By her friends?
5. What personal arguments does Ingrid present in opposition to getting a driver's permit herself?

Queries on the Writer's Techniques

1. How does Ingrid order her own and opposing arguments?
2. How does Ingrid's conclusion add to her original thesis?

Writing Topics

1. Should students who get good grades be rewarded with special privileges, such as lower-cost driver's insurance?

2. Would students become more mature if they were required to provide national volunteer service for two years following high school?

The following selection is from an exchange of letters between Darcy Peters, a Camas, Washington, homemaker, and her representative in the state legislature, Marcus Boldt, a Republican. Peters wrote to Boldt in March, saying she opposed a plan to eliminate the state's Readiness to Learn program, which finances her town's Family Learning Center, an adult-education and preschool center that Peters and her three sons attend. On April 3, Representative Boldt responded.

Words to Define
eliminate: to get rid of, wipe out

ineligible: unqualified, ruled out

budgetary: involving expenses and income

instability: uncertainty, not dependable

mandated: required by law

requirement: necessity, demand

subsidies: government payments to groups or individuals

perspectives: viewpoints, outlooks

constituency: voting group, following

discernible: observable, obvious

proposition: proposal, plan

Prereading
1. On what issues have you disagreed with a lawmaker from your area or district? How and why? (Consider the lawmaker's views as well as your own.)
2. Should lawmakers closely reflect the wishes of those who elect them on all issues, or should they vote as their consciences dictate?

THE NEW RIGHT WRITES BACK

Representative Marcus Boldt:
Please do not cancel funding for the Readiness to Learn Family Learning Center.

Our family came to the learning center frustrated. Barely self-supportive, we were struggling but living with no outside assistance. My husband was frequently laid off from work, and I was a full-time mother, not working outside the home. With four-year-old twins and another child, age three, we couldn't afford to pay for a preschool program. When I went to the Head Start program, I was told that we were ineligible because we made too much money. I felt like a victim of the system.

I was thrilled to find out we were eligible for the Readiness to Learn program. My children could all attend, and so could I. My sons, Caleb, Zachary, and Nathan, have learned so much at the center. They constantly surprise me with skills I didn't even know they had. I am so proud of their success. I myself have learned a great deal as well. Being challenged academically has sparked a thirst for learning that I never knew existed in me. I have seen the world open up before me, and I feel capable of meeting any academic challenge. Furthermore, using one of the agencies I learned of at the center, my husband is making a career change, having decided to leave the construction business to become an electrician.

This has been such a valuable experience that I hope many other families are able to attend the center. Abolishing Readiness to Learn might rob another family of the chance to improve itself and reach its long-term goals. We need this program in our area.

Sincerely,
Darcy Peters

Harper's

Queries for Understanding

1. What family circumstances justify Peters' request for funding for the Readiness to Learn Family Learning Center?
2. What benefits have Peters' family members gained by their attendance at the Readiness to Learn Family Learning Center?

Queries on the Writer's Techniques

1. What is Peters' thesis, and where does it appear?
2. How does Peters' portrayal of the family's problems combine logic with an emotional appeal?
3. How does Peters combine logic with an emotional appeal in her description of the benefits her family have received from attendance at the Readiness to Learn Family Learning Center?
4. How does Peters conclude her appeal?
5. After reading Peters' appeal and *before* reading Representative Boldt's response, how persuasive did you find it, and why?

BOLDT'S RESPONSE

Dear Ms. Peters:

Thank you for writing to me about your concerns regarding funding for the Family Learning Center. Your letter goes to the heart of the matter in the area of budgetary reform. My positions on budget expenditures are well known, and served in large measure to assure my election to this office.

I see that you have three children, ages three and four. You wrote that your husband is subject to frequent layoffs. You indicate that you are a "full-time mother, not working outside the home."

The concerns expressed by the taxpayers over your situation are as follows:

a. If your situation was subject to so much financial instability, then why did you have three children?

b. Why is your husband in a line of work that subjects him to "frequent lay-offs"?

c. Why, in the face of your husband's ability to parent as a result of his frequent layoffs, are you refusing to work outside the home?

d. Since there is no state or federally mandated requirement that children attend these programs, why should the taxpayer foot the bill for them?

e. Since your family apparently makes too much money for assistance, why should you receive subsidies of any kind?

f. How much of the situation outlined in your letter should be the responsibility of the people of this state?

g. What arrangements have you made to repay this program at some future date?

I do not necessarily agree with all of these perspectives. But I must contend with the expectations of a constituency that is tired of paying for so many programs without any discernible return.

The voters have made it clear that, in this era of personal responsibility, life must become a more "pay-as-you-go" proposition. To put it bluntly, the taxpayers' perspective says, "This program is something that Darcy *wants* to have, and not something that she *must* have."

Thank you for your time.

Marcus Boldt
State Representative

Harper's

Queries for Understanding

1. Boldt suggests three actions the Peters should have taken to avoid the family's "financial instability." What are they?

2. Boldt suggests that "self-supporting families" deserve no subsidies of any kind from government. How does his choice of a term like *subsidies* distort Peters' argument?

3. To what extent *are* the people of the state responsible for the problems faced by the Peters family?

4. Should the Peters family be expected to repay the state for services such as those rendered by the Readiness to Learn Family Learning Center?

Queries on the Writer's Techniques

1. What is Boldt's thesis, and where is it?

2. Is Boldt's technique—a series of leading questions—more or less persuasive than a series of assertions or statements? Why or why not?

3. What reasons does Boldt have for asking questions that clearly place the blame for the Peters' "financial instability" squarely on decisions made by the family?

4. Does Boldt have an open mind regarding Peters' letter? How do you know?

5. Are Boldt's questions seeking a reasoned response from Peters, or does he have some other purpose?

6. After reading both Peters' appeal and Boldt's response, how persuasive did you find Boldt's response, and why?

Writing Topics

1. Argue for or against: the state should help families protect themselves against unwanted children by providing birth control education and devices.

2. Argue for or against: the state should provide educational opportunities to help people move from part- to full-time, temporary to permanent employment.

In the following selection, a student argues that a time-honored remedy, herbal healing, has worked for her and should be taken more seriously by doctors.

Words to Define

nutrients: something that nourishes

extract: a concentrated form, something gotten by pressure

pulmonary: related to the lungs

practitioner: someone trained to do a specialized task

cholesterol: a fatty substance carried by the blood

cardiovascular: the body's system of heart and blood vessels

tannin: brownish acid

saponin: an alkali (sometimes used to make soap)

alkaloid: a group of substances found in plants; many cause nervous system damage if taken in large doses.

volatile: evaporates quickly when exposed to air

HERBAL HEALING

Student Essay (Tonya)

The world has many health disorders which could be cured by herbs. While many people are skeptical about the value of herbal healing, it has been used in the Far East, especially China, for centuries. If doctors would study and practice herbal healing, it could help a lot of sickly people.

By definition, herbal healing uses plants' nutrients to cure illnesses. Particular sorts of plants help specific disorders. For example, the herb borage can help not only ulcers and frazzled nerves, but can also treat symptoms of PMS (premenstrual syndrome). Borage can be obtained as extract or capsules. Another herb, Jamaican dogwood, helps with migraine headaches and nervous tension. The bark and root of this tree are crushed into powder and used in capsules. When I was younger, my mother gave me garlic for the common cold; it stimulates the immune system to help fight off colds and other pulmonary problems. It also lowers the cholesterol level in blood and reduces risks of heart attacks. Garlic can also be crushed and smeared on skin irritations. Although many people dismiss herbal healing, they probably haven't given it a chance. Herbal healing has had too many successes to be dismissed lightly.

In Eastern countries, such as China, this ancient system of healing has been traced back as far as 2500 B.C. Practitioners still study texts on herbal healing. The Chinese see health disorders as a sign of disharmony. Thus, they use herbs to help the body's natural healing mechanisms work more efficiently. The Chinese first discovered ginseng, which has almost the same effects as garlic. It lessens problems with the cardiovascular system and soothes skin irritations. It also strengthens the immune system. Because Chinese herbal healing isn't often used here in the United States, many people are skeptical about its effectiveness. However, the success which the Chinese have enjoyed over the centuries should lead us to consider their medical beliefs more seriously.

If doctors and scientists would take more time to study herbs, they could broaden medical knowledge, even find the cure for AIDS. Some doctors reject herbal healing because they fear their patients would suffer allergic reactions. It is true that most herbs contain tannins, saponins, alkaloids, and volatile oils. However, only a limited number of people are allergic to these ingredients. Patients already answer doctors' question, "Are you allergic to anything?" Herbal healing can help many people in this country if we would only agree to give it a chance.

Queries for Understanding

1. What examples of healing herbs does the writer cite?
2. How long have the Chinese used herbal healing, and why?
3. For what reasons have ordinary people and doctors resisted the use of herbal healing?

Queries on the Writer's Techniques

1. What is the writer's thesis, and where is it found?
2. What is the writer's plan, and where does she state it?
3. Find the topic sentences: where are they placed in each paragraph of the body?
4. How does the writer support the value of each herb she mentions?
5. What action by the reader does the writer call for?

Writing Topics

1. What information about your body and medical cures have you gained?
2. Why would this information be useful to others?
3. How could medical professionals improve the ways they treat patients, both medically and personally?

According to the author of the following selection, one day soon, computers and automation could eliminate your job forever—and you could be better off for it.

Words to Define

entrepreneur: person who takes business risks, usually in start-ups

voucher: document entitling a person to payment

imposition: a burdensome or unfair demand

value-added taxes: taxes added at each stage of the creation of a product or service

gamut: complete range, extent

productivity: the cost of goods or services resulting from labor

systematically: step-by-step, methodically

sophisticated: very complicated

automation: the use of electronics to control machines and do work

acknowledged: agreed, recognized

efficiency: the amount of energy needed to do work

transformation: a change in form or appearance

encroaching: intruding, going beyond limits

spawning: creating a product or outcome

synthesizers: electronic devices for mimicking musical tones

equitable: fair, impartial

generate: to produce, bring into being

deconstructing: getting rid of, flattening

hierarchies: people or things organized by rank or authority

obsolete: out-of-date and, hence, useless

transnational: organized across national and geographic boundary lines

concerted: planned or done together

contractual: by written, legally enforceable agreement

alternative: option, choice

onerous: unpleasant, repulsive

preoccupied: too concerned with other things

abyss: a bottomless pit, disaster

Prereading
1. What steps should be taken by both government and individuals to prepare people for a highly technical world?
2. What technological changes have affected the work you have done, or are doing, and in what ways?

NO MORE WORK

Jeremy Rifkin

The year is 2045.

Life for most Americans is quite different from what it was a half-century ago. Now that we are deep into the Information Age, most of the world's goods and services are produced in nearly workerless factories and marketed by small companies run by teams of entrepreneurs and highly trained professionals. Computers, robots, and telecommunications technologies have replaced the "worker" of the industrial era.

Less than 20 percent of the adult population works full time. Most Americans receive their economic livelihood, in the form of voucher payments, from their local governing body in return for community service work in nonprofit organizations. The vouchers are financed by the imposition of value-added taxes.

Their projects run the gamut from helping take care of children and the elderly to working in preventive health programs, local art galleries, community gardens, and neighborhood.

Because of productivity gains resulting from technological advances, people's work takes up fewer than five hours a day, leaving more time for family, friends, personal projects, and relaxation.

This is one possible vision of a not-too-distant future. The seeds for this very different world are already planted.

From the beginning, civilization has been structured in large part around the concept of work. But for the first time, human labor is being systematically eliminated from the economic process.

In the coming century, employment, as we have come to know it, is likely to be phased out in most of the industrialized nations of the world. A new generation of sophisticated information and communication technologies is being introduced into a wide variety of work situations. These machines, together with new forms of business reorganization and management, are forcing millions of blue- and white-collar workers into temporary jobs and unemployment lines—or worse, bread lines.

Our corporate leaders, economists, and politicians tell us that the rising unemployment figures represent only short-term "adjustments" that will be taken care of as the global economy advances into the Information Age. But millions of working people remain skeptical.

In the United States, corporations are eliminating more than 2 million jobs annually. Although some jobs are being created, they are for the most part in the low-paying sectors, and many are temporary or part-time positions.

We are in the early stages of a long-term shift from "mass labor" to highly skilled "elite labor," accompanied by increasing automation in the production of goods and the delivery of services.

These developments do not have to mean a grim future. The gains from this technological revolution could be shared among the people with a reduced work-week and opportunities to work on socially useful projects outside the realm of the market economy. But before any such sweeping reforms can take place, it must be acknowledged that we face a future in which the traditional role of private-sector jobs as the centerpiece of our economic and social life will be gone.

Nowhere is the effect of the computer revolution and re-engineering of the workplace more pronounced than in the manufacturing sector. In the 1950s, 33 percent of all U.S. workers were employed in manufacturing. Today less than 17 percent of the work force is engaged in blue-collar work.

Although the number of blue-collar workers continues to decline, manufacturing productivity is soaring. From 1979 to 1992, productivity rose by 35 percent in the manufacturing sector while the work force fell by 15 percent.

Many economists and elected officials hope that the service and white-collar sectors will be able to provide jobs for the millions of unemployed blue-collar laborers. Their hopes are likely to be dashed.

Andersen Consulting Co., one of the world's largest corporate restructuring firms, estimates that in just one service industry, commercial banking and thrift institutions, technological and management changes will eliminate 30 percent to 40 percent of the jobs over the next seven years. That translates into nearly 700,000 jobs. The number of U.S. banks is likely to decline by 25 percent by the turn of the century, and this, along with automatic teller machines and financial transactions via computer networks, will reduce significantly the number of employees.

Changes also have been dramatic in the wholesale and retail sectors. Typical of the trend is retail giant Sears, Roebuck and Co. Sears eliminated 50,000 jobs from its merchandising division in 1993, reducing employment by 14 percent. The cutbacks came in a year when Sears' sales revenues rose by more than 10 percent.

In most retail outlets, the use of electronic bar codes and scanners has increased the efficiency of cashiers and thereby reduced the number of positions available. Some fast-food drive-through restaurants are beginning to replace order-takers with touch-sensitive menu screens. And many industry analysts predict that electronic home-shopping will take more and more of the nation's trillion-dollar-a-year retail market.

It's not just low-level jobs that are disappearing. A growing number of companies are deconstructing their organizational hierarchies and eliminating middle management. They use computers to do the coordinating that people—often working in separate departments and locations within the company—used to do.

Harvard business professor Gary Loveman points out that while better jobs are being created for a fortunate few at the top levels of management, the men and women in "garden-variety middle-management jobs" are "getting crucified" by corporate re-engineering and the introduction of sophisticated information and communications technologies. Eastman Kodak Co., for example, has reduced its management levels from 13 to four.

"Intelligent" machines are encroaching on the professional disciplines, education, and the arts. A robot that will perform hip replacement surgery is being developed in California, and some firms use a computerized hiring system to screen job applicants.

Even in the arts, jobs are disappearing. Synthesizers are fast replacing musicians in theaters, clubs, and even opera houses. The Washington Opera Company's recent production of "Don Carlo" had in the pit only the conductor, two pianists, and a synthesizer player.

Optimists counter with the argument that the new products and services of the high-technology revolution will generate additional employment. They point to the fact that earlier in the century, the automobile made the horse and buggy obsolete but created millions of new jobs. Although it is true that the Information Age is spawning a dizzying array of new products and services, they require far fewer workers to produce and operate than the products and services they replace.

We are being swept into a technological revolution that will set off a great social transformation unlike any in history. It is time to prepare ourselves and our institutions for a world that will phase out mass employment.

A fair and equitable distribution of the productivity gains from this new industrial revolution would require a shortening of the workweek worldwide and a concerted effort by central governments to provide alternative employment for workers whose labor is no longer required in the marketplace.

In the United States, the argument persists that fewer hours at existing pay could put companies at a competitive disadvantage globally. A recent survey soliciting the support of 200 business leaders for a shorter week did not receive a single positive response. One Fortune 500 CEO wrote back, "My view of the world, our country, and our country's needs is dramatically opposite of yours. I cannot imagine a shorter workweek; I can imagine a longer one . . . if America is to be competitive in the first half of the next century."

One way to address this concern is being advocated in France. French business and labor leaders and politicians from several parties have embraced the idea of the government taking over employers' burden of paying for workers compensation in return for an agreement by companies to shorten the workweek. French policy-makers calculate that the hiring of additional workers will significantly reduce welfare and other relief payments, canceling out any additional costs the government might have to assume by absorbing the payroll tax for unemployment compensation.

U.S. business leaders' opposition to a shorter workweek also might be overcome by extending generous tax credits to companies that shift to a shorter workweek and hire additional workers. The loss of government revenue up front, some argue, would be offset by the taxable revenue generated by more workers bringing home a paycheck.

The 30-hour workweek is likely to enjoy widespread support among Americans harried by the stress of their work schedules. A growing number say they would readily trade some income gains for increased time to attend to family responsibilities and personal needs. According to a 1993 survey conducted by the Families and Work Institute, employees said they are "less willing to make sacrifices for work" and "want to devote more time and energy to their personal lives."

The foundation for a strong, community-based social force in American life already exists. The "third sector"—also known as civil society, the social economy, or the volunteer sector—is the realm where contractual arrangements give way to community bonds, and giving one's time to others takes the place of market relationships based on selling one's time. It also offers great potential as a source of work and livelihood for the millions who can't find traditional employment.

Voluntary organizations are serving millions of Americans in communities across the country. There are more than 1.4 million nonprofit organizations in the United States whose primary goal is to provide a service or advance a cause. Also, the third sector is where people relax and play, and more fully experience the pleasures of life and nature.

Americans ought to consider making a direct investment in expanded job creation in the third sector, as an alternative to welfare, for the increasing number of jobless who find themselves locked out of the global marketplace. State and local governments could provide an income voucher for permanently unemployed Americans willing to be retrained and placed in community-building jobs in the nonprofit sector. The government also could award grants to nonprofit organizations to help them recruit and train the poor for jobs.

Paying for a social income and for training men and women for a career of community service would require significant government funds. Some of the money could come from savings brought about by gradually replacing welfare programs with direct payments to community-service workers.

Government money also could be freed by discontinuing costly subsidies— tens of billions of dollars in 1993 in the form of direct payments and tax breaks— to transnational corporations that have outgrown their domestic commitments and now operate in countries around the world. Additional money could be raised by cutting military expenditures and placing a value-added tax on all high-tech goods and services.

Although powerful vested interests are likely to resist the idea of providing a social wage in return for community service, the alternative—ignoring the problem of long-term unemployment—is even more onerous. A growing underclass of unemployable Americans could lead to widespread social unrest, increased violence, and the further disintegration of American society.

Up to now, the world has been so preoccupied with the workings of the market economy that focusing attention on the social economy has been virtually ignored. This needs to change. The road to a near-workerless economy is within sight; whether it leads to a safe haven or a terrible abyss will depend on whether civilization prepares for what is to come. The end of work could signal the death of civilization—or the beginning of a great social transformation. The future lies in our hands.

The End of Work: the Decline of the Global Labor Force
and the Dawn of the Post-Market Era,
Jeremy P. Tarcher/Putnam, 1995

Queries for Understanding

1. In Rifkin's vision of the year 2045, who will produce most of the world's goods? Who will market these goods? What will the rest of us do for our "economic livelihood"? What will those of us without jobs do with our leisure time?

2. How many jobs are being eliminated each year in the United States? Where are the new jobs coming from?

3. How does Rifkin define the term *Information Age*, and what stage are we now in?

4. What view of the future must we accept in order to accept Rifkin's solution to coming problems?

5. What trends have appeared in the last several decades in U.S. manufacturing employment and productivity?

6. What changes are likely to occur in banking employment in the next several years?

7. What changes in employment have occurred at Sears, and how are these changes typical?

8. In retail outlets other than Sears, what changes in technology are likely to reduce the number of jobs?

9. According to Harvard business professor Gary Loveman, where are new jobs being created, at whose expense?

10. How are "intelligent machines" getting rid of jobs in the professional disciplines, education, and the arts?

11. Why do American business leaders oppose a shortening of the workweek to extend employment?

12. With what three arguments does Rifkin counter opposition to shortening the U.S. workweek?

13. What basis for a replacement of "market employment" already exists in the United States, and how is it defined?

14. What social advantages are offered by employment in the volunteer sector? What financial advantages?

15. What three reasons make the volunteer sector a viable employment alternative to jobs in the market?

16. What sources of funds does Rifkin identify for jobs in the volunteer sector?

17. How does Rifkin counter the opposition of powerful vested interests to providing a social wage for community service?

18. Why, according to Rifkin, has the world ignored the workings of the "social economy"?

Queries on the Writer's Techniques

1. In what way is Rifkin's title, "No More Work," misleading?

2. Does Rifkin want (a) to get something done by passing a law, (b) to persuade someone he has the best solution to a problem, or (c) to change someone's point of view on his chosen topic, or all three?

3. What is Rifkin's thesis, and where is it?

4. Why does Rifkin's thesis—a plan for the future—come so late in the essay?

5. The first section of Rifkin's essay deals with a vision of the future: why does he begin with this sketch?

6. The second section of Rifkin's essay argues that machines are replacing people. How does this section logically follow his vision of the future?

7. In an attempt to cover all sectors of U. S. employment, what sectors of American business has Rifkin surveyed?

8. How does Rifkin respond to the argument by "optimists" that the new technology will create new jobs to replace those being lost?

9. Why does Rifkin acknowledge the widespread nature of U.S. business leaders' opposition to shortening the workweek?

10. Why does Rifkin order his arguments in favor of a shorter workweek as he does?

11. When Rifkin sketches the alternatives to adopting his proposal, does he use logic, statistics, or emotion, or a combination of these? Why?

12. How is Rifkin's conclusion designed to stress the urgency of the problems he foresees?

13. How persuasive is Rifkin's essay? Why or why not?

Writing Topics

1. What presently unmet "social needs" mentioned by Rifkin could be met by funding the volunteer sector?

2. What changes should schools make to train men and women for community service careers?

THE WRITING PROCESS

In the following selection, Sonya, the author, decided to write about the music available to young people on the radio. Not only she but the parents of listeners are disturbed by rap lyrics.

STUDENT PERSUASION ESSAY: FIRST DRAFT

A listen to the radio will reveal a most interesting concern of many Americans. It's not the D.J. A great deal of these songs being played on the radio are filled with very explicit lyrics. Parents feel that music should be rated and not be allowed to be sold to anyone unless their a certain age. The singers argue that it is taking away their right of freedom of speech and that people just can't face hearing about what really is happening in todays society. Also, the singers say that singing is their own ticket out of the slums. Some of the lyrics are not suitable for little children to be listening to. For Example: when rap singer Ice-T released his song "Cop Killer." Not only this but children look up to singers and see them as role models and if a singer does something bad like kills hisself, then a fan might go out and do the same thing. Of course the singers have freedom of speech, but should there be a limit on what they are allowed to sing about and sell on tapes? With just a simple rating system, it would make everyone happy. The singers would be allowed to sing about what ever they wanted to and the parents would be happy because children wouldn't be allowed to buy certain tapes until there a certain age.

REVISING THE FIRST DRAFT

To revise her first trial draft, Sonya looks most closely at its organization. She'll ask the following questions about it and write in notes on her first draft:

1. Is the thesis clear to the reader at the beginning of the paper? Is it clear to the reader why the writer's viewpoint matters?
2. Do the sentences in the draft grow out of the thesis, in the right order? Are the sentences carefully linked together, with helpful transitions, pronouns, and repeated words or synonyms?
3. Has the writer used enough specific, concrete details? Do the details effectively support the paper's main idea?
4. Does the paper's conclusion clearly grow out of the essay?

After answering these questions on organization, Sonya marks up her draft, like this:

A listen to the radio will reveal a most interesting concern of many Americans. It's not the D.J. A great deal of these songs being played on the radio are filled with very (explicit) lyrics. Parents feel that music should be rated and not be allowed to be sold to anyone unless their a certain age. The singers argue that it is taking away their right of freedom of speech and that people just can't face hearing about what really is happening in todays society. Also, the singers say that singing is their own ticket out of the slums.

Some of the lyrics are not suitable for little children to be listening to. For Example: when rap singer Ice-T released his song "Cop Killer." Not only this but children look up to singers and see them as role models and if a singer does something bad like kills hisself, then a fan might go out and do the same thing. Of course the singers have freedom of speech, but should there be a limit on what they are allowed to sing about and sell on tapes? With just a simple rating system, it

---

Margin annotations:

Tell how explicit: about drugs, getting drunk, sex, killing →

Clarify: parents concerned about "children" →

Start new paragraph focusing on issue of rating. →

Name other rap singers, indicate topics of lyrics. Indicate how easy for children to listen to music, buy it.

Quote lyrics to Ice-T song. →

Give example of fan's action →

Need new argument by singers →

Add argument by singers: they're just making a legal living, better than selling drugs or thievery. →

Explain more fully: rating system like that used in movies would protect children and encourage singers to handle other topics. ──────▶

would make everyone happy. The singers

would be allowed to sing about what ever

they wanted to and the parents would be

happy because children wouldn't be allowed

to buy certain tapes until there a certain age.

Based on her responses to the questions and her markings on the first draft, Sonya writes an improved second draft of her persuasion paper. However, her essay is not yet complete. She needs to proofread it, asking these questions:

Proofreading Queries

1. Have I corrected grammatical problems such as noun/verb agreement?
2. Have I corrected the spelling, particularly with words that sound alike or look alike but are not spelled alike?
3. Have I corrected the punctuation, separating word groups to clarify meaning?

A listen to the radio will reveal a most inter-

no appostrophe for plural "Americans"

esting concern of many (American's.) It's not

"many" clearer than "deal"

the D.J. A great (deal) of these songs being

played on the radio are filled with very

wrong word: should be "explicit"

(explicated) lyrics. The songs are talking about

doing drugs, getting drunk, having sex, and

some even about killing people. The parents

should be possessive "their"

are concerned about (there) children listen-

wordy: replace with "buying"

ing to this music and ~~also about them being~~

~~able to go out and buy~~ it at any age.

Parents feel that music should be

unclear:
replace with "its
sale restricted"

replace wrong word
with "they're"

rated and ~~not be alowed to sale to anyone~~ un-

correct misspelling: "certain"

less their a (certian) age. The singers argue

replace misspelled "it's" and "their"

that (its) taking away (they're) right of free-

misspelled contraction "can't"

dom of speech and that people just (cant)

misspelled "really"

Misspelled
possessive, but
take out wordy
today's

face hearing about what (realy) is happening

in todays society.

misspelled "whether"

The key issue is (weather) or not the

no apostrophe in plural "parents"

lyrics of the song should be rated. (Parent's)

replace with right name: "Snoop Doggy Dog"

feel that such artists as (Snoop Dog,) Dr. Dre,

and Ice-T are encouraging people to go out

and get high, get drunk, or kill someone in

their songs. Little children are able to turn

replace misspelled "hear"

the radio on and (here) this music and are

replace misspelled "buy"

able to go to the local music store and (by)

replace misspelled "violence"

these tapes, that are describing (vilence,)

drugs, and sex. Some of the lyrics are not

replace mispelled "suitable"

Fragment
resulting from use
of When. Connect
to next
sentence?

(sutable) for little children to be listening to.

no capital for "example"

For (Example:) when rap singer Ice-T re-

leased his song "Cop Killer." Some of the

lyrics of the song went like this, "I got my

12-gauge sawed off and I got my headlights

turned off I'm bout to bust some shots off

I'm bout to dust some cops off. . . . Die, die,

Fragment missing subject or verb: get rid of Not to mention?

die, pig, die!" Not to mention how a

(policemen) would feel knowing a rap artist is

no plural for "policeman"

singing about how to kill a cop.

Replace awkward phrase

Not only this but children look up to

replace misspellings: "role models"

Break up long, unclear sentence here

singers and see them as (roll modles) and if a

replace dialect term with more acceptable "himself"

singer does something bad like kills (hisself,)

then a fan might go out and do the same

replace faulty punctuation and capitalization: "example, last . . ."

thing. For example: (Last) week a rock star

Replace misspelled "committed"

comitted suicide. One of his fan who was so

replace misspelling with "wrapped"

(rapped) up in the singer went out and comit-

ted suicide the exact same way as the singer

just two days after.

replace with plural "singers"

However, the (singer's) say there just

Replace with "they're"

replace misspellings "real" and "aren't"

singing about the (rael) world and (arent)

trying to make children to go out and use

replace with contraction "they're"

Comma splice: replace comma with period, followed by capital letter

drugs or kill someone, (there) just singing.

Punctuation spelling problems: change to "It's" and "their"

(Its' they're) right to sing about whatever they

Comma splice: replace comma with period

want, it is their freedom of speech. Singers

misspelling: change to "scared"

such as Ice-T say that people are just (scarred)

to hear about what really goes on in the

streets. In addition, the singers argue that by

Revise awkward unclear sentence: censoring and rating their albums would hurt their

censoring and rating their albums, would

cause them not sale, which would make the

replace misspelling
with "lose"

singers (loose) money. They say that singing

misspelling: replace with "their"

is (they're) own ticket out of the slums, (were)

replace misspellings with "where" and "no"

they have (know) other way of making money

replace with more formal "thievery"

than selling drugs or (thieving.)

Exercise: Proofreading

Proofread the following paragraph:

> Of course the singers have freedom of speach,
> but with just a simple rating system, it would
> make everone happy. The singers would be al-
> lowed to sing about what ever they wanted to
> the parents wuld be happy because children
> wouldnt be allowed to buy certian tapes until
> they where a certain age. We don't let children
> go see are rated movies until their seventeen,
> why should they be allowed to by tapes that
> describe the same things that are in the
> movies when they're just ten years old? Maybe
> by rating the music. It would encurage the
> singers to sing about other things. The world
> is already bad enough, we don't need children
> growing up thinking it is alright to do drugs,
> have sex, and kill someone just becuase their
> favorite singer was sing about it.

After solving her problems with organization and proofreading, Sonya writes a final version of her persuasion paper:

STUDENT PERSUASION ESSAY: FINAL VERSION
RATING THE LYRICS OF RAP MUSIC

Many Americans who have listened to the radio have become concerned with the explicit lyrics of rap music. Parents have been offended by invitations to do drugs, get drunk, have sex, and even kill people. Some parents have even been outraged by the possibility that their children would listen to this music or buy it, no matter how young. Some parents have even demanded government censorship of obscene or violent lyrics. In their own defense, singers argue their lyrics mirror reality. In describing what's really happening in society, they are exercising their rights to free speech, as well as making a living. Perhaps a rating system like that applied to movies would protect the rights of both sides in this controversy.

Most important, many parents feel singers like Snoopy Doggy Dog, Dr. Dre, and Ice-T are encouraging children to act immorally, even break the law. For example, rap singer Ice-T urged listeners to murder policemen in his song, "Cop Killer." Some of the lyrics went like this: "I got my 12-gauge sawed off and I got my headlights turned off I'm 'bout to bust some shots off I'm 'bout to dust some cops off. . . . Die, die, die, pig, die!" Children can listen to these lyrics not only by simply turning a dial, but by walking into a music store anywhere. Aside from encouraging children to disrespect the law, these lyrics might lead some deranged listener with a gun to kill policemen and other law enforcement people.

In addition to resenting the messages sent by their lyrics, many parents think the rap singers are poor role models. If a singer takes drugs or acts violently, young fans might be tempted to imitate their behavior. For example, a rock star committed suicide last week with a drug overdose. One of the star's fans was so upset that, just two days later, he committed suicide the same way. These examples of bad behavior, in singers' daily lives as well as in their lyrics, have disturbed many parents.

In defense of their songs, however, many singers point to their rights to free speech. Their lyrics do no more than describe what really goes on in the streets, they argue. Censorship of their songs is not only illegal, they say; it would deprive them of album and record sales. Singing is one of their few tickets out of the slums, they argue. It is one of the few ways they have of making a living other than selling drugs or thievery.

To protect the interests of both sides in this argument, the music industry should agree to a rating system like the one used for movies. It would label songs which include obscenity or violence and prohibit the sale of unacceptable songs to young children. A rating system would not only protect youngsters from lyrics praising sex, drugs, alcohol, and violence. It might even encourage singers to deal with more wholesome ideas in their songs. The world is already bad enough without exposing children to immoral or illegal temptations.

PERSUASION WRITING TOPICS

The following are some possible topics for a persuasion paragraph or paper. Limit your topic to fit your instructor's requirements. Tell the reader *why* you have chosen your topic, and link your details closely to your topic.

1. Consider how students should be made ready for a technical world.
2. Consider whether all or most companies should require on-the-job drug tests.
3. Consider whether advertising of alcohol and tobacco should be limited or prohibited.
4. Consider whether standardized tests should be required for all diplomas and degrees, on the high school and college levels.
5. Consider whether members of controversial organizations should be allowed to speak on campus.
6. Consider whether women should be allowed to perform all tasks open to men in the military.

Handbook

Grammar and Mechanics

This handbook will refer to the following grammatical definitions:

Sentence: Complete sentences include both a subject and a verb. The *subject* tells us *who* or *what* is doing or being. The *verb* describes the action or state of being.

Main Clause: A *main* or *independent* clause is a simple sentence that may stand alone.

Subordinate Clause: A *subordinate* or *dependent* clause is a simple sentence that may not stand alone. It must be connected to a main clause by a *subordinating conjunction* like *because, although,* or *since.*

SENTENCE FRAGMENTS

A sentence fragment is an incomplete sentence. The following are the most common reasons why a fragment is not a complete sentence:

- The fragment is missing a subject or verb.
- The fragment begins with the word *to* or a word ending in *ing*.
- The fragment begins with a connecting word.
- The fragment begins with a subordinating word.

FRAGMENTS MISSING A SUBJECT OR VERB

It is easy to omit a subject in a sentence, and the resulting fragment may sound all right if you read it in context. In fact, we often *speak* in fragments. However, fragments are not acceptable in written communication.

In 1980, four death row inmates quietly strolled out of Georgia's maximum security prison. *Disguised as correctional officers after using carbon paper to dye mail-order pajamas to look like guard uniforms.*

In the preceding sentence, the fragment is italicized. It lacks a subject. The subject is *death row inmates*—we know this from the first sentence. The subject doesn't carry over into the next group of words because each sentence must have its own subject. How can you find this kind of fragment? Look at the following words:

For a time banned in Georgia prisons.
What was banned? The word group doesn't say. The *what* word is missing. Look at the next sentence:

Are able to make something out of practically nothing.
Who was able to make something out of practically nothing? The word group doesn't say. The *who* word is missing. If you can't answer the *what* or *who* in a sentence, the subject is missing. Look at the following word group:

The Department of Corrections on their "least wanted" item list.
This word group lacks a *verb*. What did the Department of Corrections do? You can't answer the question with the information given. The word group doesn't tell us what they did.

> *Always read your document sentence by sentence. You may want to begin at the end and work your way back to the beginning. Reading each sentence separately and out of context will help you spot fragments.*

> *Always put the subject close to the beginning of the sentence as possible. Then follow it as closely as possible with the verb.*

How can you fix this kind of fragment?

    1. Join it to the sentence before or after it.

In 1980, four death row inmates quietly strolled out of Georgia's maximum security prison disguised as correctional officers after using carbon paper to dye mail-order pajamas to look like guard uniforms.

    2. Add a subject.

As a result, carbon paper for a time was banned in Georgia prisons.
The prisoners are able to make something out of practically nothing.

    3. Add a verb and, if necessary, more explanatory words.

The Department of Corrections has included on their "least wanted" item list carbon paper as well as many other common items. (*has included* is the verb)

FRAGMENTS BEGINNING WITH THE WORD *TO* OR A WORD ENDING IN *ING*

These fragments usually belong in the sentence preceding or following the fragment. They can begin with a word ending in *ing*.

Crafty criminal minds have found unusual and dangerous uses for a wide variety of common objects. Using their creativity to help them escape.

The second word group, *using their creativity to help them escape*, is a fragment. It doesn't have a subject and is missing part of the verb.
    It can be fixed in the following ways:

    1. Add a subject and a helping verb: [Note: A *helping verb* is a form of verbs like *have, do,* or *be*. It comes before the main verb to help it show time or emphasis, like the verb *are* in the following example.]

They **are** using their creativity to help them escape.

    2. Connect it to the sentence that comes before or after, whichever seems appropriate:

Using their creativity to help them escape, crafty criminal minds have found unusual and dangerous uses for a wide variety of common objects.

> *When you're connecting an "ing" fragment, watch your punctuation. Your failure to connect the "ing" word group to the next clause may confuse your reader.*

If you're connecting the fragment with the sentence that follows, use a comma after the fragment.

Using their creativity to help them escape, crafty criminal minds have found unusual and dangerous uses for a wide variety of common objects.

If the fragment is connected to the sentence that goes before it, don't use a comma:

Crafty criminal minds have found unusual uses for common objects applying the criminals' creativity to escape.

A fragment may begin with the word *to*:

The prisoners use anything they can lay their hands on. To escape from prison.

In the preceding sentence, the fragment is missing a subject, a verb, or both, depending on how you fix it.

To escape from prison is the goal of most inmates.

The word *to* plus a verb (such as *write* or *escape*) is called an infinitive. An infinitive can be used as a subject in a sentence, but of course the sentence must have a verb:

Is is the verb in this sentence.
Another way to fix this fragment is to simply add a subject and a verb:
To escape from prison, prisoners use innocent items like plastic wrap, which can be melted into a blade.

Prisoners is the subject and *use* is the verb.
Finally, we can combine the fragment with the next sentence:
The prisoners use anything they can lay their hands on to escape from prison.

Clearly, you have several choices when repairing fragments. Any of your choices will be correct as long as you create complete sentences.

FRAGMENTS BEGINNING WITH A CONNECTING WORD

Some fragments begin with connecting words (such as *also*, *and*, and *for*) or articles (such as *a*, *an*, *the*). These fragments may lack subjects, verbs, or both. Here are some problem words:

also,	and	but	especially
for,	for example	for instance	just,
mainly	like	such as	

This type of fragment occurs easily in any writing. Look at these word groups:

The warden says that nearly anything prisoners lay their hands on can be converted into something dangerous.

Like knives or bombs. (Missing a subject and a verb.)
For example kitchen matches and aerosol spray. (Missing a verb.)

Only the first word group is a sentence. The other word groups are missing either subjects or verbs. Unfortunately, reading these word groups out loud—one way to spot fragments—doesn't work too well for this type of fragment. You might hear all three word groups as one thought and think that nothing is wrong.

> *Always read your document sentence by sentence. Begin at the end and work your way back to the beginning. In other words, read each sentence separately and out of context. This process will help you spot fragments.*

> *Pay close attention to word groups starting with the word "to" or a word ending in "ing." Make absolutely certain that they contain both a subject and a verb.*

How can you fix this kind of fragment?

1. Drop the period. Then join the fragment to the sentence before or after it.
2. To complete the sentence, add the missing verb or subject or both.

The warden says that nearly anything prisoners lay their hands on can be converted into something dangerous like knives or bombs. (*Like knives or bombs* has been joined to the preceding sentence.)

For example, kitchen matches and aerosol spray cans can be used to make fire bombs. (The verb *can be used* is added along with an infinitive, *to make*, and an object, *fire bombs*.)

The first fragment was joined with the preceding sentence. A verb was added to the final fragment to create a complete sentence.

FRAGMENTS BEGINNING WITH A SUBORDINATING WORD

Subordinating words or subordinating conjunctions make clauses dependent by connecting them to main clauses with words like *because*, *since*, and *although*. They sometimes cause problems because writers don't understand them. The following are subordinating conjunctions:

after	although	so that	before
until	as	as if	if
how	when	while	that
because	where	which	whenever
wherever	through	even though	so

Remember, a conjunction joins a word group's two equal parts. (*Con* means "with," and *junction* means "joining.") The parts can be nouns or even sentences. A subordinating conjunction also joins parts in a word group. However, these parts are not equal. A subordinate belongs to a lower class or has a lower rank. (*Sub* means "beneath or lower," and *ordin* refers to "rank or order.") A subordinating conjunction joins a word group to a sentence. In fact, placing a subordinating conjunction in front of a sentence lowers its rank to that of a nonsentence or fragment.

Prisoners can wear watches, rings, and other jewelry.
Although prisoners can wear watches, rings, and other jewelry.

In the preceding example, the first word group is a sentence. In the second word group, placing *although*, a subordinating conjunction, at the beginning, created a fragment.

When you begin a sentence with a subordinating conjunction, be sure you are not writing a fragment:

Be especially careful when beginning a sentence with the word "because."

Because larger pieces of jewelry can be filed into deadly daggers. A cross can be no longer than 15 inches.

In the preceding example, the first word group is a fragment. The second is a complete sentence.

Note that when you begin a sentence with a subordinating conjunction, you will follow this introductory word group with a comma:

Because larger pieces of jewelry can be filed into deadly daggers, a cross can be no longer than 15 inches.

How can you fix this kind of fragment?

1. Combine it with the sentence that comes before or after.
2. Omit the subordinating conjunction. Don't write too many short, choppy sentences:

Pens that have a stiff metal barrel to contain the ink are forbidden. Because they can be turned into a "zip-gun" or single-shot weapon. (The second word group is a fragment.)

Pens that have a stiff metal barrel to contain the ink are forbidden because they can be turned into a "zip-gun" or single-shot weapon. (Combined with the previous sentence.)

Pens that have a stiff metal barrel to contain the ink are forbidden. They can be turned into a "zip-gun" or single-shot weapon. (Subordinating conjunction omitted and the fragment turned into an independent sentence.)

> *Remember: If you begin a sentence with a subordinating conjunction, you'll have two subjects and two verbs in the sentence.*

Because liquid shoe polish contains alcohol, it can be used to make a fire bomb. (Subjects: *shoe polish* and *it.* Verbs: *contains* and *can be used.*)

Applying What You've Learned

Underline the fragments (three of them) in the following paragraph. Then rewrite, replacing the fragments with complete sentences.

Joseph Curtis and Stephen Sanders think trash bags ought to be different. And invented ways of holding it. Draw strings around the edge that pull up to form a bag. Tubular necks, stiffeners and drawstrings, according to manufacturers, are great. But cost more than regular bags to make.

RUN-ON SENTENCES AND COMMA SPLICES

Run-on sentences and comma splices are two common sentence errors. In a run-on sentence, one sentence follows the other with no punctuation or conjunctions to join them. In a comma splice, two sentences are joined with a comma. In the following example, the first sentence literally runs on into the second:

Recording machines are prohibited authorities don't want inmates secretly taping conversations of cellmates or guards.

The first sentence is *Recording machines are prohibited;* the second sentence is *authorities don't want inmates secretly taping conversations of cellmates or guards.*

The following two sentences are joined only by commas and create a comma splice. If you splice two wires, you join them together. If you use a comma splice, you join two sentences with a comma.

Recording machines are prohibited, authorities don't want inmates secretly taping conversations of cellmates or guards.

These sentences are very hard for the reader to understand. To correct either a run-on sentence or comma splice, use either punctuation or a conjunction.

Recording machines are prohibited; authorities don't want inmates secretly taping conversations of cellmates or guards.

Recording machines are prohibited because authorities don't want inmates secretly taping conversations of cellmates or guards.

How can you find a run-on sentence or a comma splice?

1. Read your document aloud. If you run out of breath after a word group, or your voice drops, or a pause seems appropriate, you may need some punctuation.
2. Make sure each sentence has one subject and one verb. If it has two subjects and two verbs, make sure you've used either some kind of conjunction or a period or semicolon.

Electric razors are not allowed they can be converted into weapons or tattoo machines.

In the preceding example, the subjects are *electric razors* and *they*. The verbs are *allowed* and *can be converted.*

Electric razors are not allowed; they can be converted into weapons or tattoo machines.(Corrected with punctuation.)

Electric razors are not allowed because they can be converted into weapons or tattoo machines. (Corrected by adding a subordinating conjunction, *because.*)

3. Count your sentences. If you have very few in a medium-length document, look for run-ons or comma splices.
4. Some words attract run-ons and comma splices like magnets. These words include both connectives and pronouns:

consequently	finally he	she	it	however	I
moreover	now	then	suddenly	there	therefore
they	we	who	you		

Look for patterns in your writing. Frequently your mistakes are variations of one problem—fragments beginning with *and*, perhaps, or run-ons beginning with pronouns.

FIXING SENTENCE ERRORS

1. Use a period to create two sentences:

In 1967, inmates escaping from a prison used leather dye as a fuel for a bomb they threw it into a guard tower. (run-on sentence)

In 1967, inmates escaping from a prison used leather dye as a fuel for a bomb, they threw it into a guard tower. (comma splice)

In 1967, inmates escaping from a prison used leather dye as a fuel for a bomb. They threw it into a guard tower. (corrected with a period)

> *Be careful about splitting a word group into two sentences. If you do this too often, your writing will sound choppy and abrupt.*

2. Separate the sentences with a semicolon. Use this option only if the thoughts are closely related. It would not work, for example, for the following run-on:

Ski masks can hide inmates' faces the warden also prohibited publications that depict violence or graphic sex.

These two sentences are not closely related. Therefore, a period would be more appropriate:

Ski masks can hide inmates' faces. The warden prohibited publications that depict violence or graphic sex.

3. Separate the sentences with a connector and a semicolon. Conjunctive adverbs are the only connectors you can use this way. Unlike a *subordinate conjunction*, these words do not connect two clauses; they merely interrupt a thought to add emphasis. They are *throw-away* words that can be omitted without changing the sentence's meaning. They include the following:

Words that show something added:

also	besides	in addition
likewise	moreover	similarly

Words that show something different:

however	despite this	instead
nonetheless	on the other hand	still

Words that show a result:

therefore	as a result	accordingly	thus
because of this	consequently	hence	

Words that point out:

for example	for instance	afterwards	that is
namely	then	to illustrate	eventually

Words that tell when something happens:

later	meanwhile	presently	thereafter
sometime	soon	subsequently	

The following word groups use conjunctive adverbs:

Shellac was used in prison factories to refinish furniture; however, now it is banned. (The two sentences are separated by a connector (a conjunctive adverb) and a semicolon.)

> Use a semicolon with a conjunctive adverb **only** if you have a sentence on either side. The following sentence does not require a semicolon.

The phosphorous on kitchen matches can be scraped off, however, to make a fire bomb. (The word group *the phosphorous on kitchen matches can be scraped off* is a sentence. *However, to make a fire bomb* is not.)

4. Use a comma and a coordinating conjunction.

Shellac was used in prison factories to refinish furniture, but now it is banned. (A comma and a coordinating conjunction—*but*—join the sentences.)

5. Begin one of the sentences with a subordinating conjunction:

Although shellac was used in prison factories to refinish furniture, now it is banned. (A subordinating conjunction—*although*—comes first in one of the sentences, joining both of them together.)

The following words all serve as subordinating conjunctions:

after	if	even if	when	whenever

although	though	in order that	so that	even though
as since	whether	that	while	what
whichever	before	unless	how	because
until	who	whoever	wherever	
whatever	whose	where	which	

Applying What You've Learned: Errors with Run-on Sentences

Correct the following run-on sentences by using the principles you learned in the preceding section:

1. Most people in the world do without forks they prefer chopsticks or fingers.
2. It is reasonable to ask why we have found them essential three reasons suggest themselves.
3. First, our diet is unlike that of the rest of the world it is very meat-heavy.
4. We can eat a chunk of meat with our fingers the grease and burn factors are great.
5. Forks have become popular here they let greedy diners spear big chunks more easily.
6. Second, Westerners are less comfortable with close contact the fork helps us keep our distance.
7. Last, the fork has many spin-offs they include the dessert fork, the salad fork, and the oyster fork.
8. Many of these forks serve no useful purpose perhaps the rise of new money explains their attractiveness.
9. Renaissance fat cats may have started the tradition the true flowering of table utensils came during America's Gilded Age.

Applying What You've Learned: Errors with Comma Splices

Correct the following comma splices by using the principles you learned in the preceding section:

1. Toothbrushing makes good sense in America, we are widely addicted to sugar.
2. This custom is not widespread, the Romans, for example, rinsed their mouths with urine instead of brushing.

3. Many Asian peoples chew betel nuts, many people do nothing at all.

4. Toothbrushing is, therefore, not natural, it should be seen as a strange Western habit.

5. Horace Miner spoofed the body ritual of North Americans, he described our tooth brushing as a "mouth rite."

6. We insert a small bundle of hog hairs into our mouths, along with it go magical powders, we then move the bundle in a series of gestures.

7. We also pay regular visits to a "holy-mouth-man," he drills holes in our teeth.

8. The "holy-mouth-man" also fills our teeth with magical substances, they stop decay and attract friends.

9. Natives return to holy-mouth-men year after year, this is in spite of the fact that our teeth keep decaying.

SUBJECT–VERB AGREEMENT

In all writing, the subjects and verbs should "match" or agree in number. If the subject of a sentence (the *who* or the *what* in a sentence) is singular, the verb, or action word, must also be singular. If the subject is plural, the verb must be plural. (Singular comes from the word *single* and means "one." *Plural* means "more than one.") As a general rule, use a singular verb when the subject is *he*, *she*, or *it* or the equivalent; in other words, one person, place, idea, or thing takes a singular verb. The verb will usually end in *s* or *es*. Frequently, though not always, if your subject ends in an *s*, your verb should not.

The World Future Society publishes a magazine with forecasts about the future.

The subject *World Future Society* is singular; it is one group.
The verb *publishes* ends in an *es*.

The editors of the magazine believe that many strange events will happen in the future.

The word *editors* is plural—more than one person—and the verb, *believe*, matches the subject. Note that the verb *believe* does not end in *s*.

The English language has some "troublesome" verbs that are called "irregular." That is, they don't follow the pattern for pluralizing regular verbs, which is simply to add an *s* or *es* ending to the verb.

Regular Verb Patterns

Singular Plural

I believe

you believe

he, she, it believes

we believe

you believe

they believe

Irregular Verb Patterns

Singular	*Plural*
I am, I have, I do	We are, we have, we do
you are, you have	you are, you have
you do	you do
he, she, it is	they are
he, she, it has	they have
he, she, it does	they do

Present Tense	*Past Tense*
be, am, is	was, were
become	became
begin	began
bend	bent
bite	bit
blow	blew
break	broke
bring	brought
bought	bought
build	built
catch	caught
choose	chose
come	came
creep	crept
cut	cut
do	did
draw	drew
drink	drank
drive	drove
eat	ate
fall	fell
feed	fed

feel	felt
fight	fought
find	found
fly	flew
forget	forgot
forgive	forgave
freeze	froze
get	got
give	gave
go	went
grow	grew
have	had
hide	hid
hit	hit
hold	held
hurt	hurt
keep	kept
knew	knew
lay	laid
lead	led
let	let
lie	lay
lose	lost
make	made
meet	met
pay	paid
put	put
read	read
ride	rode
rise	rose
run	ran

see	saw
sell	sold
send	sent
set	set
shine	shone
shrink	shrank or shrunk
sing	sang
sit	sat
sleep	slept
speak	spoke
speed	sped
spend	spent
stand	stood
steal	stole
stink	stank or stunk
strike	struck
swim	swam
take	took
teach	taught
tear	tore
tell	told
think	thought
throw	threw
wake	waked, woke
wear	wore
win	won

Because subject–verb agreement is so important, be very careful when you edit sentences. Sometimes it is difficult to identify the subject of a sentence. Problems can develop when a phrase (a group of words) or a clause (a group of words that contains both a subject and a verb) separates the subject from the verb.

The electronic human like one of the many science fiction ideas is a real possibility.

The idea that people may someday be part human and part electronic is one of the forecasts of the Futurists.

In the first sentence, the subject *human* is separated from the verb *is* by the phrase *like one of the many science fiction ideas*. In the second sentence, the subject *idea* is separated from the verb *is* by the clause *that people may someday be part human and part electronic*.

To check your agreement, first find the subject. Ask *who* or *what* is acting in the sentence. See if any of the following words, which are prepositions, come after the subject (the noun following a preposition is never the subject):

to

for

over

in

on

with

of

like

Next cross out prepositional phrases or relative clauses following the subject. Note: a *prepositional phrase* consists of a preposition like *as, to* or *for* followed by a noun: *over the fence*. A *relative clause* is a dependent clause beginning with a pronoun such as *who* or *that* acting as an adjective.

Finally, identify the verb and make sure it matches the subject.

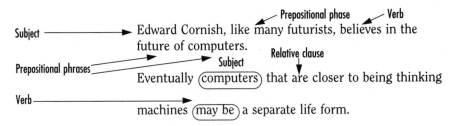

When a sentence begins with *there* or *here*, the normal word order is reversed and the verb comes before the subject.

Verb ↓   ↓ Subject
There are no jobs that last a lifetime anymore.

Verb ↓   ↓ Subject
Here is the reason why this is true.

Sentences beginning with *there is* or *there are* are generally boring and often wordy. The word *there* is not a person, place, or thing. Furthermore, using this construction is dangerous because it so easily can create a subject–verb agreement problem.

Put whoever or whatever does the action in a sentence at the beginning of the sentence and follow it as closely as possible with the verb. For example, the real subject of the following sentence is *job.*

No job lasts a lifetime.

SPECIAL CONSTRUCTIONS

Each of the following words needs a singular verb:

either (one of)

each (one of)

every (one of)

neither (one of)

one (of)

which (one of)

When you use the combinations *either/or* and *neither/nor*, the verb agrees with the closest subject:

Neither the boss nor the employees have secure jobs.
(The verb *have* agrees with employees.)

Either those three or Corey needs to find another job. (The verb *needs* agrees with Corey.)

VERB AGREEMENT IN RELATIVE CLAUSES

Dependent clauses beginning with *who, which,* or *that* are called relative clauses. The verbs in these clauses must agree with the word referred to by *who, which,* or *that.*

In the future, virtual reality experiences *that lead to personality afflictions* will send people to psychiatrists.

The relative clause is italicized. The verb in the clause, *lead,* must agree with the subject *experiences.*

COLLECTIVE NOUNS

Collective nouns refer to a group of something. Usually these nouns take a singular verb. The following are some collective nouns:

class committee	group	company	family
government	team	jury	school

The jury agrees that insanity caused by virtual reality is not a good defense.

In this sentence, the jury completely agreed; it acted as a unit. If however, members of the group do not agree or act independently, the collective noun will use a plural verb:

His family put on their virtual reality visors.

Since each family member puts on his or her visor separately—they all can't wear the same one—we use a plural verb and plural pronoun.

Applying What You've Learned: Errors with Subject–Verb Agreement

Correct the subject–verb agreement problems in the following sentences:

1. The number of Americans who is seriously overweight jumped to one-third in the 1980s. Some 58 million people in the United States weighs at least 20 percent more than their ideal body weight.
2. This make them, in the terms of science, obese.
3. "All of us was stunned," says Dr. Albert Stunkard, a psychiatrist and food expert.
4. "It run counter to what we as a nation seems to be doing."
5. The extra baggage are not just unsightly but unhealthy as well.
6. There is alarming signs that the next generation may be in even worse shape.
7. "The kids eats nothing but junk food," says Lia Hennessey, a special-ed teacher.
8. She watch students on school trips open the lunches their parents packs for them, gobbles up the Oreos and Pop-Tarts and tosses out the sandwiches.
9. Just before the holidays, most Americans takes it for granted they would puts on weight.
10. However, those pounds just gets harder and harder to lose.
11. Weight-loss tycoon Jenny Craig blame the news media. "Now they broadcasts that diets don't work."

12. Those tubs of greasy movie-theater popcorn packs four days' worth of fat into a container as big as a fire bucket.

13. Each of those servings of extra-rich Häagen-Dazs Triple Brownie Overload contain 44 grams of fat—the equivalent of half a stick of butter.

14. Before we wins the food battle externally, we must fights them internally—one bulge at a time.

ACTIVE AND PASSIVE VOICE

Verbs are said to be either active or passive. An active verb is briefer and more direct. In the active voice, the subject of the sentence carries out the action of the verb in the sentence. In the passive voice, the subject receives the action. A passive verb includes a form of *to be* with a past participle (for example, to be heard). (See the section "Verb Forms" for more information.)

In the future, terrorists can wipe out half a city's population with superplagues. (active voice)

In the future, half a city's population can by wiped out by terrorists with superplagues. (passive voice)

Using active or passive voice creates different effects in a sentence, changing emphasis. Whether to use it or not depends on who or what the real actor is, not necessarily the grammatical subject. Remember, sentences with simpler verb forms are easier to read. Ask yourself *who* is doing *what* in the sentence. Who can wipe out half a city's population? The answer is *terrorists*. Therefore, make *terrorists* the subject, as in the preceding example.

Avoid the passive voice, if possible. The passive voice is useful in the following cases:

• When the doer is unknown:

Millions of trading cards are printed and sold every year.

• When the action or object is more important than the doer:

Bat-themed trading-card sets based on the new Batman movie were released this summer.

• When you want to make the action impersonal or to soften the tone:

Two card manufacturers were signed on to print collectibles.

VERB TENSES

For regular verbs in the present tense add an *s* or *es* to the third-person form (he, she, it).

The 100-card Batman set features original artwork based on the newest movie.

If the verb ends in *y*, change the *y* to *i* and add *es*. For example, I *fly* becomes he *flies*.

For regular verbs in the past tense, add a *d* or *ed* to the third person form.

These cards started as original penciled drawings by top comic artists.

If the verb ends in *y*, change the *y* to *i* and add *ed*.

For the future tense of all verbs, simply add *will* to the basic verb:

Packets of these cards will sell for $2.99.

IRREGULAR VERBS IN PRESENT, PAST, AND FUTURE TENSES

Irregular verbs change form from present to past tense. For example, *become* changes to *became*, *break* changes to *broke*, and *go* changes to *went*. In the future tense, the verb returns to the original form and, as with regular verbs, adds *will*—*will become, will break*, and *will go*.

If you are unsure how or if a verb changes form when the tense changes, check your dictionary. The principal parts of all verbs are listed after the word itself in this order:

past tense

past participle

present participle

third-person singular present tense

For example, the verb *go* looks like this in a dictionary:

go (gō) *v.* went, gone, going, goes.

The letters in parenthesis tell how the word should be pronounced, and the abbreviation *v.* tells us that it is a verb.

The past participle is yet another form that a verb might take. With a regular verb, the past participle looks just like the past tense. In irregular verbs, however, the past participle has a different form. The past participle is combined with a helping verb like *has* or *have* to form the present perfect tense. With this tense, we describe an action that began in the past and is still going on in the present:

Millions of collectors have waited anxiously for these new Batman cards.

Remember: *has* is the third-person form of the verb *have* and agrees with *he, she,* or *it; have* agrees with everything else.

The past perfect tense tells us that one particular action that occurred in the past happened earlier than another action. It uses *had,* the past tense of *have,* along with the past participle:

The artists had drawn the penciled images by hand before the images were transformed by the computer.

PRONOUNS

Pronouns are the words that we use instead of repeating the noun. The following are pronouns:

I	you	she	it
we	they	who	whoever
me	him	her	us
them	whom	whomever	my
mine	your, yours	his	her
hers	its	our	ours
their	theirs	whose	he

A sentence that does not use pronouns may be awkward and wordy:

Collectors are anxious to get the "metal cards," which the collectors believe will be a good investment for the collectors' collection.

If we substitute the correct pronouns, the sentence is shorter and easier to read:

Collectors are anxious to get the "metal cards," which they believe will be a good investment for their collection.

Pronouns should refer to only one word. In the preceding example, all of the pronouns refer to *collectors.*

"Metalcards" have drawings over a foil backdrop to create the effect they want.

In this sentence, we are not sure exactly who the word *they* refers to: *cards, drawings* or someone not mentioned in the sentence, the artists or the collectors. The confusion can be very frustrating to a reader. The following sentence clarifies the meaning:

"Metal cards" have drawings over a foil backdrop to create the effect the artists want.

PRONOUN ANTECEDENTS

Pronouns replace nouns, other pronouns, or even phrases in sentences. We noted earlier that a pronoun can only refer to one word or phrase. We call what the pronoun refers to the antecedent. Making pronouns agree with their antecedents is usually easy:

Collectors who put together a collection of movie photo stickers can put them in an official collectors' album.

In this sentence, the pronoun *them* clearly refers to the stickers.

Applying What You've Learned: Pronoun Antecedents

For the following sentences, write the pronouns and their antecedents in the blanks at the right.

	Pronoun	*Antecedent*
Example: Thomas Hardy lived to be 200 years old, or so it seemed to his competitors.	his	Thomas Hardy
1. Hardy viewed biographers as cannibals, and he worked hard to ward them off.	_____	_____
2. Hardy's second wife, Florence, reworked his biography to make his first wife seem guileful.	_____	_____
3. Florence opened herself up to accusations of dishonesty.	_____	_____
4. The poems are full of squabbling, but mostly it's the poet arguing with himself.	_____	_____
5. Hardy's biographer treats the poems as interesting mostly for their personal revelations.	_____	_____
6. Although Emma was a trial in life, in death she became a perfect angel.	_____	_____
7. Hardy changed Emma's personality to her benefit, a surprise given his sorrowful temperament.	_____	_____
8. Hardy had to lose everything before he could find himself.	_____	_____
9. In Hardy's case, everything had to be lost before he could find its value.	_____	_____

PRONOUN AGREEMENT

Problems with pronoun agreement primarily develop when we use indefinite pronouns (for example, *anybody, both,* and *none*). Some indefinite pronouns take singular verbs and pronouns, some take plural verbs and pronouns, and some take either depending on the position of the indefinite pronoun in the sentence.

The following indefinite pronouns are singular and take both singular verbs and singular pronouns:

anybody	anyone	everybody	everyone
one	nobody	no one	somebody
someone	something	each + noun	every + noun
another	either	neither	much

The subject of the following sentence is the indefinite pronoun *anybody*:

Anybody who likes Batman wants to add these cards to his or her collection.

In this sentence, the singular verbs *likes* and *wants* and the pronoun *his* agree with *anybody*.

The following indefinite pronouns are plural and take plural verbs and plural pronouns:

any of	both of
few of	many of

Some indefinite pronouns can be either singular or plural depending on the noun to which they refer:

all	most	none
any	more	some

Some of the trading cards are due for shipment in June.

Some of the pack is printed on foil.

In the first sentence, *some* refers to *trading cards* and needs the plural verb *are*. In the second sentence, *some* refers to *the pack* and needs the singular verb *is*.

MODIFIERS

A modifier is a word that tells us something about another word:

Designers of cards try hard to create affordable, playable games.

In this sentence, *hard, affordable,* and *playable* are modifiers. *Hard* tells us how much the designers are trying to create good games. It is an adverb because it tells us about the verb *try. Affordable* and *playable* tell us what kinds of games they're trying to create. These words are adjectives because they tell us about a noun, *games.*

Adverbs describe or tell us about the action of verbs, adjectives, other adverbs, and even whole word groups. Adverbs answer the questions how, why, where, and when. Sometimes adverbs end in *ly.*

Adverbs

Wizards of the Coast, the designers who started it all, *always* try *really* hard to eliminate the "Mr. Suitcase Factor." (The adverbs are italicized.)

Adjectives tell us something about nouns and pronouns. They tell us, for example, how many or what kind:

With the "Mr. Suitcase Factor, " a *tournament* player can't be *competitive* without investing thousands of dollars in *powerful* playing cards. (The adjectives are italicized.**)**

Adjectives and adverbs can show comparisons between people and objects. Use the *comparative degree* to describe a greater or lesser amount of the quality you're describing. For example, you may be describing something that is better, bigger, or nicer:

The better game cards are collectible because they have something unique printed on them.

The *superlative degree* describes the greatest or least degree of the quality you're describing. For example, you may be describing something that is best, worst, or slowest:

One of the best, most popular games is "Magic: The Gathering."

For short adjectives and adverbs, form the comparative by simply adding *er.* Form the superlative by adding *est:*

slow, slower, slowest

green, greener, greenest

ugly, uglier, ugliest

For some two-syllable adjectives that end in a vowel, such as *dirty, ugly, crazy,* or *smelly,* change the *y* to *i* and add *er* or *est:*

dirty, dirtier, dirtiest

ugly, uglier, ugliest

Adjectives and adverbs with two or more syllables usually form the comparative by using the words *more* or *less* and the superlative by using *most* or *least.*

wonderful, more wonderful, most wonderful

horrible, less horrible, least horrible

Be careful not to use *more* and *er* together to form the comparative or *most* and *est* for the superlative:

Incorrect: That is the most slowest game I've ever played.

Correct: That is the slowest game I've ever played.

SPECIAL CASES

Don't confuse the words *good* and *well*. *Good* is an adjective that describes a noun or pronoun. *Well* is an adverb that describes verbs. For example, "He does *good*" means that he performs good works. "He dances *well*" means that he dances in an expert way. Both are also irregular modifiers; that is, they change form in the comparative and superlative degrees.

Adjective	*Comparative*	*Superlative*
good	better	best
bad	worse	worst

Adverb	*Comparative*	*Superlative*
well	better	best
badly	worse	worst

Always put your modifiers close to the words they modify. Otherwise the results might be confusing, awkward, or even oddly funny:

They sold the new packs to the collectors wrapped in colorful foil.

In this sentence, it appears that the collectors were wrapped in foil. If the modifying phrase *wrapped in colorful foil* is placed close to the words it modifies, the sentence becomes clear:

They sold the collectors new packs wrapped in colorful foil.

Limiting modifiers, such as *almost, even, exactly, just, only,* and *simply,* should fall right before the word or word group they modify:

Millions of people play only SimCity on the computer.

The preceding sentence implies that SimCity is the only game played on the computer by millions of people.

Millions of people only play SimCity on the computer.

This sentence implies that the game SimCity can be played on the computer, which millions of people do, but it may be played another way—for example, with cards.

Sometimes modifiers may dangle. That is, they don't refer exactly to anything in the sentence. Dangling modifiers usually begin sentences, contain a verb, and imply a subject:

Sitting alone at the computer, SimCity is a one-person game.

The preceding sentence implies that SimCity is sitting alone at the computer, which doesn't make sense. Correct the sentence by turning the dangling modifier *Sitting alone at the computer* into a dependent clause. In other words, use a subordinating conjunction, subject, and verb:

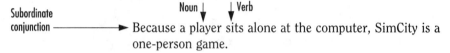

Subordinate conjunction ——→ Because a player sits alone at the computer, SimCity is a one-person game.

COMMONLY CONFUSED WORDS

A number of words sound alike but have different meanings and spellings. Some of the most common mistakes involve misusing vowels and apostrophes. The following are commonly confused words.

AFFECT/EFFECT

The "AE" rule: The verb *Affect* begins with an *a* and means "act on" or "influence." The verb *Affect* is an action word.

The manufacturer believes that the SimCity card game will affect sales of the computer game.

Effect begins with an *e* and means "end result." *Effect* is a noun and can have *a*, *an*, or *the* in front of it.

They handed out free playing cards but still don't know the effect of this strategy.

ITS/IT'S

It is easy to confuse *it's* and *its*. However, the real cause of confusion is the apostrophe. When *its* indicates ownership or possession, do not use the apostrophe:

SimCity handed out "personalized" promo game cards to its customers.

In the preceding sentence *its* refers to the customers of SimCity.
When *it's* means "it is," use an apostrophe, as you would in a contraction, because the *i* is left out of the word *is:*

Despite the unusual nature of their distribution, it's [it is] unclear whether the SimCity promos could be called "ultra-rare."

THERE/THEIR/THEY'RE

To decide which of these word to use, ask the following questions:

1. Am I pointing to a place or direction? If so, use *there*:

She simply wanted to know if she could find the cards over there.

2. Am I using the word to begin a sentence? If so, use *there:*

There are 90 cards in the core set of "Flights of Fantasy.

Note, however, that *there* is not the real subject of the sentence. *Flights of Fantasy* is the subject. As discussed earlier, overusing this word can cause you to make serious writing errors. Rewriting the sentence by putting the real subject first makes the sentence stronger.

"Flights of Fantasy" has 90 cards in the core set.

3. Am I writing about what something or someone owns or has possession of? If so, use *their*.

Their core set is divided into three 30-card subsets.

4. If I put *they are* in the sentence, would it still make sense? If so, use *they're*. Remember, *they're* is a contraction of *they* and *are*.

They're not just promo cards; they're actually rule-altering and playability cards.

TWO/TOO/TO

To decide whether to use *two, too,* or *to,* ask the following questions:

1. Are you writing about a number? If so, use *two.*

Two players reviewed the most popular games, on the market.

2. Could you substitute the words *also, as well,* or *extremely* and still have the sentence make sense? If so, use *too.*

They liked the new Star Trek game, too.

3. Is the word followed immediately by a verb (action word)? If so, use *to.*

Most of the games were fun to play.

   4. Is the word followed by a noun (name word) or an adjective and a noun? If so, use *to*.

They gave promo cards from all the games to their friends.

APOSTROPHES: POSSESSIVES AND CONTRACTIONS

Apostrophes show either that a word is possessive (has ownership) or is a contraction. The following rules will help you use apostrophes correctly.

USING APOSTROPHES TO SHOW POSSESSION

   1. Apostrophes may show ownership. When someone or something owns someone or another thing, use the apostrophe.

Price's game cards
Ben's collection
The card's artwork

   2. If the word already ends in *s* or *es*, simply add an apostrophe.

Students' collections
Players' cards

   3. Use the apostrophe and *s only* with a noun (name word).

   • If the noun is singular, show possession by adding an apostrophe and *s* (for example, *Jim's coat*).
   • If the noun is plural and ends in *s*, add an apostrophe after the *s* (for example, *Dickens' novel*).
   • If the noun is plural or does not end in *s*, add an apostrophe and *s* (for example, geese's flight).

   4. Don't use an apostrophe with possessive pronouns (my, mine, his, hers, its, ours, theirs, yours, whose) because these pronouns already show ownership.

   5. Never use an apostrophe to form the plural of a word:

Incorrect: Destini Productions also distributed promotional *card's* from its new game.
Correct: Destini Productions also distributed promotional *cards* from its new game.

Using Apostrophes to Make Contractions

1. Apostrophes are used in contractions to indicate a missing letter. For example, in the contraction *don't*, which is a contraction of the words *do* and *not*, the apostrophe replaces the letter *o* in *not*.

   isn't (contraction of *is not*—the *o* is missing)
   can't (contraction of *can not*—the *n* and *o* are missing)
   it's (contraction of *it is*—the second *i* is missing)

PUNCTUATION

COMMAS

Coordinating Conjunctions   Use a comma with a coordinating conjunction (*and, but, or, nor, for, yet, so*) that separates two independent clauses or sentences.

Tobacco cards were printed between 1909 and 1914, and they are very valuable to collectors.

Introductory Elements   A comma always follows an introductory phrase or clause.

In those days, it was understood that women were primarily concerned about the care and appearance of their homes. (Introductory phrase *In those days* is followed by a comma.)

Designed to appeal to men, tobacco cards were inserted into packs of tobacco products. (Introductory phrase *Designed to appeal to men* is followed by a comma.)

Although the market for tobacco products consisted primarily of men, some manufacturers designed cards to appeal to women. (Introductory clause *Although the market for tobacco products consisted primarily of men* is followed by a comma.)

Manufacturers hoped that women could influence their husbands to buy certain brands because this would increase sales. (In this sentence, no comma is used to set off the clause *because this would increase sales* because it comes in the middle of a sentence.)

Items in a Series   A comma separates words, phrases, or clauses in a series.

Military figures, actresses, history, and travel were popular subjects.

The comma before *and* in a series may be omitted. However, if you decide to use this style, be consistent throughout your paper.

When Not to Use a Comma   Do not use a comma in the following instances:

1. If you begin sentences with introductory phrases or parenthetical elements.

Fabric tobacco inserts were made of a felt-like material and *could be used to make pillow cases and other household items.* (The italicized word group is not a sentence and therefore no comma is needed.)

2. After a conjunction:

Incorrect: They were produced in many different sizes and, the designs were unusual.
Correct: They were produced in many different sizes, and the designs were unusual.

3. If all the items in a series are joined by *and*:

The so-called tobacco blankets depicted pets and Indian patterns and butterflies.

4. With only two items:

They also depicted flags and "Persian rug" motifs.

5. Between very short clauses in a sentence:

Tobacco blankets were attractive and they were useful.

6. Between clauses not joined by a coordinating conjunction:

Incorrect:"National Flags" is one of the most available blankets, It presents colorful flags of the world.
Correct: "National Flags" is one of the most available blankets. It presents colorful flags of the world.(The sentence was corrected by substituting a period for the comma.)

Other corrections might include adding a coordinating conjunction or substituting a semicolon for the comma. You can also insert a subordinating conjunction in front of one of the clauses. The following are possible corrections:

"National Flags" is one of the most available blankets, and it presents colorful flags of the world.

"National Flags" is one of the most available blankets; it presents colorful flags of the world.

"National Flags" is one of the most available blankets because it presents colorful flags of the world.

Word Groups That Interrupt the Flow in a Sentence Sometimes words or groups of words interrupt the flow of a sentence. They may provide additional information within the sentence, or they may be transitions from one sentence to another. However, if they were omitted from the sentence, the meaning of the sentence wouldn't change. These are called parenthetical expressions, and they are set off by commas. In the following sentences, the parenthetical expressions are italicized:

By the way, these felts were used in quilt-making.
"Miniature Indian Blankets," *in my opinion*, are noteworthy for their historical content.
The Native American-style blanket, moreover, includes the swastika symbol, *which means "good luck" or "well-being" in Sanskrit.*

Note that conjunctive adverbs, such as *however, moreover*, and *nevertheless*, are surrounded by commas *only* if they do not have a sentence on either side. See the section on semicolons if you are unsure how to punctuate these words.

Some collectors, on the other hand, prefer the wildly colored "Butterfly Designs."

Other interrupting words or group of words are called appositives—words that substitute for or describe other words:

One design, "Persian Rugs," has fringed ends to simulate real rugs.(*Persian Rugs*, an apositive, describes the subject, *design.*)

If you can leave out a word group that interrupts a sentence without affecting a reader's understanding of the sentence, set it off by commas.

Their primary function, then and now, was to add to the decor of dollhouses.

Then and now can be omitted without changing the meaning of the sentence.
    Sometimes, a word group interrupts a sentence but is essential to the meaning. In other words, the meaning of the sentence will change if the word group is omitted. Don't use commas to set off these essential word groups.

"Persian Rugs" are in high demand among collectors who specialize in dolls and dollhouses.

The preceding sentence implies that these rugs are in high demand primarily with *specific* collectors: those who specialize in dolls and dollhouses. If we omitted *who specialize in dolls and dollhouses*, we would change the meaning of the sentence.

SEMICOLONS

A semicolon is like the balance point of a scale.

You need balancing sentences on both sides of a semicolon.

Tobacco blankets are collectible because of their attractive designs; they also appeal to collectors of all tobacco memorabilia.

The sentences on either side of the semicolon balance each other. You do not need a coordinating conjunction (such as *and, but, for, or, yet, so*) between the sentences.

PUNCTUATING CONJUNCTIVE ADVERBS

Conjunctive adverbs, such as *therefore, however*, and *nevertheless*, often cause problems for students. However, their punctuation is not difficult if you can identify them and you can recognize a complete sentence. The following are some of the most common conjunctive adverbs (see the section "Fixing Sentence Errors" for a more complete list):

therefore

however

nevertheless

consequently

hence

accordingly

moreover

furthermore

besides

indeed

in fact

When a conjunctive adverb has a sentence on either side, use both a semicolon and a comma. Note that the semicolon comes before the conjunctive adverb:

Tobacco blankets aren't cards exactly; however, their distribution, variety, and function were like tobacco cards.

Be sure to follow the conjunctive adverb with a comma. (Note that if you use only commas, you may create a comma splice.)

Remember: If you use a semicolon, a sentence must appear on both sides of the adverbial connective. Otherwise, simply use commas:

Many groups of blankets, however, can be found by asking a dealer who displays tobacco cards.

Many groups of blankets is not a sentence, nor is *can be found by asking a dealer who displays tobacco cards*. Consequently, we use commas and not semicolons because the word *however* interrupts the flow of the sentence.

COLONS

A colon introduces a formal list. (When typing, always leave two spaces after the colon.)

Tobacco cards were designed around the following subjects: comic scenes, birds, dog and fish series, colleges, historic homes, state seals, and coats of arms.

Even if you decide to indent and bullet the list, you will still use the colon.

Tobacco cards were designed around the following subjects:

- comic scenes
- bird, dog, and fish series
- colleges
- historic homes
- state seals
- coats of arms

A colon introduces an important piece of information:

When collecting Tobacco cards, always remember: none of the cards in any issue are numbered.

Use the colon to introduce a formal quotation:

At a recent convention, one collector said the following: "Cards are the best collectibles because they take up very little space, are affordable, and are interesting."

When writing a business letter, use a colon, not a comma, at the end of the salutation if you aren't on a first-name basis with your reader:

Dear Dr. Moneyminder:
Dear Ms. Pfeiffer:

If you use a courtesy title such as *Dr., Professor, Mr., Mrs.,* or *Ms.,* use a colon:

> Dear Dr. Moneyminder:
> Dear Ms. Pfeiffer:

If you know someone well enough to use his or her first name, use a comma:

> Dear Bedelia,
> Dear Lenny,

Avoid using doing the following:

> Dear Mr. Flackfinder,
> Dear Albert:

Colons separate hours from minutes and chapters from verses:

> 9:15 p.m.
> John 3:15

QUOTATION MARKS

Quotation marks enclose direct quotations taken from writing or speech. The words must be exactly what was written or said.

> "Beautiful day, isn't it," said Kirk as he chopped some wood.
> "Yes, it is," replied Picard just before he handed Kirk another log.

This is a direct quotation, stating the words just as Kirk and Picard said them. Notice that the punctuation that belongs with the quoted words goes inside of the quotation marks. Each new quotation by another person is put in a separate paragraph. However, if you are using a quotation of several sentences by the same person, don't put each sentence in a separate paragraph. Also, don't put separate quotation marks around each sentence unless it is interrupted by a "stage direction" such as *he said.*

> "I don't have a cat, unlike my character," said Brent Spiner, who plays Data on *Star Trek: The Next Generation.* "But, then, unlike my character, I'm not that smart, either. My musical tastes are grounded in Tin Pan Alley. Basically, I like '20s music."

Do not use quotation marks with an indirect quotation:

> Brent Spiner told the reporter that he didn't have a cat.

In this sentence we are not quoting the exact words that the actor spoke. Thus, we need no quotation marks.

Use single quotation marks to enclose a quotation within a quotation:

"I've gotten tons of mail to clarify some of the mistakes Data has made, and the only thing I can say is, 'I hadn't a clue,' you know. I'm really just a dumb actor who memorizes brilliant dialogue."

"I think my impetus for being an actor began somewhere in the middle of the Lucy episode in Hollywood with William Holden," Spiner commented. "I watched that and said to my mother, 'I gotta do that one day.' "

In the second example, two different quotation marks appear at the end of the sentence—one single finishing the inside quote and one double finishing the main quote.

Use double quotation marks as follows:

- For short works such as songs, short stories, short poems, article or essay titles, or TV programs

"The Circle of Light" (song)

"The Bear" (short story)

"Captain" (article)

"Encounter at Farpoint" (TV episode of *Star Trek: The Next Generation*)

- For words being used in a special sense or being defined.

"Runabout" refers to a small spaceship used between space stations and planets.

Do not use quotation marks in the following instances:

- The title of your essay
- Nicknames
- Slang

Putting quote marks around slang does not permit you to use it in your paper.

Incorrect: I think Captain Kirk is a "dork."
Correct: I think Captain Kirk is unattractive.

Remember that commas and periods go inside quotation marks:

"Jean-Luc," said Dr. Crusher, "there's something I've been meaning to tell you."

Dashes, question marks, and exclamation points go inside quotation marks only if they are part of the quotation:

"I could have been talking about my character's love for the captain—who knows?"

Colons and semicolons go outside the quotation marks.

Most trekkies know the "Prime Directive": Starfleet personnel and ships cannot interfere with the normal development of any society.

UNDERLINING AND ITALICS

Use underlining or italics when naming long works such as books, plays, movies, TV programs or series, works of art, magazines, long poems, pamphlets, published speeches, or long musical works. Put shorter works like short stories, poems, articles in magazines, and episodes of TV series in quotation marks.

My favorite episode in *Star Trek: The Next Generation* is "The Naked Now."

Finally, underline or italicize the names of planes, ships, spacecraft, and trains; also italicize foreign words that are not commonly used in English:

> *Air Force One* (plane)
>
> *Titanic* (ship)
>
> *Enterprise* (spacecraft)
>
> *Best Friend* (train)
>
> *persona non grata* (Latin phrase)

CAPITALIZATION

Capitalize the following:

- The first word in every sentence or question
- Proper nouns and adjectives made from proper nouns (such as Shakespearean and Mexican). Do not capitalize the articles *a, an,* and *the* that go in front of these words unless they begin a sentence.
- The pronoun *I*

ABBREVIATIONS

You will probably use very few abbreviations in your writing. Generally, avoid them, especially *etc.*, unless absolutely necessary. You can and should, however, abbreviate titles immediately before and after names:

Dr.	Mrs.	Ms.
Mr.	Rev.	Gen.

| St. | B.A. | M.D. |
| Ph.D. | Sr. | Jr. |

Note the position of the periods in these abbreviations. Don't use such abbreviations unless they appear immediately before or after a proper name.

Dr. Al Aboard

Rev. William von Malottke

Many abbreviations and acronyms (words created from the first letters of a name) are familiar to everyone:

USC, UCLA, SMU (schools)

FBI, YMCA, NOW(organizations)

IBM, NBC, AT&T (companies)

FDR, JFK (people)

AIDS, TB (diseases)

ICBM, TCBM (missiles)

TV, VCR (entertainment machines)

These abbreviations do not require periods. Most abbreviations of three or more words also do not require periods. Use all capital letters for acronyms. To form the plural, add *s* (for example, TVs and VCRs).

Use periods in the following abbreviations:

Latin abbreviations, such as i.e. and etc.

Time designations: a.m. and p.m. When abbreviating the word *number*, as in "no. 12"

Dates: B.C., A.D. (as in A.D. 456 or 12,000 B.C.)

If an abbreviation might be confusing, spell out its meaning the first time you use it and place the abbreviation in parentheses; from then on you may simply use the abbreviation:

He needed to consult the Consumer Price Index (CPI).

If you are unsure about an abbreviation, check the dictionary—many of them are listed. Some dictionaries, like *The American Heritage Dictionary*, contain a list of abbreviations at the end of the book.

Credit List

Index